DATE DUE		

THE HANDBOOK OF
NON-VIOLENCE

THE HANDBOOK OF
NON-VIOLENCE

By ROBERT A. SEELEY

Including Aldous Huxley's
An Encyclopedia of Pacifism

Lawrence Hill & Company, Westport, Conn.

Lakeville Press, Great Neck, N.Y.

Library of Congress Cataloging-in-Publication Data

Seeley, Robert.
    The handbook of non-violence.

    Bibliography: p.
    Includes index.
    1. Peace. 2. Pacifism. I. Huxley, Aldous, 1894–1963.
Encyclopedia of pacifism. 1985. II. Title.
III. Title: Encyclopedia of pacifism.
JX1952.S43   1986   327.1'72   85-27044
    ISBN 0-88208-208-6
    ISBN 0-88208-209-4 (pbk.)

Published in the United States of America by
Lawrence Hill & Co., Westport, Conn, and
Lakeville Press, Great Neck, N.Y.

1 2 3 4 5 6 7 8 9

Printed in the United States of America

Contents

Acknowledgments

This book could not have been completed without the help and support of many people. Work on the project would not have begun without Murray Polner, who secured publication rights, gave many helpful comments on the manuscript, and helped in many other ways—too many to enumerate here. Winston Potter designed the book; Coghill Book Typsetting did the typesetting.

I also owe thanks to Lisa Price, who helped to obtain needed source material; to Michael Barba, who sorted through thousands of clippings and articles and shared the most important ones with me; and to James Feldman, Jr., who provided information on the law of war and the army's AirLand Battle program. Barbara Smith of the American Friends Service Committee provided essential information on Central America and the nonviolent movement in Brazil. Marian Neudel and Carol McNeill helped me formulate the ideas in the article on Women and War.

In preparing this manuscript I have drawn heavily upon many written sources. This would not have been possible without the Philadelphia Yearly Meeting Library and the Free Library of Philadelphia. The Center for Defense Information was also a resource whose value is impossible to overstate. The articles on Combat and on Conventional War drew on the work of John Keegan, a compassionate and perceptive observer of military history.

Special thanks, too, to the Central Committee for Conscientious Objectors for giving me the chance to talk with those people—soldiers, sailors, and potential draftees—who are most immediately affected by military policies. I have

vi

learned far more from my counselees, I think, than they learned from me.

And finally, I am grateful to Ruth Seeley, my wife, and Laura Jane Seeley, my daughter, for providing support and for so much else. A project like this is difficult; it would have been far more so without my family's encouragement.

Foreword

Aldous Huxley's *Encyclopedia of Pacifism* was edited for the Peace Pledge Union and was published in 1937. At once it became a major statement of the pacifist position. Those who have read it since have found it both challenging and inspiring. Those who had not read it—and they were the majority, even within the peace movement—had often heard about it and tried in vain to find it at libraries and bookstores. The *Encyclopedia* was published in a new edition by Garland Publishing Company in 1972, but even the new edition was hard to find.

Until recently I had never seen the book. My work on this edition thus became a dual opportunity: on the one hand, to write about war, peace, and nonviolence in an intensive and wide-ranging way, and, on the other, to read, finally, Huxley's *Encyclopedia* about which I had heard so much. In the process I came to appreciate the power of Huxley's mind and the magnitude of his achievement in ways I might not have done otherwise. What Huxley did was difficult, and he did it well. The *Encyclopedia* is not perfect, but few books are. It deserves to join the small shelf of pacifist classics.

The work is reprinted here. So much of the *Encyclopedia* speaks forcibly to our problems today that it could easily stand alone. But much has happened since Huxley's edited version. He could not have known in 1937 about nuclear weapons, Gandhi's liberation of India, King's nonviolent campaign in the South, "smart" weapons, the Indochina War, the Holocaust, and many other future events and issues. When the *Encyclopedia* was published Europe was the center of the political and military world, and—to name but one issue—counterinsurgency warfare was little known and had not yet acquired a name. Thus I have prepared a series of additional articles which, for the most part, do not overlap with Huxley's entries.

The new sections do not attempt to reproduce Huxley's reasoning or editing style. Even if I had wanted to, I could not have done so. Instead I have tried to choose significant topics, to provide some information on them, and to reflect on their meaning. This I think is what Huxley himself would have done if he had prepared new sections for the *Encyclopedia*. I would also like to thank The Peace Pledge Union and Chatto & Windus, The Hogarth Press for permission to reprint the *Encyclopedia*.

At the end of this book the reader will find a selected bibliography and a list of major peace groups. The bibliography will facilitate further study on topics considered in the body of the book; it is confined almost exclusively to books, with a few major articles from readily available periodicals. While the list of peace groups makes no attempt to be all-inclusive, the groups listed will provide readers with the names of local contacts.

Robert A. Seeley

Philadelphia, PA.
July 31, 1985

PART ONE

Aldous Huxley's
An Encyclopedia of Pacifism

An
Encyclopædia of Pacifism

Armaments, Private Manufacture of

The desire of arms manufacturers to make profits is a standing menace to world peace. It is in their interest to work for policies which are likely to produce dangerous international situations and to work against disarmament and the establishment of world peace, which would spoil their trade.

This trade is a very profitable one. Between 1915 and 1918 the American munition firm of Dupont de Nemour paid dividends amounting to 458 per cent of the part value of the original stock. According to British history of the Ministry of Munitions, the profits of J. P. Morgan & Co. amounted from 1914 to 1918, to more than $2,000 million. Recently British rearmament has brought substantial profits to manufacturers and especially financiers. In the *Daily Telegraph* of March 11, 1935, we read that Vickers Ltd. is giving a free three-fourths share for every six-eighth share held. The ordinary dividend for 1935 was raised from 6 per cent to 8 per cent. Writing in the *Peace Year Book*, Mr. Francis Williams estimates that the total profit to armament share interests during 1935 was more than £32 millions. More than £5 millions of this went into the pockets of the promoters who floated new aircraft companies.

The cynically anti-social attitude of the arms manufacturer is well expressed in the following remark, which is cited from an article in *The Aeroplane* for March 15, 1933. "The manufacturers of both aeroplanes and engines may hope for increased turnover and profits a year or so hence, when the Disarmament Conference has faded out and the programme of expansion is allowed to proceed."

In a Memorandum addressed to the Admiralty in 1919, Admiral of the Fleet Lord Wester Wemyss summed up the case against the arms manufacturer as follows: "Every firm engaged in the production of armaments and munitions of any kind naturally wants the largest output. Not only has it a direct interest in the inflation of the Navy and Army Estimates and in war scares, but it is equally to its interests to push its foreign business. For the more armaments are increased abroad, the more they must be increased at home.· This interrelation between foreign and home trade in armaments is one of the most subtle and dangerous features of the present system of private production. The evil is intensified by the existence of international armament rings, the members of which notoriously play into each other's hands. So long as this subterranean conspiracy against peace is allowed to continue, the possibility of any serious concerted reduction of armaments will be remote." In the United States an inquiry into private arms manufacture was held in 1934 and 1935, and in England a Royal Commission sat in 1935. Private manufacture still continues.

For the arms manufacturer, profit comes before patriotism. He will sell his products to any one who is prepared to buy, even though the buyer be an actual or potential enemy. In his evidence before the Arms Commission (1935) Mr. W. Arnold Forster mentioned the fact that a gun captured by the Bedfords in Palestine had the words "Made by Sir W. G. Armstrong Whitworth & Co." inscribed on it.

Agreement between arms manufacturers may even survive the outbreak of hostilities. During the World War, the Briey basin was not bombarded, because French and German armament makers had a gentlemen's agreement that neither side should be embarrassed in its production of munitions. The war was con-

2

sequently prolonged; but the profits of the manufacturers were increased.

That armament firms may take active steps to sabotage attempts at disarmament was demonstrated in the notorious Shearer case. In 1929 Mr. Shearer sued the three largest American shipbuilding companies for a quarter of a million dollars for services rendered at the Geneva Naval Conference of 1927. (They had already paid him fifty thousand dollars.) His duties at the Naval Conference were as follows: to work up fear of the British Navy by means of anti-British propaganda; to entertain naval officers and newspaper correspondents; to get big-navy publicity into reputable American journals in the guise of news; to discredit American peace organizations. Meanwhile, at home, he was to organize a lobby at Washington for the purpose of influencing federal legislation in favour of a big navy and merchant marine; he was to have articles inserted in magazines and lectures and addresses delivered before patriotic organizations, American Legion branches, Chambers of Commerce, etc. In brief, Mr. Shearer's business was, by all means in his power, to make it appear that the interests of the Bethlehem Shipbuilding Corporation, the Newport News Shipbuilding and Drydock Company, and the American Brown Boveri Corporation, were identical with the interests of the American people. (Cf. *Patriotism Ltd.* published by the Union of Democratic Control.)

The two points to notice here are these:

(1) Industrialists and financiers brought up in the capitalist ethic will behave (probably with a perfectly clear conscience) in ways that are morally outrageous and socially mischievous.

(2) Ordinary people, who stand to make no profit out of war, can be swept off their feet by bellicose propaganda, however discreditable its origin. Exploiters and Exploitees are equally the victims of their upbringing in a society which esteems above everything success, possessions, triumph at the expense of others. Not only the economic system, but also what may be called the psycho-

logical system of our societies requires changing. The two are related, and yet in some measure independent of one another. A desirable change in the economic system would not automatically produce a change in the psychological system sufficiently great to make war impossible. That is why it is essential that there should be associations of men and women specifically pledged to put pacifist principles into action in all the circumstances of life in personal relations, in economic relations, in politics, in education.

(See *Arms Trade, Nationalization of; Economic Reform and Pacifism; Education and Peace.*)

Armaments Race

The two points to be noticed in regard to the Armaments Race are the following:

(1) All statesmen insist that the armaments of their own nation are being prepared solely for reasons of defence.

(2) All statesmen insist that the existence of armaments in a foreign country constitutes a reason for the immediate creation of new armaments at home.

"Germany is making her preparations not in order to *attack* anyone, but to insure that no one shall be able to attack or bully our country again" (Dr. Rudolf Kircher, Editor of the *Frankfurter Zeitung*, in a letter to the *Spectator*, November 11, 1936).

"We should never use our forces for aggression. They threaten no-one, and no-one is afraid that they do. We do not desire forces greater than are necessary for our own defence and to enable us to fulfil our responsibilities" (Mr. Neville Chamberlain in a speech at Kelso, September 21, 1935).

Such quotations could be multiplied indefinitely. Every nation is defending itself against the defensive measures of all the other nations. (See *Example.*)

4

Arms Trade, Nationalization of

The private manufacture of armaments is morally disgraceful, and at the same time, as has been shown in the article on the subject, politically dangerous. Reformers have, therefore, proposed that the manufacture of armaments should be entirely nationalized. (In recent years the State has manufactured about five-twelfths of the armaments used by Great Britain—private firms about seven-twelfths.) This would certainly liberate governments from the influence of socially irresponsible profit-makers. But it must not be imagined that nationalization is a complete solution of the problem. Private manufacture of armaments is morally outrageous and politically dangerous; but so, in its own way, is the manufacture of armaments by the nation.

(1) Instruments of murder are always instruments of murder, whether privately or publicly manufactured.

(2) State manufacture would give a certain legal sanction to the production of these instruments. The mass of unthinking public opinion would feel that an officially sanctioned armament industry must somehow be respectable. The total abolition of the evil thing would consequently become more difficult.

(3) Nationalization of the armament industry would lead to an undesirable strengthening of the already too powerful authority.

(4) The State is more powerful than any private employer. The personnel of a nationalized arms industry could be dragooned and bribed so as to become a kind of technical army at the disposal of the executive.

(5) The armament industries of highly industrialized States would be in a position to supply or withhold war material from less-developed States. In this way it would be possible for States with efficient arms monopolies to exercise political pressure upon their neighbours. (See *Economic Reform and Pacifism.*)

Nationalization or armament manufacture is merely the substitution of one evil for another. What is needed is complete abolition. If machinists, railway workers and dockers were to refuse to co-operate in the manufacture or transport of armaments, and if this movement were supported by a refusal to co-operate in the production of militaristic propaganda on the part of the writers, printers and teachers, the iniquitous preparations for mass murder would soon be effectively brought to a stop. (See B. de Ligt, *Mobilisation contre toute guerre.*)

Biology and War

War is often described as a Law of Nature. This is not true. Among the lower animals war is unknown. True, there are carnivores which prey upon other animals; but their activities are no more war-like than are the activities of fishermen or butchers. Moreover, the existence of carnivores should not blind us to the fact that there is at least as much co-operation in nature as strife.

Individuals of the same species often fight together; but these fights are seldom pushed to a finish; the conquered is rarely killed or even permanently hurt. Such duels waged in the heat of passion, under the stress of hunger or sexual impulse, are quite unlike war, which is mass murder, scientifically prepared in cold blood.

In nature, it is only among the social insects, such as the ants and termites, that we meet with anything resembling war. And even here the resemblance is only superficial. Insect wars are conducted by members of one species against members of another species. Man is the only creature to organize mass murder of his own species.

It is often argued that war is inevitable, since man is descended from pugnacious ancestors, akin to the gorilla. This is probably not the case. Most zoologists are now of the opinion that man's ancestors was not a gorilla-like ape, but a gentle, sensitive creature, something like a tarsier. In any case, the gifts which brought man his extraordinary biological success were not ruthlessness and brute strength (plenty of animals are much stronger and fiercer

6

than he is), but co-operation, intelligence, wondering curiosity and sensitiveness. In the words of Charles Darwin, "The small strength and speed of man and his want of natural weapons are more than counterbalanced firstly, by his intellectual faculties (chiefly or exclusively gained for the benefit of the community), and secondly, by those social qualities which led him to give and receive aid from his fellowmen."

Another biological argument often invoked in defence of war is the following: War is civilization's equivalent of natural selection; it acts as nature's pruning-hook, ensuring the survival of the fittest. This is obviously untrue. War tends to kill off the young and healthy and to spare the unhealthy and those who are too old to beget children. In the second place, there is no reason to suppose that warlike peoples are superior to unwarlike peoples. Even if the violent were to survive (and war is just as likely to kill them off as to ensure the persistence of their stock), this would not necessarily mean the survival of the most satisfactory type of human being. The most violent are not the best human beings; nor, conversely, are the most valuable necessarily the strongest. In so far as war is an agent of selection it selects dysgenically, ensuring the survival, not of the more desirable, but of the less desirable human strains. In the past war's capacity to do harm was limited by the fact that the instruments of destruction at men's disposal were crude and inadequate. Today, thanks to technological progress, they are enormously efficient. War, therefore, has now become as dangerous to human societies, and even to the whole human species, as cancer is to the human body. War is "natural" to exactly the same extent as cancer is "natural."

British Empire

An area comprising about one-quarter of the land surface of the world, and about one-quarter of its population, which is either

controlled by, or associated with, Great Britain, and which oc-
cupies this position as a result of various historical causes. Chief
among these causes are (a) that we were victorious in the great
wars of the sixteenth, seventeenth and eighteenth centuries; (b)
that we preceded all the other nations in the development of the
modern industrial system, which creates a demand for markets
and fields of investment outside the mother-country, and so led
to the imperialist aggressions of the nineteenth century.

The claims of British colonists to self-governing institutions,
which caused the loss of the American colonies in 1782, raised
a problem which was solved, partially at least, by granting self-
government to Canada, Australia, New Zealand, and the white
population of the Union of South Africa.

There are, therefore, speaking broadly, two distinct parts of
the Empire: (a) a "White Empire," which might fairly be called
a "Commonwealth of Nations," comprising a population of about
65 millions, and (b) a "Dark Empire," which is ruled from
above with about 385 millions. In effect, there is a Commonwealth
ruling an Empire; though in India, Burma, Ceylon and the West
Indies some steps have been taken towards self-government for
the "Dark" populations. (See *Mandates; Imperialism and Colonies; Defence.*)

British Influence,
Effect of Pacifism on

It is often stated, as an argument against pacifism, that a disarmed Britain would lose all influence in world affairs and that,
since this influence is an influence for good, the world would
suffer. Britain should be strong for the benefit of humanity in
general.

In regard to this contention we may make the following
remarks:

8

(1) The identical argument was used by Hitler to justify German rearmament. A weak Germany, he proclaimed, was a source of general insecurity; a strong Germany would be a blessing for the whole world. We regard Hitler's argument as a tissue of sophistries. Why should our own exactly similar argument deserve to be regarded differently?

(2) All countries regard themselves as virtuous; all take it for granted that any war in which they take part will be a war of defence, not of aggression; all believe that it is only the imperialism of other nations that is bad. British aims, motives and methods are not regarded by others with the same admiration as we give to them ourselves. We may think that the influence which our enormous navy allowed us to exercise throughout the world was wholly good; others are not of this opinion. The truth of the matter would seem to be that any imperialism, including our own, is bad.

(3) British influence upon the world was based upon sea power. Because Britain was invulnerable and because the British Navy controlled the seas, we were able, during the eighteenth and nineteenth centuries to add colony to colony, to seize strategic ports and establish naval bases and coaling stations throughout the world. In narrow seas the navy is now an ineffective instrument. Sea power has therefore lost most of its significance. If we imagine that we can continue to have the kind of influence that was ours during the nineteenth century, we are cherishing an illusion. The foundations of that power—domination of the sea—have slipped away from under us. The game of imperialism is one which, whether we like it or no, we are no longer in a position to play. To make believe that we are what we were during Queen Victoria's reign is merely silly. The facts of the contemporary world are such that we cannot hope to go on having the kind of influence we once possessed.

(4) If we really wish to exercise a beneficent influence upon the world (and, incidentally, at the same time to save our own country from irremediable ruin) we should do all in our power

to induce the government to get rid of its armaments and either to liberate outright its subject people or else, where this did not seem practicable, to hand over the administration of them to a genuinely international authority. Such a policy would do more for peace than any other that a British government could pursue. Our present policy, which consists in combining vulnerability at home with menaces abroad, is a policy that fairly invites war—a war in which, owing to the rise of air power, we shall suffer more than any other nation. Menacing rearmament is our surest way of losing whatever influence we ever possessed; disarmament, even unilateral disarmament, is our surest way of regaining influence—a genuinely beneficent influence for peace. (See *Defence*.)

Causes of War

The main causes of war are of three kinds: (1) the pursuit of wealth, (2) the pursuit of glory, (3) the advocacy of a creed. Usually all three are combined in varying proportions, as, for example in the Book of Joshua. The economic motive has various forms:

(a) Occupation of fruitful territory—e.g. Whites and Indians in United States.

(b) Plunder—e.g. Romans in Asia Minor; Cortez and Pisarro.

(c) Trade—e.g. English and Dutch in seventeenth century.

(d) Markets and fields for investment—most modern imperialist wars.

(e) Raw materials—e.g. Japan in China, France and Germany as regards Lorraine.

The motion of glory is usually dynastic or governmental—for example, the ancient Assyrians and Persians, and eighteenth-century wars so far as the Continent of Europe is concerned. But it can be made popular by propaganda, and always has been made so since the French Revolution.

Creed wars may be religious or political; usually they are both. They almost always also have economic motives. The early Mohammedans, for example, had economic motives (*a*) and (*b*); the Protestants wished to secure church lands and revenues; and so on. The English Civil War combined religious and political motives in equal measure. The Albigensian crusade was, on the part of the instigators, more economic than political. The French revolutionary wars, the American Civil War, and the various civil wars since 1815, involved important politico-economic issues, and were all, in a greater or less degree, creed wars.

The main causes predisposing to modern war are: first, the competition between States for markets and raw materials; secondly, the competition between classes as regards the distribution of the national wealth. These two causes are intertwined, because different governments stand for different economic systems. (See *Economic Reform and Pacifism; Education and Peace.*)

Chemical Warfare

During the Crimean War Lord Dundonald proposed that sulphur fumes should be used against Sebastopol. The War Office rejected the proposal on the grounds that "an operation of this nature would contravene the laws of civilized warfare."

Gases much more poisonous than sulphur fumes were used in the last war, first by the Germans, then by all the combatants. In 1925 the Powers met at Geneva and signed a Protocol completely prohibiting the use of gas in warfare. It is clear, however, that no nation considers itself bound by its pledges in this matter. Chemical research is carried on by the military authorities in every country. Everywhere it is taken for granted that, in the next war, open towns will be subjected to intensive chemical bombardment from the air. The Geneva Gas Protocol of 1925 is treated in advance as merely a scrap of paper.

The principal chemicals used in the last war were as follows:

Chlorine. The gas first used by the Germans. Attacks the air cells of the lungs.

Chloropicrine. Attacks lungs and eyes. It is a liquid and, when scattered, continues to give off poisonous vapours for many hours.

Phosgene. Similar to chloropicrine, but more poisonous. From the military point of view it is not very satisfactory as it is a gas, not a liquid; consequently does not poison the ground, but is blown away by the wind.

Mustard Gas. This is a liquid and can contaminate ground for days and even weeks. Two or three hours after exposure to mustard gas the patient begins to cough and vomit; his eyes are inflamed; his throat is parched. Next the skin begins to itch and large blisters form all over the body. At the end of the first day "the patient lies virtually blinded, with tears oozing between bulging œdematous eyelids." After the second day acute bronchitis develops. Second-day infections then set in, causing broncho-pneumonia. Death occurs at any date from the second day to the fourth week. "With ill-protected troops the death-rate may be very high." (*Note.*—The civilian population is not protected at all.)

Lewisite. Similar to mustard gas, but more poisonous, owing to its arsenic content. It has been calculated that fifty bombers each carrying five thousand pounds of lewisite could, under perfect conditions, poison an area fifty miles long and thirty-five miles wide.

Thermite. A mixture of powdered aluminum and iron oxide. When ignited, rises to a temperature of 5000° centigrade—nearly as hot as the surface of the sun. A small thermite bomb, no bigger than a cricket ball, is enough to start a fire. A single plane could carry many hundreds of such bombs.

All the foregoing substances were known in 1918. Much research has been devoted to chemical warfare since that date and it is certain that considerable improvements have been made both in the substances themselves and in the methods of using them.

How is it proposed to defend civil populations against chemical attacks?

In 1932 Mr. Baldwin said: "The only defence is in offence, which means that you have to kill women and children more quickly than the enemy if you want to save yourselves." In 1936, Colonel Lindbergh affirmed that there was now no such thing as a defensive war. It is significant that the main increase in the Air Force is an increase in bombers—that is to say in instruments of aggression, not of defence.

Meanwhile, there is talk of gas masks, gas drill, and the like. Gas masks cannot be worn by young children, by the aged, or by those with any weakness of the lungs. Moreover, even if they could be supplied to all those physically capable of wearing them, they would be perfectly useless against mustard gas or lewisite, which do not affect the lungs alone, but the entire body. Why should an enemy obligingly use chemicals against which some protection exists, when he can drop other substances against which there is no protection?

A bombardment with a mixture of thermite, high explosives and vesicants would kill large numbers outright, would lead to the cutting off of food and water supplies, would smash the system of sanitation and would result in general panic. There will be a frantic rush out of the towns. Those who are not crushed to death in this first rush will die of starvation and disease later on. The chief use of the army will be, not to fight an enemy, but to try to keep order among the panic-stricken population at home.

China, Pacifism in

Confucianism holds up the ideal of the just, reasonable, humane and cultivated man, living in an ordered and harmonious society. Europeans have always unduly admired the military hero and the martyr. Not so the Chinese. "The traditional conception of Confucianism," writes Max Weber, "tends to prefer a wise prudence to mere physical courage and to declare that an untimely sacrifice of life is unfitting for a wise man." The European preference for military heroism and martyrdom is a most unfortunate one; for it has tended to make men believe that death was more important than life and that a long course of folly and crime could be cancelled out by a single act of physical courage. In this way it has provided justifications for every kind of atrocity, from religious persecution to aggressive imperialism. Plato was of the same opinion as Confucius. "Many a mercenary soldier will take his stand and be ready to die at his post; and yet they are generally and almost without exception insolent, unjust, violent men and the most senseless of human beings." To die courageously is less important (though of course a man should be ready, if necessary, to sacrifice his life in a noble cause) than to live humanely, harmoniously, intelligently. Such is the teaching of Confucianism.

Confucius was a rationalist. Lao Tsu, or whoever was the author of the *Tao Te Ching*, was a mystic. The Tao, or way, is an eternal, cosmic principle, which is at the same time the inmost root of the individual's being. Philosophically, the doctrines expressed in the *Tao Te Ching* are akin to those current in Indian thought. Its ethical teachings—the command to return good for evil, to cultivate humility, to refrain from assertiveness and self-importance—are similar in many respects to those of Jesus.

Since the time of Confucius and Lao Tsu, Chinese ideals have been essentially pacific. European poets have glorified war; European theologians have sanctified religious persecution and nationalistic aggression. This has not been the case in China. Chinese religion, whether Confucian, Taoist or Buddhist, has always been anti-militarist. So have the majority of the great Chinese poets. The soldier was regarded as an inferior being, not to be put on the same level with the scholar or the administrator.

The Chinese have shown themselves capable of carrying out very effective non-violent resistance to aggression. During the World War, for example, Japanese aggression was resisted by non-co-operation in the form of a boycott of Japanese goods. In 1925, a number of Chinese students were shot by British troops. The reply was a boycott which caused the English to lose nearly three-quarters of their trade with China.

In recent years, the great tradition of Chinese pacifism has shown signs of weakening. China is being Westernized. This means, in practice, that its inhabitants are being supplied with modern weapons, conscripted (the law was promulgated in 1936) and drilled. (See *Christ, The Teaching of; Christian Church's Attitude to War, The; India, Pacifism in.*)

Books: the most complete history of Pacifist ideas and practice is *La Paix Créatrice*, by B. de Ligt, published by Marcel Rivière, rue Jacob, Paris.

Christ, The Teaching of

For the teaching of Christ in regard to war and the overcoming of evil the chief authorities are the several elements which are contained in the Synoptic Gospels, the relevant passages in St. Paul's Epistles and such evidence as can be found elsewhere in the New Testament. His teaching has been too frequently sought only in isolated sayings divorced from their setting and interpreted as legislative enactments. But for Christians who believe that His intention was never legislation, that His character is a consistent whole, and that His authority depends upon the quality of His person and the spirit of His actions rather than upon isolated and edited utterance, it is more important to consider the significance of His crucifixion than to debate particular points, such as the alleged use of a whip in the Temple-market (John ii, 15), or the cryptic and despairing "It is enough!" (Luke xxii. 38), or the parable of the strong man armed—who is obviously the devil! (Luke xi, 21).

In any case it is not easy as the whole record of the Church's attempts to justify war proves (the *Summa Theologiæ* falls back upon a quotation from John the Baptist) to quote any authority from Christ. If we appeal to isolated sayings, such words as "Do not offer violence in opposing evil" (Matt. v, 39) which St. Paul explains by adding, "But overcome evil with good" (Rom. xii. 21), or "They that take the sword shall perish by the sword" (Matt. xxvi. 52), are at once more explicit and more representative: and the principle that the more unconventional the sayings are the less likely are they to be later, or edited, is a sound one. For those who cling to the supposed sanction of one or other of the familiar "pro-war" sayings Dr. G. H. C. MacGregor's recent volume provides a full examination of them.

In considering the general meaning of Christ the following points are surely indisputable: (1) He regarded God as always and everywhere the Father whose dealings with His creatures are motivated only by love: to assert that God uses alternative methods—love and justice—and that love is not always applicable is to deny either that God is what Jesus taught or that He is in any real sense God. (2) In consequence men are persons, not pawns or slaves, and their freedom to reject must never be overborne by force whether of violence or of bribery or of the supernatural. At His temptation (Matt. iv. 1-11, Luke iv. 1-13) Jesus repudiated these three ways of coercing men. The method of His whole ministry is consistent with this repudiation; He rejected the nationalist policy of the Zealots, the cheapening and materializing of His own demands, the use of psychic or miraculous powers to enforce assent. (3) In presenting His call to His people He refused to admit either by resistance or by flight that the last word lay with armed force: indeed, by accepting the Cross He challenged this common assumption and disproved it. Non-resistance, seeming at first to fail, actually and signally triumphed. His crucifixion transformed His disciples and changed the course of history. The Cross, the symbol of non-resistance, has been, however, inappropriately, the Church's sacred emblem ever since.

The new way of life thus initiated was accepted and proclaimed by the earliest disciples. Love, joy, peace, fortitude were acknowledged as the fruit of Christ's spirit: martyrdom was the Christian

16

answer to militarism: warfare was with the powers of evil—
of the spirit not of the flesh. The only book in the New Testament that shows evidence of another way, the Revelation, is a
product rather of Jewish apocalyptic than of Christian patience,
and was in fact regarded as non-canonical by the best minds of
the early Church. For them military service was a thing impossible: violence was condemned: and war was an outrage against
God. (See *China, Pacifism in; Christian Church's Attitude to
War, The; India, Pacifism in.*)

Christian Church's Attitude to War

Contrary to the widely-held and oft-repeated view that Jesus
himself gave no verdict on the rightness or wrongness of war, it
is clear on several grounds that He was convinced of its wrongness, and that He taught, acted, and suffered accordingly. Several
conditions, however, impeded the clear grasp of this verdict on
the part of His early followers, for example, the remoteness of
the whole question (as a practical issue) from the lives of most
of them, their consequent absorption in many more immediate
spiritual and moral questions, the war-stories in Scripture, the
difficulty of seeing how the Emperor (regarded by all as God-
ordained) could get on without an army, and the tendency of
simple-minded Christians to take the line of least resistance in
face of a complex problem. Hence during the first three centuries, we see two processes going on side by side: (1) the expansion of the Church leading first to the conversion of soldiers
who remained soldiers, and then to the enforced or even voluntary enlistment of Christians in the army: and (2) the Christian
ethic of love making it increasingly clear to the thoughtful Christians that the profession of Christianity was incompatible with a
military life. There probably existed a few Christian soldiers from
the very first, but we do not hear of them in any numbers until

A.D. 170. Most early Christian authors, on the other hand, speak of gentleness, bloodshed, etc., in such a way as to suggest that, if consistent, they must have held that no Christian could fight: yet we find no explicit mention of this precise issue till A.D. 177–80, when Celsus' attack on Christianity seems to presuppose a general refusal on the part of Christians to serve in the legions. This refusal was expressly approved and defended by Tertullian (even in his pre-Montanist days), Hippolytus, and Origen in the third century, and Lactantius early in the fourth century. Of these the most significant is Origen, who writes as if a refusal to fight were the normal Christian position, bases this refusal not on any dread of contamination from idolatry, but on Jesus' ethical teaching, and defends it (with a theory of the special function of Christians in the world) against the current charge of incivism. Round about A.D. 300 we get cases of men punished for refusing, when required, to serve as soldiers: the best known is that of Maximilian, martyred in Northern Africa in A.D. 295.

When Constantine became supreme in A.D. 313, the Church was so grateful to him for delivering her from prolonged and crushing persecution and for graciously and generously patronizing her, that it would have been exceedingly difficult—even if her mind had been clearly and unanimously made up—for her to adhere to a strictly pacifist attitude. As Christian feeling was far from being unanimous, such an adherence was out of the question. There is no need to doubt the sincerity of Constantine's conversion: but his alliance with the Church necessarily committed her to a willingness to allow lay-Christians to fight under him and his successors. This turnover in conviction did not indeed come all at once. During the fourth century, individual Christians refused service, individual writers expressed approval of such refusal, and —more significant still—certain codes of Church-procedure in the East still maintained the old pacifist rigour. But, broadly speaking, the case had gone by default. Henceforth, for many centuries—though from time to time the Church exerted herself in the cause of peace—the only surviving trace of the Origenist position was the rigid refusal to allow *the clergy* to shed blood in war: but ways were found now and then for evading even this restriction. The refusal of a layman to serve as a soldier became a mark of heresy: it was one of the characteristics of the Cathari or Albigenses, who were so mercilessly persecuted in the thirteenth century.

When the Reformation came—early in the sixteenth century—the return to Biblical religion re-opened the problem. Erasmus gave a strong lead by his eloquent denunciations of war. Luther at first was strongly inclined to a strict obedience to the Sermon on the Mount: but he entirely gave this up (except as purely abstract theory) after 1525, and taught that Christians must accommodate themselves to the needs of an imperfect world so far as to fight when required. Calvin, by a different theoretical route, arrived at a similar result even less reluctantly. The pacifist practice was, however, maintained by the Anabaptist groups up and down Europe, and defended both by them and by Faustus Socinus. Its positive service to human progress was totally overlooked. It was felt to be socially so dangerous that it greatly embittered the persecution to which Anabaptists and Socianians were subjected by both Catholics and Protestants.

Since the sixteenth century, pacifist practice has been maintained for the most part only by comparatively small non-Catholic sects —such as the Doukhobors in Russia, the Mennonites in the Low Countries, and the Quakers in England. Individuals in other Protestant bodies have from time to time revealed the uneasiness of the conscience of Christendom by advocating pacifism as the truly Christian way: but it was not until the Great War (more particularly the introduction of conscription in England) that Christian men on any large scale were roused to face the issue afresh. The conscientious-objection-movement, and all the discussion that has gone on concerning it since 1914, have introduced a fresh chapter in the history of Christian ethics, and necessitated a deeper consideration of the issues involved than has ever been given to them since the days of Origen.

Civil War

Societies cannot hold together without traditional loyalties and habits of confidence, kindness and forbearance. More even than international war, civil war destroys these essential conditions of a tolerable social life. England has had no foreign invasion since 1066 and no considerable revolution since 1688. That is why democratic institutions have been able to flourish here. They cannot flourish in countries where civil wars are frequent.

Once civil war has actually begun, it is hard for the pacifist to act with much effect. He must therefore do all he can, while peaceful conditions prevail, to prevent civil war from ever breaking out. He must refuse to join political parties pledged to intolerance and the persecution of their enemies; and he must do his best to dissuade others from joining such parties.

If the pacifist finds himself confronted with the *fait accompli* of civil war, what should be his policy? In his pamphlet on Spain, Mr. Runham Brown has written on this problem as follows: "I am not opposed to the use of a certain measure of physical force; but that force must be a restraining force and not a destructive one. . . . If I found that the reactionaries were in such numbers or possessed of such weapons as to make restraint impossible and that mass destruction was the only means of subduing them, I should definitely reject that method, even if I had to allow them to take control; but if they did take control, it would not be with my help. I should refuse them all co-operation, refuse to become their tool and should use my best efforts to bring everything to a standstill." Summing up, we may say that the pacifist's policy in regard to civil war should be as follows: pacification of mutually intolerant groups in time of peace; restraint of the war-makers at the first outbreak of civil strife; then, if that proved impossible without mass murder, non-co-operation. (See *Revolution*.)

Class War

The pacifist does not ignore the existence of the so-called Class War in modern capitalistic society. Nor is he indifferent to it. Without necessarily accepting the Marxian analysis of our social order, it is evident that just as there are "Haves" and "Have-nots" among the nations, so there are among the social strata within the nations. The wealthier and more powerful classes tend to live by the exploitation of their fellows. Such a state of affairs is contrary to pacifist principles. It involves moreover much unnecessary suffering and even death through conditions of starvation or semi-starvation, inadequate precautions against accidents (because these would involve a reduction of profits), sweated employment, etc. Modern industry takes a huge toll of life and health, most of which could be avoided. Employers exercise economic power over employés (which is essentially non-moral). Friction and hatred result.

The pacifist's sympathy is naturally with the exploited and the down-trodden. The spirit of the class war and particularly any recourse to violence in the furthering of it are, however, anathema to him. He must seek a solution of the social conflict along other lines. An important step forward is to show to all concerned that the idea of the class war is based on conditions which no longer exist. In a world of economic scarcity, the wealth of one group means the poverty of another. But we live in an age of potentially unlimited plenty. There is, therefore, no economic reason for the class struggle. There is however a psychological factor. Some men desire power over others. This lust for power is the principal source of evil and it is essential to combat it by every means, psychological as well as political. The educational system must be so designed that it shall turn children into free and responsible human beings, not into militarists. (See *Education and Peace*.) Executive power must be decentralized, so that there shall be genuine democracy and widespread self-government. (See *Political Implications of Pacifism*.) The economic power in the hands of individuals must be limited and the principle of co-operation extended. (See *Economic Implications of Pacifism, Consumers' Co-operative Movement, The*.) The power-religions of nation, race and class must be combated. (See *Nationalistic Religion*.) In the meantime we must do everything we can to secure a decent standard of life for every human being.

In the social struggle, as in the international field, the problem needs deep study of possible ways of transforming our present chaotic system into an orderly one based on the pacifist principle of co-operation for the common good. As in the international field, the technique of non-violence will prove the most effective weapon. (See *Civil War; Economic Implications of Pacifism*.)

Communism and Fascism

The way in which violence begets violence is very clearly illustrated by the history of the rise of Communism and of Fascism. The Communist revolution in Russia was the fruit of violence. Tsarist tyranny had prepared the ground, sowing hatred and resentment among the oppressed masses. In 1917 the fabric of Russian society had been reduced to chaos by the impact of war. Military violence gave the revolutionaries their opportunity; violently, they seized it. More military violence, in the shape of the White Russian and allied attacks upon the Bolshevists, confirmed the new régime in its essentially anti-pacifist principles. Marxian theory had from the first insisted upon the necessity of violence; but even if they had not desired to do so, circumstances would have compelled the Bolsheviks to put the Marxian theory of violence into practice. Communism became a militant, even a militaristic creed.

22

Communist violence in Italy, itself produced in large measure by the disruptive violence of war, evoked violent reaction. Fascism was born and, after a period of civil strife, came to power.

In the case of Germany, the allies were given ample opportunity to behave with justice and generosity; but, during the fifteen years which preceded the accession of Hitler, Germany was treated with consistent injustice. Such concessions as were made were always made reluctantly and so late that they never did anything to allay the bitterness of German public opinion. In Nazism, Frenchmen and Englishmen are reaping the fruits of their governments' stupid inhumanity and injustice. Hitler's violence is the answer to the arrogance of France and England and, to a less extent, to the militant propaganda of Russian Communism—itself, as we have seen, a product of earlier violence.

Anti-Communists call upon us to suppress Communism by violence; anti-Fascists exhort us to answer the threats of Nazism with counter-threats. Both parties would have us reply to violence with violence. In other words both would have us do precisely those things which, as the history of the last twenty years makes so abundantly clear, are certain to produce the greatest possible amount of tyranny, war and civil strife. Pacifists are people who profit by the lessons of history; militarists, whether of the right or the left, are people who are determined not to learn by experience. (See *Revolution; Civil War.*)

Consumers' Co-operative Movement

The Consumers' Co-operative Movement must not be confused with the "Army and Navy" or any other stores. Nor must it be looked on as just a prosaic method of thrift, nor dismissed because of its imperfections.

It is, as a matter of fact, an economic and ethical revolution, and a colossal structure, existing in over thirty countries, for carrying on trade and industry by organized consumers. It is

23

built up by working-class capital, and is therefore free from capitalist control and speculation.

The watch-words of the Movement are "Production for Use, not for Profit," and "Government by the People for the People." Its motto is "Each for All and All for Each."

What is familiarly known as the "divi" is the method by which capitalist profit-making is abolished, because the surplus on trading does not go to the owners of capital, but is in the main (after paying a fixed interest on capital) returned to the purchasers according to the amount of their purchases.

The British and Irish Movement has 7½ million members. Membership of local "Co-ops" is open to everyone who takes up a £1 share (payable by instalments). Shares are withdrawable and no one can hold more than 200. Members elect the Management and other Committees, and, through the Quarterly Meetings, control the general policy. Voting is on the principle of "one person, one vote," whatever the number of shares held.

These societies form a network over nearly the whole of the country. In 1935 their trade was nearly £221 millions. They have proved a valuable check on the raising of prices by local rings, for example, in bread, coal and milk. In the milk trade, they have been the pioneers in many places of the latest hygienic methods. Most societies give grants for education and recreation, amounting in 1935 to over £251,000. Since these figures were published, striking progress has been made; for example, in London (which was a co-operative desert in 1900) a trade of £28 millions is done by about 1¼ million members.

The distributive societies have formed themselves into *Federations* for national purposes, with thoroughly democratic constitutions. On the trading and manufacturing side, the most important are the English, Scottish and Irish *Co-operative Wholesale Societies*. Their trade amounted in 1935 to nearly £117½ millions. The English C.W.S. also carries on Banking and Insurance at its headquarters in Manchester, the Mecca of Co-operators from all over the world. Its soap production makes a breach in the Soap

24

Monopoly. Altogether the C.W.S. is the largest business dealing in domestic supplies in Britain. It has carried on friendly trade and other relations with the Russian Co-operators for the last fifteen years.

The Co-operative Union deals with legal matters, parliamentary legislation, propaganda, agriculture, etc. It holds the Annual Co-operative Congress of delegates from affiliated societies. Its educational work comprises a College, with training for teachers, research and statistical work.

An additional feature of the educational and propaganda doings of the movement is the un-official "Guilds," the largest of these being the Women's Co-operative Guild, with nearly 80,000 members. It is recognized by the official bodies, but is independent in its action. It has specialized in rank and file co-operative education and policy, and on the reforms needed in married working women's lives, for example, its successful campaign for a co-operative women's minimum wage and for Maternity Benefit. It strongly supports complete pacifism.

The British Movement which employs about 300,000 workers has a good record as regards hours and wages. It originated the weekly half-holiday in shops, pays trade union (or higher) wages; and the C.W.S. and many of the large societies require their employés to be trade unionists; there is a system of arbitration in disputes. It is a splendid stand-by for the workers in lock-outs and strikes.

Owing to capitalist attacks, co-operators have formed a political party and entered Parliament, where they work with the Labour Party.

The Co-operative Press publishes a variety of periodicals, including the *Co-operative News*, and it now owns *Reynolds' News*, the old radical Sunday paper.

A world-wide Federation, the International Co-operative Alliance, has been formed by the movements of thirty countries, laying the foundation of an Economic League of Peoples. It was the only organization which maintained contact with all its members during the War. (See *Economic Implications of Pacifism*.)

Cost of War

The cost of the Great War has been reckoned at about four hundred thousand million dollars, or eighty thousand million pounds. According to figures quoted by Dr. Nicholas Murray Butler in his 1934 report to the Carnegie Foundation this sum would have sufficed to provide every family in America, Canada, Australia, Great Britain and Ireland, France, Belgium, Germany and Russia with a five-hundred pound house, two hundred pounds worth of furniture, and a hundred pounds worth of land. Every town of twenty thousand inhabitants and over in all the above-mentioned countries, could have been presented with a library to the value of a million pounds and a university to the value of two millions. After which it would have been possible to buy the whole of France and Belgium, that is all the land, houses, factories, railways, churches, roads, harbours, etc., in these countries. In 1914 the total value of France was, according to official statistics, sixty-two thousand million dollars; the total value of Belgium, twelve thousand million dollars. This means that, with the money required to impose the Treaty of Versailles upon Germany, one could have bought, lock, stock and barrel, five countries as large as France and five others as large as Belgium. To impose this same Treaty of Versailles thirteen millions of human beings were killed outright, while war conditions were responsible for the death of many millions more.

Defence

Most military experts are agreed that it is impossible to defend large cities, such as London or Birmingham, against attack from the air. A cynically frank article in the *Army, Navy and Air Force Gazette* informs us how the fighting forces regard our anti-aircraft defences. "However completely we may guard our country in the air, it is more than likely that enemy bombers will get through. If they are permitted to carry out destruction unimpeded, the great danger is that the will of the people to continue the struggle, which is the mainspring of victory, will give way. If, on the other hand, the searchlights are playing and the guns are banging, they will not feel that they are the victims of Government incompetence and neglect as well as of unprovoked aggression, and will be willing to continue the struggle." The guns must bang, not because the banging will prevent women and children from being massacred, but because the noise will encourage people to go on with the war, that is, consent to the massacre of yet more women and children.

Anti-aircraft guns and interceptor planes cannot prevent all the bombers from reaching their destination. (Air-Marshal Sir Robert Brooke Popham goes so far as to say that "in the next war enemy aeroplanes will only meet one another by accident or by mutual design.") Some of the raiders will doubtless be brought down; but enough will get through to spread death, destruction and panic. The chief result of anti-aircraft fire and interceptor attack will be to make the raiders drop their bombs hurriedly and therefore inaccurately. An unopposed raid might, if the raiders so desired, be directed against particular military objectives, such as government offices, barracks, aerodromes, factories, railway stations and the like. An attack opposed by guns and interceptors would not be stopped, it would merely be made indiscriminate. In their anxiety to get out of the danger zone, raiders will content themselves with dumping their fire and poison at any point on the enormous targets spread out beneath them. By compelling raiders to fly higher than they would otherwise do, balloon barrages will produce the same result as anti-aircraft guns and interceptors. So will black-outs. From a great height you cannot trace the topography of a darkened city in detail; but you can see

27

the city as a whole. All the anti-aircraft defences hitherto devised guarantee only one thing; that the aerial bombardment shall have the maximum of imprecision—in other words, that the civil population, and not any specifically military objective, shall be the principal target.

It may be remarked that defences against land attack tend to produce the same results. Thus, there is reason to believe that the Maginot line of fortification which guards France's eastern frontier and which is now to be extended to the Channel, is practically impregnable. If the Germans were to attack France, would they waste their resources in storming defences which cannot be taken? Obviously not. The very strength of France's purely military defences makes it certain that any attack against her will be directed against the civil population from the air. The existence of the Maginot line is the guarantee that in any future war Paris will be bombed.

In a recent series of articles the military correspondent of *The Times* pointed out that, so far as land warfare is concerned, the power of defence has increased more rapidly than the power of attack. It is unlikely that a land offensive could succeed against troops armed with the weapons which modern technology has placed at their disposal. This being so, it is obvious that strategists will not waste their resources in attempting the impossible. They will strike where the enemy's armour is weakest—that is to say, at the civil population in large cities.

Because it is an island, because it is not self-supporting, because it is densely populated, England is more vulnerable than any other European country. Paris and Berlin are far from the frontiers of France and Germany; London, a far larger city, is situated within a few miles of the frontier of England. Most of our food comes from abroad, and the ships carrying it have to pass through narrow seas which no navy can defend from air attacks. One port, that of London, supplies a quarter of the whole population. Nothing would be easier than to paralyse the port of London. If this happened, those eleven millions who are fed from London

28

would have to subsist on accumulated supplies. But the accumulated supplies of food in this country are very small and most of them are stored at the ports, where they could be destroyed easily.

As things are at present we combine the maximum of vulnerability (due to our geography and the distribution of our population) with the maximum of potential aggressiveness (due to our armament policy). We are more open to attack than any other nation and we now ourselves are trying to make ourselves more formidable than others as a potential attacker. Our new air-fleets contain far more bombers than interceptors, that is, far more instruments of attack than instruments of defence. Our whole defence policy is based on the threat of aggressive retaliation.

But, in the nature of things, we cannot inflict as much damage on an enemy as the enemy can inflict upon us. Foreign populations are not so dense as our own; foreign capitals are smaller and farther from the frontier than is London. Numerical parity and even numerical superiority in the air would do nothing to diminish our intrinsic vulnerability. In any war of aggression and counter-aggression, we should inevitably come off worse than any of our potential enemies or allies. And we should come off worse, even though our air-fleet might be larger than theirs. Our present policy, which consists in combining vulnerability with aggressive rearmament, is merely suicidal.

A Genuine Defence Policy. At least a year's supply of food must be kept in store and, to avoid the danger of destruction, the stores should be in small granaries scattered widely over the countryside. Essential services should be duplicated, dispersed and protected. Fire-fighting services should be enlarged and a corps of technicians organized for repairing damages done. Finally, the heavy industries should be decentralized and the cities rebuilt, so as to consist of a series of tall blocks of buildings, each with its bomb-proof roof and each standing in its area of open space. This rebuilding would provide a fair measure of security from air attack and would, at the same time, vastly increase the amenity of our at present monstrously ugly, unhygienic and inefficient cities. The expense would, of course, be very great, but not much greater than the expense of aggressive armaments and incomparably less than the expense of the war which those armaments invite.

Meanwhile, our huge fleet of bombers should be completely scrapped. By reducing simultaneously our vulnerability and our power of aggression, we should make it quite clear that we were concerned solely with our own legitimate defence. In this way, we should make a real contribution towards the safety of our people and the peace of the world. A well-defended, unaggressive Britain would not provoke attack nor offer a temptingly easy target.

Along with these purely technical measures would have to go a complete reorientation of policy. It is clear, for example, that a hopelessly vulnerable Great Britain cannot expect to preserve a large colonial empire for its own exclusive benefit. During the nineteenth century, when our command of the sea was undisputed, we followed the policy of the open door. During the twentieth, when sea power has lost most of its importance and when, from being the least vulnerable country in Europe, we have become the most vulnerable, we have chosen to place barriers in the way of free trade. Such a policy is an invitation to other nations to attack us. Its reversal is desirable not only on moral grounds, but also as a simple measure of national self-preservation.

The conclusions we have reached may be summed up as follows:

(1) Existing passive defence methods serve only to make attack indiscriminately destructive.

(2) Our policy of defence by means of threatened attack can only serve to alarm foreign nations and ultimately to invite aggression; for, however great our air forces, we cannot, owing to the facts of geography, inflict as much damage as can be inflicted on us.

(3) Technical measures for passive defence can be taken.

Pacifists may legitimately support a policy of genuine defence without aggression.

Disarmament Conference

The associated powers who were victorious in the Great War promised in Article 8 of the Covenant, incorporated in the Treaty of Versailles (1919), that the Council of the League would "formulate plans" for "the reduction of national armaments to the lowest point consistent with national safety and the enforcement by common action of international obligations." But it was not till 1932 that the question of an all-round reduction of armaments was referred by the League of Nations to an international conference for consideration. The Disarmament Conference, over which The Right Hon. Arthur Henderson was selected to preside, first sat in February 1932 and continued its deliberations for over two years, the last full session being held in June 1934. A tentative draft agreement drawn up previously by the British Government in which many blanks were left to be filled in came under discussion, attempts were made to differentiate between offensive and defensive armaments and various suggestions were made for the limitation of armaments and for the abolition of certain war weapons. The Soviet suggestion of complete disarmament had been ruled out of order at a preparatory conference held before the Disarmament Conference itself had been convened. It soon became clear that with the aid of the experts who attended the conference anything like a unanimous decision on any point was impossible. The discussions showed clearly that an attempt was being made not to prevent war but to decide how the next war should be waged.

The powers were beginning at the wrong end. Armaments depend on policy and until the causes of war have been examined and complaints, claims and grievances have been fully stated, it is

31

useless to lay down arms regulations which would certainly be broken by any nation which imagined itself in danger.

Economic Implications of Pacifism

Constructive pacifism is more than a mere objection to war; it is a complete philosophy of life and as such, has important political, sociological and economic implications. The capitalist system is essentially militaristic. Competition between small profit-making enterprises may be compared to inter-tribal warfare. The rise of the huge company and the amalgamation of companies into trusts and cartels are phenomena analogous to the emergence of national communities. There is conflict between these large economic groups, just as there is conflict between nations. There are also treaties of alliance, made for the purpose of exploiting the consuming public. At this point the analogy with nationalism ceases to hold good. Singly or in groups, nations fight with one another; there is no common enemy against whom they can all combine. For capitalist concerns, a common enemy exists in the shape of the consumer. They can make peace and come together in order to despoil that common enemy.

Pacifists are equally opposed to the inter-tribal conflicts of small competitive concerns, to the large-scale conflicts of great trusts (conflicts which, when the trusts are organized on a national crisis with the support of the national government, are the preliminaries of military warfare between nations), and to the exploitation of that common prey of all profit-making enterprises, the consumer. Capitalism, at any rate in its present socially irresponsible form, is incompatible with pacifist principles. The philosophy of pacifism insists that to employ good means is of greater practical importance than to pursue good ends. This is so, because good means can only result in good ends, whereas good ends cannot be achieved by bad means. Pacifists reject the revolutionary's theory that violence and tyranny are justified when used for a good cause.

On this point they part company with communists, fascists and all others who believe that the world can be bludgeoned into the likeness of Utopia. Their political philosophy is democratic.

Some few attempts have already been made to modify the militaristic character of capitalism, to limit opportunities for private profit-making and to protect the consuming public. The London Transport Board and the Port of London Authority are essays in the limitation of capitalism. The Post Office, municipal services for transport, light, water, roads and the like are examples of full-blown socialism already at work. The Co-operative Movement has shown that, without violence and even without the backing of state or municipality, private individuals can create, in the midst of capitalist surroundings, a flourishing island of non-competitive, non-exploiting, non-profit-making economic activity. Co-operation is applied pacifism. The more widely the application can be made the better. In the British Isles co-operation has tended to confine itself too narrowly to the preparation and distribution of foodstuffs. The experiments in the various Scandinavian countries have, however, made it clear that the principle can be extended much more widely. To increase the membership and enlarge the activities of the Co-operative Movement is work of an essentially pacifistic nature. (See *Consumers' Co-operative Movement; Economic Reform and Pacifism; Revolution.*)

Economic Reform and Pacifism

The causes of war, it is often argued, are predominantly economic; these causes cannot be removed except by a change in the existing economic system; therefore pacifist movements, like the P.P.U., are useless.

Those who use such arguments belong to two main classes: currency reformers and socialists.

(1) Currency reformers, such as Major Douglas and his followers, point to the numerous defects in our present monetary

system and affirm that, by remedying those defects, prosperity could be made universal and war eliminated. This is over-optimistic. Defects in the monetary system may intensify economic conflicts in general. But by no means all economic conflicts are conflicts between nations. Many of the bitterest economic conflicts are between rival groups within the same nation; but because these rival groups feel a sentiment of national solidarity, their conflicts do not result in war. It is only when monetary systems are organized in the interests of particular groups of nations that they become a potential cause of war. So long as nationalism exists, scientifically managed currencies may actually make for war rather than peace. "Once the controllers of national monetary systems begin to apply their power self-consciously for the betterment of their people, we have monetary conflicts arising on strictly national lines, such as we see today in competitive exchange depreciation and exchange control" (quoted from *Economic Cause of War,* by Kenneth Boulding). The greater the conscious, scientific control exercised by national monetary authorities, the greater the international friction, at any rate until such time as all nations agree to adopt the same methods of control.

(2) The present economic system is unjust and inefficient, and it is urgently desirable, as the socialists insist, that it should be reformed. But it must not be thought that such reforms would automatically lead to universal peace. "In so far as the socialization of a single nation creates truly national monopolies in the exports of that nation, so the power of the government increases, and the national character of economic conflicts becomes intensified. Thus the socialization of a single nation, even though the rulers of that nation be most peaceably minded, is likely to intensify the fears of other nations in proportion as the control of the socialist government over its country's economic life is increased. . . . Unless they are supported by a strong conscious peace sentiment, they (the socialist régimes of individual nations) may be turned to purposes of war just as effectively—and indeed probably more effectively—than capitalist societies." It will thus be seen that

34

pacifist movements have an important part to play. That changes in the present system must be made is evident; and it is also clear that, in the long run, these changes will make for the establishment of peace. But meanwhile, so long as nationalistic sentiment persists, reforms in the economic and monetary system may temporarily increase international ill feeling. The function of pacifist movements is to prevent, if possible, the desirable changes in the economic and monetary systems from resulting in discord. To renounce war personally and to stand by that renunciation is the best propaganda that individuals can make in favour of peaceful internationalism and against a nationalism that may be bellicose even under a socialist régime.

Economic Warfare

The causes of war are of various kinds, political, economic, psychological, etc., but it is clear that at the present time the economic factor is a very important one. The struggle for markets and for raw materials is openly declared by governments to be the reason for their war preparations, and has been an important factor in the several wars which have been waged during recent years. The desire of certain nations to obtain colonies is partly a matter of prestige, but partly also a matter of economic necessity. It is useless to say that such and such a country does not need colonies because it can freely buy all the raw materials it needs in the world's markets. Actually it is often unable to do so. Its currency is unacceptable beyond its own frontier and the world supply of gold is ludicrously inadequate for the amount of modern international trade. Goods can only be paid for by goods. Imports must be balanced by exports. But when such a nation seeks to export its manufactured goods, it is met everywhere by tariff barriers which make its task an impossible one.

There are 7,000 miles of new tariff-walled frontiers in Europe since the War. Everywhere tariffs have steadily increased, often as

35

measures of economic retaliation. The British Empire, which in pre-war days was a free-trade Empire, where all nations could buy and sell on equal terms, is now a tariff-bound territory, in which nations outside the Empire are at a considerable disadvantage.

Quotas and restrictions add their effect to tariffs in strangling international trade, and countries without colonies feel the effect of this in a steady forcing down of their standard of life. In such circumstances even the manufacture of armaments may appear to have an economic justification in increasing the home market and lessening unemployment, quite apart from their use as an international bargaining weapon, or their use in a war for colonial territory.

The tariff war, which has been raging in the world for the past fifteen years and shows little sign of becoming less acute, is a potent cause of international friction which is leading to war. Although the world's economic experts have repeatedly declared that there can be no return to prosperity without a lowering of tariff barriers, no government is prepared to take the first step. In tariffs, as in armaments, a policy of example is needed. Britain might well take the lead by giving to all nations equal trading rights in those territories over which she has control (i.e. India, the Crown Colonies and the home country). It is significant that discriminatory tariffs are forbidden in the mandated territories. The alternative to economic disarmament (if necessary unilateral), is the continuation and intensification of tariff war until it produces armed conflict. (See *Example; Haves and Have-nots.*)

Education and Peace

In totalitarian states all education is avowedly an education for war. The military training of children in these countries begins almost before they are out of the kindergarten. The period of compulsory military service at eighteen or twenty is merely the culmination of an educational process which has been going on for years.

Military discipline and training in the use of arms is accompanied by a training in nationalistic fervour. This is carried out mainly by means of the teaching of history. The art of distorting history in favour of one's own country or race has been carried to extraordinary lengths under the dictatorships. Young Germans are taught that art, science, philosophy and ethics are purely Aryan and Nordic products; young Italians are taught to worship the Roman Empire; young Turks learn that the world owes its civilization to the Seljuks. And so on.

To a less extravagant degree, the same is true even of the liberal democracies. History, as taught in English and French schools, for example, is history with a strong national bias. Even when the facts are not distorted, they are selected—and the selection is in favour of militarism. Thus, in a *History of Great Britain and Ireland* for use in lower forms, sixty-six pages out of one hundred and sixty dealt with wars, while only one page was given to the Industrial Revolution, and three-quarters to social conditions after 1815. Trades Unions, Co-operative Societies and the Labour Party were not mentioned at all; nor, except for Chartism, was there any reference to any working-class movement of the nineteenth and twentieth centuries.

Nationalism is the most powerful of contemporary religions, and in all countries children are systematically instructed in the tenets of the local nationalist creed. Like the Jesuits and, more recently, the psycho-analysts, the rulers of modern states realize the importance of catching the human animal while it is young and plastic.

In the education of children, the manner of teaching is at least as important as the matter taught. Dr. Montessori, the pioneer of modern pedagogical methods, has written on this subject as follows: "The child who has never learned to act alone, to direct his own actions, to govern his own will, grows into an adult who is easily led and must always lean upon others. The school child, being continually discouraged and scolded, ends by acquiring that mixture of distrust of his own powers and of fear, which is called shyness and which later, in the grown man, takes the form of discouragement and submissiveness, of incapacity to put up the slightest moral resistance. The obedience which is expected of the child both in the home and in the school—an obedience admitting neither of reason nor of justice—prepares the man to be docile to blind forces. The punishment, so common in schools, which consists in subjecting the culprit to public reprimand and is almost tantamount to the torture of the pillory, fills the soul with a crazy, unreasoning fear of public opinion, even of an opinion manifestly unjust and false. In the midst of these adaptations and many others which set up a permanent inferiority complex, is born the spirit of devotion—not to say of idolatry—to the "condottieri," the leaders. . . ." Dr. Montessori might have added that the inferiority complex often finds expression in compensatory brutality and cruelty. The traditional educational methods are calculated to form a hierarchical society in which people are abjectly obedient to their superiors and inhuman to their inferiors. Each slave "takes it out of" the slave below.

Bertrand Russell has an interesting paragraph in his book, *Which Way to Peace?* on the relation between education and militarism. "Schools," he writes, "have very greatly improved during the present century, at any rate in the countries which have remained democratic. In the countries which have military dictatorships, including Russia, there has been a great retrogression during the last ten years, involving a revival of strict discipline, implicit obedience, a ridiculously subservient behaviour towards teachers and passive rather than active methods of acquiring knowledge. All this is rightly held by the governments concerned to be a method of producing a militaristic mentality, at once obedient and domineering, cowardly and brutal. . . . From the practice of the despots, we can see that they agree with the advocates of 'modern' education as regards the connection between discipline in schools and a love of war in later life."

It is a significant fact that Montessori methods are discouraged and even prohibited in the principal dictatorial countries. The Montessori Society of Germany was dissolved by the political police in 1935; and in July 1936 the Fascist Minister of Education decreed the abolition of all official Montessori activities in Italy. Governments that desire to raise up a population of soldiers cannot afford to tolerate a system of education designed to produce free, intelligent and self-reliant individuals.

Ethics and War

Pacifism is the application of the principles of individual morality to the problems of politics and economics. In practice we have two systems of morality: one for individuals and another for communities. Behaviour which, in an individual, would be considered wrong is excused or even commended when indulged in by a national community. Men and women who would shrink from doing anything dishonourable in the sphere of personal relationships are ready to lie and swindle, to steal and even murder when they are representing their country. The community is regarded as a wholly immoral being and loyalty to the community serves to justify the individual in committing every kind of crime.

The wars of earlier days were relatively harmless affairs. Few conquerors were systematically destructive; Jinghiz Khan was an exceptional monster. Today, scientific weapons have made possible indiscriminate and unintentional destruction. Most military experts are agreed that a large-scale war waged with such weapons will be the ruin of European civilization. War was always wrong, and war-makers have always been men of criminal intentions; science has now provided the war-makers with the power of putting their intentions into destructive action on a scale which was undreamt of even a quarter of a century ago. In the past, national communities could afford to behave like maniacs or criminals. Today the costs of lunacy and wickedness are excessive; nations can no longer afford to behave except like the sanest and most moral of beings.

Example

The advocates of a policy of unilateral disarmament believe that a genuinely pacifistic gesture by one of the great powers would profoundly affect public opinion throughout the world and would lead to a measure of general disarmament. Non-pacifists deny that such an example would be efficacious and insist that the only hope of security lies in the piling up of armaments and their pooling, if possible, for use by the League.

It is, of course, impossible exactly to forecast what would be the effect of unilateral disarmament by a great power, which could only be done in a democratic country with the consent of the majority of the electors. All that can be said is that, when the militarist denies the effectiveness of example, he is saying something which is completely belied by the facts of contemporary history. By retaining their armaments after the World War, England and France set an example which was followed by all the lesser allied powers and, later, by Germany and the other countries which had been disarmed under the provisions of the Treaty of Versailles. The rapid rearmament of Germany has manifestly served as an example for the recent rapid increase in French and British armaments. All armaments races are essentially the fruit of example. Under the pressure of fear, suspicion and desire for prestige, each competing nation feels bound to imitate the others. Gun is pitted against gun, plane against plane, poison bomb against poison bomb. In the end, one of the competitors finds that the strain is too great, and trusting in a momentary superiority, precipitates the catastrophe; or else there is an "incident"—a political assassination, such as that which served as pretext and occasion for the World War, a frontier skirmish, an insult to the flag; accidentally and against the conscious wishes of all concerned,

40

the machinery of destruction is set in motion. The longer the competing nations have gone on following one another's example in piling up armaments, the more numerous and efficient will be the weapons of destruction and the more disastrous, in consequence, the effects of the conflict.

As already shown, each government explains the piling up of armaments as a precaution of "defence" against an aggressor. A disarmed nation could not conceivably be accused of being an aggressor. Complete disarmament would therefore mean absolute security.

We see then that example is enormously potent in the matter of armament. There is no reason to suppose that it will not be equally potent in the matter of disarmament. An act of unilateral disarmament would relieve international tension, allay fear and suspicion, calm the susceptibilities of those who feel that their prestige demands an army, navy or air force as big as the other fellow's. There is every reason to believe that a lead towards sanity would be followed. At present we prefer to give a lead towards insanity.

Unilateral disarmament by our country is the natural and consequential public policy which follows from the individual pledge of war resistance.

Force

Pacifism is often opposed on the ground that "civilization is based on force," "there cannot be justice unless it is imposed by force," and so on. What exactly does this word "force" stand for? The answer is that, when used in reference to human relations, it has no single definite meaning. "Force" is used by parents, when, without resort to any kind of physical compulsion, they make their children obey them. "Force" is used by the attendants in an asylum, when they restrain a maniac from hurting himself or others. "Force" is used by the police when they control traffic and "force" of another kind and in greater quantity is used by them when they make a baton charge. Finally, there is the "force" that is used in war. This varies with the mentality of the combatants and the weapons and other technical devices at their disposal. Chivalry has disappeared and the "rules of war" are coming to be ignored; in any future war "force" will probably mean violence and fraud used to the extreme limit of the belligerents' capacity.

"Force" used by armies making use of modern weapons is morally unjustifiable and is not even likely to secure its object, for the simple reason that these weapons are so destructive that a war cannot now preserve any of a nation's vital interests; it can only bring ruin and death indiscriminately to all who come within its range, innocent and guilty, attacker and attacked, soldier and civilian alike. Merely in order to be effective, "force" must be used in moderation.

Experience shows that the forces which accomplish most are psychological forces—the force of persuasion, the force of loyalty, the force of social tradition, the force of good example and the like.

Haves and Have-nots

It is often said that the world is divided into two camps; that of the Haves and that of the Have-nots, that of the satiated nations, who want to keep what they already possess, and that of the dissatisfied nations, who want to increase their possessions. The mentality of the first group is summed up by the British Navy League poster, which represents a bulldog standing on a Union Jack with the caption: "What we have we hold." The mentality of the second group is expressed by the slogan which originated in Germany: "A place in the sun." It is worth noting that, of the twenty-five metals essential to the life of an industrial country, the British Empire has adequate supplies of eighteen, Japan of three, Germany of four, Italy of 4.3 (Dr. Alfred Salter, House of Commons, February 5, 1936).

Whether a colonial Empire is profitable to the colony-owning people as a whole is a question which economists find hard to decide. Certain English politicians have expressed the view that colonies do not pay. In spite of this, there are few indeed who are prepared to part with any colonial territory. But international politics are not framed on the basis of an exact accountancy. The question whether colonies pay or not is of secondary importance. The significant fact is that there is everywhere a great mass of opinion which thinks they pay and a still greater mass which associates national prestige with their possession. It may not be true that the sufferings of the Have-not nations are wholly or mainly due to their lack of colonies. But it probably is true that their peoples think that they are suffering for this reason; and it is certainly true that they regard the possession of colonies as a source of national prestige. A pacifism which consists in preserving the *status quo*, in "holding what we have," is not calculated to inspire much respect. "The implication is that England and America are the only two solvent nations in the Western world and that, since they have what they want and need, it is in their interest to preach peace" (from *A Critique of Pacifism*, by Reinhold Niebuhr).

A policy of free trade on the part of the Haves can do something to mitigate the resentment of the Have-nots. Mr. Ramsay Muir has pointed out that "between 1850 and 1900 the whole of Africa was partitioned and we got the lion's share. How was it that the world allowed us to get it almost without any kind of struggle? It was because the world knew that, if somebody else got it, the world would be excluded by tariffs, but that any territory acquired by Great Britain would be open to traders of other countries on equal terms with British traders." Today, Mr. Ramsay Muir goes on to point out, "Great Britain has reversed that policy by the Ottawa agreement."

The resentment of the Have-nots against the Haves is likely

to persist as long as the exclusive ownership of colonies persists. There can be no final solution to the problem until all colonial territories are either liberated and given their independence, or, if their peoples are really incapable of governing themselves under modern conditions, placed under the guardianship of a genuinely international body, to be administered for the benefit, first, of the inhabitants, and, second, of the world at large. (See *Economic Warfare; Imperialism and Colonies; Mandates.*)

Imperialism and Colonies

"Imperialism" is a word used in two senses. As a political principle it is often opposed to nationalism. Nationalism concentrates on the development of each nation. Imperialism concentrates on the advantage of one nation ruling over, guiding, and developing a number of other nations. The advantage claimed is that much greater political units are created under a single government. The disadvantage is that such a principle is generally accompanied by pride in mere size and grandeur, belief in the use of force, belief in the superiority of one race over others, and a habit of boasting of one's strength—all the things that are crystallized in the word "jingo."

The word "Imperialism" is more commonly used to denote the actual system of empires as it now prevails. Out of the sixty odd sovereign States of the world, only six possess considerable empires—Great Britain, France, Belgium, Portugal, Holland, Italy. These empires were acquired for a variety of reasons—as a source of raw materials, as an outlet for surplus population and surplus production, as a source of profit to a small class of speculative financiers. It is doubtful whether colonies are profitable to the colony-owning country as a whole. To certain classes, however, such as financiers and colonial administrators, they are profitable; and, since these classes rule, there is a tendency for their interest to be regarded as a national interest. Moreover, the conception

44

of prestige makes it hard for a nation to abandon even a demonstrably useless possession.

In an empire, the idea of sovereignty and possession, appropriate only to national states, has been extended to vast groupings of subject or semi-subject peoples. In the economic sphere, these great units have become more and more exclusive.

The advantage of this exclusiveness to the people of the mother country is highly questionable. It cannot be disputed, however, that in a world of economic nationalism, the closing of markets, etc., to all but the citizens of the mother country inflicts injury on the states which do not possess empires.

It is claimed by the imperial or colonial powers that they have prevented local wars, and advanced civilization among backward peoples. It is claimed, on the other side, that the advances in civilization have been far smaller than might have been achieved by a more disinterested form of government; and that the rivalries between the imperial, or would-be imperial powers, have been made far more serious by the exclusive empire system. All the wars of the past half-century, at least, have arisen out of conflicts between empires as to the control of various under-developed or "backward" portions of the world.

Imperialism is challenged from two sides. On the one hand, there is a rising tide of nationalism within the various empires, entailing demands for self-government and independence. On the other hand, there is an increasing realization that the whole idea of the exclusive empire belongs to an age that is past; and that the backward regions of the world, both in respect of economic development and cultural advance, should be regarded as a responsibility resting upon the international community as a whole. (See *Mandates*; *Defence*; *British Empire, The.*)

India, Pacifism in

Pre-Aryan India seems to have been a pacific country. The excavations at Mohenjo-Daro and Harappa have revealed no fortifications and very few weapons. At the same time there is evidence that the Yogic practices, which have played and still play so important a part in all Indian religions, had been developed as early as the fourth millennium B.C. The theology underlying such practices is a theology of immanence, which affirms that the soul of the individual is a portion of the divine soul of the world. Yogic practices are designed to make the individual become conscious of this identity between his inmost self and the spirit of the universe. This theology is summed up in the phrase: "Thou art that." Pacifism and humanitarianism are the necessary corollaries of this doctrine. The Hinduism of historical times is a religion combining elements of widely different value. For those who want such things, it provides magic and orgiastic fertility rites; for the more spiritual it provides mysticism and a high philosophy. Its caste system is a kind of static militarism, in which the position of conquerors and conquered has been petrified into an unchanging social order. The doctrine that "thou art that," with its accompanying mystical practices and its humanitarian consequences, has persisted as a standing protest against this fossilized militarism.

Humanitarian and pacifist principles were proclaimed and acted upon, often with excessive scrupulousness, by the followers of Jainisen, a dissident sect of Hinduism which came into existence in the sixth and fifth centuries B.C.

More important was the rise of Buddhism at about the same period. Like the Jains, the Buddhists taught and practised *ahimsa*, or harmlessness, refraining from doing hurt to any living being. Even Buddhist laymen were expected to refuse to have anything to do with the manufacture and sale of arms, with the making of poisons or strong drink, with soldiering or the slaughter of animals. Buddhism is the only great world religion which has made its way without bloodshed or persecution, without censorship or inquisition. It is interesting to compare Buddhist and Christian views on anger. For Buddhism anger is always and unconditionally wrong and disgraceful. For Christians, in whose bible the savage

46

literature of the ancient Hebrews is included on the same footing as the prophetic writing and the New Testament, anger may be a divine attribute. What is called "righteous indignation" has justified Christian churchmen in committing innumerable atrocities. (See *China, Pacifism in; Christ, The Teaching of.*)

Individual Disputes and National Disputes

There is a fundamental difference between war and disputes between individuals. Individuals quarrel in hot blood; war is coolly and scientifically prepared in advance and soldiers are carefully trained in order that they may overcome their natural feelings and be ready to kill and to be killed at the word of command.

Individuals fight in their own quarrels; soldiers are trained to fight in quarrels that are not their own—for the financial advantage of business interests, for national prestige, for the sake of potential military advantages. (It is worthy of note that one of the causes of war is war itself. Wars are fought in order that the victor may have a better strategic position during future wars. The possession of an army and navy is in itself a reason for going to war; "we must use our forces now," so runs the argument, "in order that we may be in a position to use them to better advantage another time.")

In some cases individuals fight in self-defence against a bully or a criminal. This fact provides the militarist with a favourite argument. "If an individual policeman is justified in arresting an individual criminal, a national policeman is justified in arresting a national criminal." The analogy is entirely false. The individual policeman arrests one man—the man who is guilty. The national policeman (represented by an army, navy and air force) uses all the means at his disposal—and these means are now diabolically effective—not to arrest one guilty person, but to destroy, maim,

47

starve and ruin millions of men, women and children, the overwhelming majority of whom have committed no crime of any sort. The process which righteous militarists describe as "punishing a guilty nation" consists in mangling and murdering innumerable innocent individuals. To draw analogies between an army and a policeman, between war (however "righteous" its aims) and the prevention of crime, is utterly misleading.

Another favourite question asked by militarists is the following: "What would you do if you saw a stranger break into your house and try to violate your wife?" This question may be answered as follows: "Whatever else I might do—and it is quite likely that I should become very angry and try to knock the intruder down or even to kill him—I should certainly not send my brother to go and poison the man's grandfather and disembowel his infant son." And that precisely is what war consists of—murdering, either personally or (more often) through the instrumentality of others, all kinds of people who have never done one any sort of injury.

International Police Force

This proposal either takes the form of a complete international force of navy and army and air force, as advocated by the New Commonwealth, or an international air police force, officially supported by the Labour Party. It is argued that instead of depending in an emergency on doubtful military contributions from various nations, a standing force under the direction of the League of Nations should be established. But apart from the doubt as to whether a declared aggressor can be thwarted and forced into acquiescence by methods of violence, there would be insuperable difficulties in enlisting, recruiting, arming, training and even locating such an armed body, and its command and release for action would require a unanimous international decision which would not be likely to be forthcoming. In the world of today it is inconceivable that French and Germans, Russians and Italians, Americans and Japanese would unite together in order to man such a force; it is inconceivable that the staff officers of the various nations would draw up in advance elaborate plans of campaign for an attack, in certain contingencies, on their own countries. If certain nations refused to participate the main purpose would not be served and if the contribution in men of any one nation or combination of nations preponderated they would be accused of trying to dominate the world.

The proposal is not only undesirable but utterly impracticable. (See *Sanctions*.)

International Politics in the Light of Christ's Teaching

It has generally been taken for granted that Jesus regarded political affairs as entirely outside His orbit. There is reason, however, to believe that this view is erroneous.

(1) The stories of the Baptism, the Temptation, the conversation at Cæsarea-Philippi, the trials before Caiaphas and Pilate, and the entry into Jerusalem, make it certain that Jesus regarded Himself as Messiah. Now, all conceptions of Messiahship had this in common: the Messiah was essentially a national figure. Questioned by Pilate, Jesus avows Himself King of *the Jews*.

(2) At the beginning of His ministry, Jesus expected that His messianic plan for Israel would be successful, as is clear from the fact towards the end (see Matt. xxiii. 37 ff.; Luke xiii. 34 f.; xix. 41 ff.). He expressed his disappointment that the Jews had refused to follow Him as leader. As "King of the Jews," what did Jesus have in mind for His people?

(3) Release from foreign domination was the great political preoccupation of the Jewish contemporaries of Jesus. All of them believed that the Gentiles would be overthrown and destroyed, enslaved or, in a few cases, converted, by divine power in the

course of a great messianic war. Jesus must have had something to say on this question. His conception of the Messiah's function was, however, very different from theirs. His plan for the Jews seems to have been that, under His leadership, they should give up their desire for vengeance against Rome and for the destruction of the Gentiles and that, trusting wholly to deeds of love, should undercut Gentile hostility by means of "non-violence" and convert enemies to friends, uniting them in the brotherhood of true religion. The Jews, in a word, were to be the pioneers of a new kind of religio-political action.

(4) In support of this contention, it may be pointed out that the injunction in the Sermon on the Mount of love for enemies does not, as has been generally supposed, refer exclusively to individual conduct in the private relationship of life. "Whoever shall compel thee" (Matt. v. 41) seems to be a reference to the forced labour imposed by Roman and Herodian officials. The word for "enemies" is perfectly general and may refer equally well to public and private enemies. The word "neighbour" is a technical term for "fellow-Israelite" (cf. Lev. xix. 18) and the exhortation to love not neighbours only is therefore an exhortation to love Gentiles. In Luke xii. 54-xiii. 9, Jesus seems to be urging the need for reconciliation with the enemy before it is too late and to be pointing out that, unless His countrymen repent and give up their ideas of violent revolt and vengeance, they will assuredly be destroyed. The lamentation over Jerusalem (Luke xix. 41-4) and the words to the woman on the road to Golgotha (Luke xxiii. 27-31) convey the same idea. The advice that Cæsar's tribute should be submissively paid is in line with the whole scheme of effecting a reconciliation between Israel and Rome.

The fall of Jerusalem in A.D. 70 followed the Jewish rejection of Jesus and His policy—followed it in virtue of an inexorable psychological law: Acts of love beget love: acts of hatred beget hatred. To the policy of Jesus the Jews preferred armed revolt; the Romans reacted against violence with violence, and, since they were the stronger, Jerusalem was sacked, even as Jesus had predicted. "If thou hadst known the things that belong unto thy peace! but now they are hid from thine eyes." Because these things were hid, because the eyes of the Jews were closed, Jerusalem suffered destruction.

(See *The Politics of Jesus*, by C. J. Cadoux, in *Congregational Quarterly*, Jan. 1936, pp. 58-67.)

League of Nations

Many rested their hopes on the establishment of an international body for the settlement of disputes as the one good feature which might emerge from the devastating conflict of the Great War. President Wilson took a leading part and the Covenant of the League of Nations was drawn up and, very unfortunately, attached as part of the Treaty of Versailles, in 1919. President Wilson was thrown over by his own people and the U.S.A. never joined the League. The so-called enemy countries, Germany, Austria, Bulgaria and Turkey, were not admitted till some years later. Germany was not invited to enter the League till 1926. The League therefore has never been complete. Soviet Russia eventually joined. But Japan withdrew in March 1933 and Germany withdrew in October 1933. The suspicion that the League had been affixed to the Treaty of Versailles in order to maintain the *status quo* as laid down by the punitive clauses in the Treaty, was not without justification.

The League has done good work in subsidiary matters and its constructive work might well be strengthened. It has also resolved minor international disputes. But the great error of its founders in proposing the use of collective force as a method of preventing or stopping aggressive warfare on the part of any one of the Great Powers has been demonstrated in the cases of Japan and Italy. The attempt to carry out this provision has greatly weakened the authority of the League. Until the League is all-inclusive and the obligation to use force in any circumstance is eliminated from the Covenant, its continued existence may be regarded as doubtful. If some nations adhere to the Covenant while others remain outside, the result can only be the establishment of two hostile camps.

(Consult *The Aims and Organization of the League of Nations* [published by the Secretariat of the League]. On the reform of the League, see L. P. Jacks, *A Demilitarized League of Nations* [*Hibbert Journal,* Aug. 1936].)

Liberty

War is incompatible with liberty. So, to a lesser extent, is intensive preparation for war. Conscription, or military slavery, is universal on the Continent of Europe. In the dictatorial states, Italy, Germany and Russia, even children are taught rifle drill and the use of the machine-gun.

Thanks to their country's geographical position, Englishmen have hitherto avoided military slavery. Navies can be manned with a comparatively small force and, except during the Great War, when conscription was temporarily introduced, England has had no need of a large army.

There are signs that this state of things may soon be changed, and that Englishmen and perhaps also English women and children will soon be subjected to some form of military slavery. This military slavery will probably not take the form of continental conscription. The rise of air power has made it very doubtful whether huge national armies will ever be used again. But at the same time air power has made it certain that the whole civilian population will be involved in any future war as it never was involved in the past. What the militarist fears above everything is that an untrained civilian population will rapidly lose its "will-to-war," if subjected to prolonged bombardment from the air. Therefore, he argues, civilians must be disciplined to endure the horrors of war, even as soldiers are disciplined. In this way and in this way only will it be possible for the military machine to score a "victory" over the military machine of the enemy. Whether this "victory" will be worth having is a matter which the militarist refuses to consider. He wants to win and he does not mind whether half the population and all the decencies of civilized life are sacrificed in the process.

In the dictatorial countries not only the young men of military age, but all civilians without exception, are subjected to military training in the form of gas drill, practice black-outs and evacuations, periodical parades, etc. There is every indication that our militarists will soon demand that similar measures should be put into force in this country. Gas drills may seem harmless enough; indeed, attempts will be made to represent them as genuine defence measures. In reality, as has been shown in the article on Defence, gas drills, black-outs and the like, are almost completely futile as defence. The military experts know that they are useless, but desire to impose them, first, because gas drills may create a consoling illusion of security and, second, because they offer a golden opportunity for imposing military control on the civil population. The truth is that these seemingly harmless exercises are only the first instalment of complete military slavery.

The militarist's ideal is a country that is one vast barrack, inhabited by well-drilled men, women and children, prepared at the word of command to "do or die" (especially to die) without ever attempting to "reason why." In the words of Mr. Jonathan Griffin, air-power threatens to "make liberty a thing of the past, and reduce the whole of Europe to the condition of those parts of it which in the 'Dark Ages' were really dark."

Mandates

The Mandate System is clearly and conveniently described in Article XXII of the Covenant of the League of Nations. It came into being after the Great War as a means of dealing with parts of the Turkish Empire, and with the German colonies, which had been occupied by the Allies. It was a compromise between those who wished to annex these territories outright, and those who (like President Wilson) wanted to place them under something like international administration. What happened was that the "Allied and Associated Powers" (a term which included the U.S.A.) allotted them to certain States—Great Britain, South Africa, Australia, New Zealand, France and (later) Belgium—as "mandated territories." These States were to exercise all the powers of governments, but subject to certain definite obligations to the League. They were to report annually to a Mandates Commission, consisting of persons chosen for their expert knowledge, but not officially representing particular Governments; the Mandates Commission being responsible to the Council of the League of Nations. They were also to fulfil the conditions laid down in Article XXII and in the separate Mandates of each territory. The chief conditions are:

(a) equality of economic opportunity for all League of Nations members;

(b) no fortifications or bases, or military training of Natives for other than police purposes and the defence of territory;

(c) justice to Natives;

(d) freedom of conscience and religion;

(e) prohibition of abuses.

The Mandates Commission has no power of enforcing its decisions, but in fact its powers of inquiry and of securing world publicity have done something to raise the standard of administration and to promote the idea of international responsibility for the "backward" areas of the world. It seems clear that the Mandate System can and should be developed. (See *Imperialism and Colonies*; *British Empire, The*; *Defence*.)

Mineral Sanctions

"Mineral Sanctions" were first proposed by Sir Thomas Holland, F.R.S., in his presidential address to the British Association in 1929. The theme was more fully developed in a small book (*The Mineral Sanction*) by the same author, published in 1935.

What follows is a brief summary of the main points in the scheme.

(1) No country is self-sufficient in regard to supplies of minerals.

(2) Minerals cannot be made artificially, nor can they be replaced by synthetic substitutes.

(3) No industrialized country can carry on without a steady and sufficient supply of minerals. In war-time the normal supply must be increased by anything from five to twenty times.

(4) Seeing that all countries are dependent upon others for supplies of certain indispensable minerals, it follows that an international agreement to refuse to sell minerals to a belligerent would be an effective method of stopping or at least shortening a war.

Let us consider a few concrete examples.

Great Britain is mainly or entirely dependent on oversea sources for supplies of copper, chrome, lead, zinc, sulphur, mercury, tungsten, nickel, molybdenum, mica, manganese, cobalt, antimony and bauxite (for the extraction of aluminium).

Germany has no bauxite, no antimony, no chrome, insufficient copper and iron, almost no manganese, no mica, no molybdenum, no mercury, hardly any nickel, sulphur, tin or tungsten.

France depends wholly on foreign sources for chrome, copper, manganese, mercury, mica, molybdenum, nickel, sulphur, tin and tungsten. She is partly dependent on foreign countries for zinc, lead, coal and antimony.

Both Japan and Italy are even poorer in indispensable minerals than the countries listed above. Even the United States, by far the richest in natural resources of all the great powers, is not self-sufficient where minerals are concerned. The same is true of Russia which, though more plentifully supplied than her neighbours to East and West, has to depend on foreign sources for supplies of antimony, copper, molybdenum, nickel, quick-silver, sulphur, tin and tungsten.

To anyone who considers these facts it must be sufficiently clear that a system of mineral sanctions offers very good prospects for shortening hostilities, when once they have broken out, and even for controlling the preparations for future wars. No attempt, however, has been made to establish such a system. The rulers of the nations prefer to carry on the traditional policy, which is to arm their own people and at the same time to sell to their neighbours the minerals which, in all probability, will be used against the sellers in the form of armaments.

Moral Equivalent of War

A common defence of war is that it is a school of virtues. In war a man learns obedience, courage, self-sacrifice; he throws away his life that a greater purpose may triumph. It is true that war may evoke these virtues. But we must not forget that it also evokes and encourages a number of vices. In war, the actual fighters learn to be inhuman and cruel, while the politicians who direct the fighters learn to lie and swindle. For the behaviour of politicians, the reader is referred to the articles *Propaganda* and *Secret Treaties*. As for the fighters, these were actually subjected during the World War to a systematic education in cruelty. Lectures on bayonet fighting were intended to heighten the bloodthirstiness of recruits. The following citation is from a military manual for use in the American Army. (The paragraph, which has now been modified, was cited in *The World To-morrow*, New York, Feb. 1926). "Bayonet fighting is possible only because

56

red-blooded men naturally possess the fighting instinct. This inherent desire to fight and kill must be carefully watched for and encouraged by the instructor. To finish an opponent who hangs on, or attempts to pull you to the ground, always try to break his hold by driving the knee or foot to his crotch and gouging his eyes with your thumbs. Men still have fight in them unless you hit a vital spot. But when the bayonet comes out and the air sucks in, and they begin to bleed on the inside, they feel the pain and lose their fight."

It will be seen then, that the military virtues have to be paid for, and paid for pretty highly. But the virtues, let us admit frankly, exist. If civil life does not evoke these virtues, then we must change civil life until it does. Otherwise war can still defend itself by being able to claim (if not actually to prove) that it is more moral than peace.

What, then, is the moral equivalent of war? It is a way of living which calls out endurance, bravery and self-forgetfulness, but for constructive ends and not for destruction. In war, a man is asked to lay down his life in defence of his country, and his natural devotion responds, and responds gladly in many cases, to that call. His sacrifice is admirable; but the accompaniments of that sacrifice and the reasons for which it is made are far from admirable. For what he is being asked to do is to go on killing other men until such time as he himself is killed by them. And when we ask for what purpose he is to kill and be killed, we find as often as not that the war is being fought for the most ignoble reasons. In all war there is a most unsatisfactory mixture of private virtue with public and private vice. Yet so strong in men is the wish to serve a cause greater than themselves and to lose themselves in that cause, and so incapable are our peace-time societies of giving us that sense of being wanted by a great and noble cause, that it is easy to persuade men to take part in war. All they wish to do is to show their devotion and courage; what they actually succeed in doing is to participate in an orgy of mass murder, a campaign against civilization.

Modern dictatorships owe much of their popularity, not to their successful campaigns abroad, but to the fact that they have been able to make so many of their peoples believe that by disciplined effort and sacrifice they could, all together, build up a united nation freed from poverty and class selfishness.

Beside the desire for discipline and self-sacrifice, there is also in healthy people, especially when they are young, a love of risk and a need to live dangerously. Our societies are not only too meaningless; they are also, for many people, too safe, too unexciting. Hard games get rid of some of this pent energy; but games are inadequate. War still attracts men because they want to risk their lives and not merely keep themselves fit. A system of peace-time national service should be organized, making it possible for every boy and young man to take his turn at one or other of the tough jobs and civilian risks that exist—fire-brigade service, life-boat service, light-house service, sea fishery, mine safety work, down to traffic direction and sewer inspection. Those whose physique would not permit such roughing could gain as much honour by offering themselves for essential scientific experiments. In some such way as this individuals would be given a cause to live for and if necessary to die for—would be enabled to practice the soldier's virtues without committing the crime of war.

Morality of Pacifism

It is often objected that pacifism is morally unjustifiable. "Your position in society," the critic of pacifism argues, "is that of a parasite. You are profiting by what the armed forces of your country are doing to preserve you and your family from danger but you refuse to undertake defence work yourself and you try to persuade others to follow your example. You have no right to take from the society in which you live without giving anything in return."

Several answers to these criticisms present themselves:

(1) In the contemporary world, the armed forces of a country do not provide its inhabitants with protection. On the contrary, their existence is one of the principal sources of national danger. There is no more effective way of provoking people to attack than to treaten them. At the present time Great Britain combines extreme vulnerability with formidable aggressive armament. Our policy of rearmament with weapons of aggression is one which positively invites attack. The pacifist is criticized as a shirker who seeks security behind a line of soldiers, sailors and airmen, whom he refuses to help. In reality, his dearest wish is to get rid of the soldiers, sailors and airmen, and all their machinery of destruction; for he knows that so long as they are there, security will be unattainable. Tanks, bombers and battleships do not give security; on the contrary, they are a constant source of danger.

(2) Those who accuse pacifists of being parasites upon the society in which they live should pause for a moment to consider a few facts and figures. Since the last war this country has spent sixteen hundred millions of pounds upon its armaments, and the rate of expenditure is now to be increased. The world as a whole spends nearly two thousand millions a year on its "defence forces." These "defence forces" live at the expense of the working community, performing no constructive work, absorbing an increasing amount of the world's energy and not only failing to provide the individual citizens of the various nations with adequate protection, but actually inviting attack from abroad. To the inhabitant of a bombarded London it will be no satisfaction to learn that the planes for which he has been paying so heavily in taxation are bombarding some foreign capital.

(3) Refusal to obey the government of the society of which one is a member is a very serious matter. Still, most moralists and political philosophers have been of opinion that individuals are fully justified in disobeying the State if the State commands them to do something which they are convinced to be wrong. Social solidarity is not always desirable. There is such a thing as

solidarity with evil as well as solidarity with good. A man who finds himself on a pirate ship is morally justified in refusing to co-operate with his shipmates in their nefarious activities. All reformers have been men who refused to co-operate, on some important issue, with the societies of which they were members. That is why so many of them have been persecuted by their contemporaries. The Christian religion takes its name from a persecuted reformer.

Criticisms and answers:

(1) The State provides free schools, libraries, pensions, etc. In return the individual should do what the State demands of him.

Answer: (*a*) The individual pays for State services in taxation.

(*b*) The State is not God and its demands are not categorical imperatives. The State was made for man, not man for the State. The State is a convenience, like drains or the telephone; its demand that it should be treated as an allwise divinity is inadmissible and leads, as the history of tyrannies and dictatorships shows, to every kind of crime and disaster.

(*c*) If the State may justifiably demand of an individual that he should commit murder for the sake of his country, then it is equally justified in demanding that he should commit lesser crimes. But we can imagine the outcry that would be raised by pious militarists if, for example, in an effort to raise the birthrate and improve the quality of the race, the State were to conscribe all women and compel them to have sexual intercourse with eugenically selected men.

(2) "The pacifist method of dealing with war is too slow and there will be another war before there are enough pacifists to stop it."

The pacifist method is certainly slow; but the militarist's method is far slower. Indeed, the militarist's method is foredoomed to make no advance whatever towards the goal of peace. War produces more war. Only non-violence can produce non-violence. Pacifism is admittedly slow and hard to practise; but the fact remains that it is the only method of getting universal peace which promises to be in the least effective.

(3) "There is something worse than war, and that is injustice." But war inevitably commits injustices far greater and more widespread than those it was called upon to redress.

(4) "Pacifism tends to increase the arrogance and power of dictators."

(a) None of the modern dictators has been faced with large-scale pacifism. Where non-violence has been used on a large scale (see *Non-Violence*) even violent and ruthless rulers have been nonplussed.

(b) What increases the arrogance of dictators is not so much pacifism as the half-hearted use of their own violent methods. The violence of dictators must be opposed either by violence greater than theirs (with the certainty of prolonging the war habit and the possibility of doing irreparable damage to civilization) or else by complete pacifism (which, however slow and difficult, will ultimately lead to the establishment of peace).

Nationalism

We cannot discuss nationalism without first defining the word "nation," and the only definition which covers the ground is "a community organized for war."

It is clear that a nation is not a racial entity, since many millions of Negroes are nationals of the United States; it is not a linguistic entity, since the Swiss nation is composed of speakers of German, French and Italian; it is not even a geographical entity, since the German nation is cut in two by Poland, and the Swiss Canton of Ticino is geographically as well as linguistically part of Italy.

The definition given above is that recognized by the League of Nations, which admits to membership a community, however small, which has an army of its own, but refuses admission to a community, however large, whose autonomous powers do not include the provision of armed forces.

California is not now entitled to membership; but if a revolution were to divide it among a dozen bloodthirsty dictators, each of these could be represented at Geneva.

A nationalist is thus a person who wishes to surround himself, and those who can be induced to conspire with him, with a closely and aggressively guarded military frontier, and incidentally to prevent as far as possible that cross-fertilization of ideas which always has been and always must be the sole insurance against the relapse into barbarism which perpetually threatens all human communities.

Nationalistic Religion

During the last hundred years Europe has witnessed a rapid and accelerating movement away from monotheism towards tribal idolatry. The place of God has been largely usurped by such deified entities as the Nation, the Race, the Class, the Party. In the totalitarian states these abstract entities are embodied in the person of a semi-divine Leader. (We are reminded of the king-worship imposed upon their subjects by the successors of Alexander the Great, of that Roman emperor-worship in which the early Christians steadfastly refused to participate.)

In every country, liberal as well as totalitarian, the local idolatry is preached in schools, in the press, over the wireless, in political speeches, very often even from Christian pulpits. In dictatorial countries this preaching is more systematic and probably more effective than in liberal countries; that is all. The dictators aim at inspiring young people with a crusading enthusiasm for the local idol and his deified vice-regent. They are trying to do what was done in the seventies of last century by the makers of modern Japan. These astute psychologists took the ancient religion of Japan, Shintoism, and adapted it for use in a modern, centralized state. The Emperor became God, and the first duty of his subjects was to live and work and, if necessary, die for the God-Emperor and his accredited representatives. "A new system of compulsory education was introduced to inculcate before all worldly knowledge the duty of unconditional obedience to the Son of Heaven, the Mikado, whose service is perfect freedom." The makers of new Japan had this advantage over the contemporary dictators: Shintoism was an existing religion with traditionally hallowed rites and beliefs. The dictators of modern Europe have to create their equivalents of Shintoism. The traditional religion of Europe is not nationalism; it is Christianity in one or other of its forms.

The churches have protested against the idolatrous deification of the State, but without much effect. For the present generation, the claim of the churches to stand for the brotherhood of man in the fatherhood of God was seriously compromised during the last war. In 1914 the ecclesiastical authorities in all the belligerent countries enthusiastically threw in their lot with their respective governments and preached a holy war against fellow Christians, merely because they happened to be living on the wrong side of the national frontier. (In a service of intercession, sanctioned by the Archbishop of Canterbury in September 1914, we find the following sentence: "We pray thee, O God, to judge between us and the enemy, and of Thy great mercy to give us the victory.")

Psychologically speaking, the strength of nationalistic idolatry lies in its power to assuage the sense of personal inferiority. Here, for example, is an individual who is poor, exploited, socially insignificant; to him come the apostles of the local idolatry, assuring him that, as a member of the divine Nation, Party, Class or Race, he is superior to everyone else in the world outside his own particular community. The nation-god is glorious and even his feeblest and most unimportant worshippers mystically participate in that glory.

Nationalistic idolatry inculcates pride and vanity, on the one hand, and hatred and contempt for foreigners on the other. It is essentially a religion of war. Pacifists should make it their business to understand the nature of this evil religion and, having understood it, to steel their minds against the emotional appeals and lying suggestions which are incessantly being made in its name.

Non-Violence

Pacifists believe—and their belief is based upon individual experience and a study of history, past and contemporary—that the most effective, the most equitable, the most economical way of meeting violence is to use non-violence.

If violence is answered by violence, the result is a physical struggle. Now, a physical struggle inevitably arouses hatred, fear, rage and resentment. In the heat of passion all scruples are thrown to the winds, all the habits of forbearance and humaneness acquired during years of civilized living are forgotten. Nothing matters any more except victory. And when at last victory comes to one or other of the parties, this final outcome of physical struggle bears no relation to the rights or wrongs of the case; nor, in most instances, does it provide any lasting settlement to the dispute at issue. (The cases in which victory does provide some kind of lasting settlement may be classified as follows: (1) Victory is final where the vanquished are completely or very nearly exterminated. In the case of war between two populous countries extermination is unlikely: one war tends therefore to beget another. (2) Victory may lead to an unquestioned settlement where the fighting forces involved are so small that the mass of the population is left unaffected by the struggle. Today the entire population is liable to be affected by war. The relatively harmless wars conducted according to an elaborate code of rules by a small warrior-caste are things of the past. (3) Victory may lead to permanent peace where the victors settle down among the vanquished as a ruling minority and are, in due course, absorbed by them.

This does not apply to contemporary wars. (4) Finally, victory may be followed by an act of reparation on the part of the victors to the vanquished. This will disarm resentment and lead to a genuine settlement. It was the policy pursued by the English after the Boer War. Such a policy is essentially an application of the principles of non-violence. The longer and the more savage the conflict, the more difficult is it to make an act of reparation after victory. It was relatively easy to be just after the Boer War; it was psychologically all but impossible to be just in 1918. That is why the pacifist insists that the principles of non-violence should be applied, wherever possible, before physical conflict has actually broken out.)

Non-violence does not mean doing nothing. It means making the enormous effort required to overcome evil with good. Non-violence does not rely on strong muscles and devilish armaments; it relies on moral courage, self-control and the knowledge, unswervingly acted upon, that there is in every human being, however brutal, however personally hostile, a fund of kindness, a love of justice, a respect for goodness and truth which can be reached by anyone who uses the right means. To use these means is often extraordinarily hard; but history shows that it can be done—and done not only by exceptional individuals, but by large groups of ordinary men and women and even by governments.

In the paragraphs which follow, a few instances are cited, illustrating the way in which non-violence has been used, first, by isolated individuals, second, by groups and, thirdly, by governments.

During the American Civil War no consideration was shown to those who objected to war on religious grounds. After being cruelly tortured, Seth Loflin, a Quaker, was offered a gun. In spite of threats and abuse, he refused to take it; whereupon he was court-martialled, and condemned to be shot out of hand. In the presence of the firing squad Loflin, who was absolutely calm, asked time for prayer, saying, "Father, forgive them, for they know not what they do." The soldiers were so much impressed that they lowered their guns and, braving the penalty for disobedience, refused to shoot on such a man.

Dr. Theodore Pennell went to India in 1892, as a medical missionary. His work lay among the wild tribes on the North-West Frontier. Dressed as a Pathan and sharing the Pathans' mode of living, he travelled about the country unarmed and unafraid, giving his services to all who needed them. Hearing that a band of warriors had been ordered to take him alive or dead, Pennell made his way directly to the Mullah who had given the order. Astonished and deeply impressed by the doctor's courage, the Mullah gave him food, listened to his account of what he was doing and, when night came, ordered that his bed should be placed between his own and that of his son, thus indicating that the stranger was under his protection.

It is in the East that we find the most striking examples of non-violence practised by large groups. In South Africa and later in India, Gandhi organized non-violent resistance to the Government. The South African experiment was remarkably successful. In India a number of very considerable successes were recorded, and it was shown that very large groups of men and women could be trained to respond to the most brutal treatment with a quiet courage and equanimity that profoundly impressed their opponents, the spectators in the immediate vicinity and, through press accounts, the public opinion of the whole civilized world. The difficulty of effectively training very large numbers in a very short time proved too great. In a number of cases, inadequately trained groups resorted to mass violence. Rather than see his movement degenerate into civil war (in which, incidentally, the British, being better armed, would inevitably have won a complete victory) Gandhi called off his movement.

In 1919 a movement of non-violent resistance to Japanese imperialism broke out in Corea. In spite of the brutality of Japanese repression, the movement remained essentially pacifistic. Unfortunately for the Coreans, their leaders were not sufficiently practical. The boycotting of Japanese goods, civil disobedience, non-co-opera-

66

tion and refusal to pay taxes were not effectively organized on a large scale. These methods, which were used so effectively in India and again in China (where the shooting of unarmed students by the Shanghai police led, in 1925, to a formidable boycott of British goods) were tried out too late in Corea. The movement was only partially successful. The Japanese repressed it with savage violence, but were compelled to make very considerable concessions. At the same time the psychological effect of the movement upon the Coreans themselves was very great; as a people they recovered their self-respect and the revolt of 1919 was followed by a kind of renaissance of the best elements of Corean civilization.

Examples of non-violent acts by governments are seldom of a very heroic kind and the motives behind them are seldom un-mixed. The tradition of politics is a thoroughly dishonourable one. The world sanctions a double system of morality—one system for private individuals, another for social groups. Men who, in private life, are consistently honest, humane and considerate, believe that when they act as representatives of a group, they are justified in doing things which, as individuals, they know to be utterly disgraceful.

During their working hours, the most high-minded politicians will practise deception and give orders for the murder of their fellows. To get rid of this odious tradition that, in politics and to some degree also in business, it may be one's duty to do what one knows to be wrong is one of the urgent tasks to which all pacifists should apply themselves. Meanwhile the tradition still persists; and it is for this reason that application of the principles of non-violence and even of plain morality by governments are so rare. At best the application is incomplete. In many cases it follows on an unsuccessful attempt to solve some thorny problem by means of violence. Such was the case, for example, in South Africa, when, as has been mentioned above, Campbell-Bannerman gave the Boers self-government. The methods of violence had been tried, during the South African War, and found completely wanting. The war had solved no problems; it had merely created a number of new problems. Campbell-Bannerman's courageous policy was crowned by a measure of success which it would have been utterly impossible to achieve by means of violent repression.

Something of the same sort happened in Ireland. After attempting, quite unsuccessfully, to compel the Irish to be loyal subjects to the Crown, the English suddenly reversed their policy and granted Home Rule. The result was, not indeed enthusiastic co-operation (after centuries of oppression, that would have been too much to expect), but at any rate peace. It did at least become possible for the English to get rid of the national disgrace of the Black-and-Tans.

In recent European history, the most complete examples of the application of non-violent principles by governments are supplied by Sweden and Norway. In 1814 the Treaty of Kiel provided that Norway should be handed over to the kingdom of Sweden. Bernadotte invaded the country; but after a fortnight, during which no serious conflict took place, opened negotiations. The union of the two countries was agreed upon, being achieved, in the words of the preamble to the Act of Union, "not by force of arms, but by free conviction." Ninety years later, in 1905, the union was dissolved. By an overwhelming majority, the Norwegians decided to become independent. The Swedes accepted that decision. No violence was used on either side. (See *Force*; *Revolution*.)

Over-Population and Food Supply

Preparations for aggressive and imperialistic wars are often excused on the ground of over-population. Rulers of countries preparing for war point out that the domestic food supply is insufficient and that their peoples must either acquire new territory or starve.

Now, much of the difficulty experienced by certain countries in

68

securing adequate food supplies is due predominantly to a faulty monetary policy, which prevents them from buying from abroad. This faulty monetary policy is due in its turn to the determination of the governments of the countries concerned to spend all available national resources on armaments. Food cannot be bought because the country is preparing to go to war; the country must go to war because food cannot be bought. As usual, it is a vicious circle.

Faulty monetary policy may prevent certain nations from buying food abroad. But even if the policy were altered, it would still remain true that food would have to be obtained from abroad. In relation to home supplies, certain countries (including Germany, Japan and Great Britain) may be described as over-populated. To what extent is this over-population a valid excuse for new agression or the continuance of long-established imperialism? According to experts trained in the techniques of modern agro-biology, imperialism has now lost its principal justification. Readers are referred to Dr. Wilcox's book, *Nations Can Live at Home*, for a systematic exposition of the agro-biologist's case. For pacifists, the significant fact is this: any country which chooses to apply the most advanced agro-biological methods to the growing of food-plants, including grasses for live-stock, can support a population far in excess of the densest population existing anywhere on the earth's surface at the present time. (The methods advocated by Dr. Wilcox have already been used commercially on a large scale. The revolutionary system of "dirtless farming" devised by Professor Gerike of California is still in the experimental stage; but if it turns out to be satisfactory, it promises a more copious supply of food, produced with less labour and on a smaller area, than any other method can offer.)

It is profoundly significant that no government has hitherto made any serious effort to apply modern agro-biological methods for the purpose of raising the standard of well-being among its subjects and of rendering imperialism superfluous. As has been pointed out elsewhere in this book, the causes of war are psychological as well as economic. People prepare for war, among other reasons, because war is in the great tradition; because their education has left them militaristically minded; because they live in a society where success is worshipped and competition is more highly appreciated than co-operation; because war is exciting and gives them certain personal or vicarious satisfactions. Hence the reluctance to embark on such constructive policies as mineral sanctions or intensive agriculture—policies which show some genuine promise of stopping war or removing its causes. Hence, too, the extraordinary energy which governments and peoples put into such destructive, war-provoking policies as re-armament, centralization and the enslavement of individuals to the state. Practical pacifists should work for any constructive policy which offers some hope of removing the causes of conflict. Among such policies, that of improving the methods of agriculture takes an important place.

Patriotism

"Patriotism," in Nurse Cavell's words, "is not enough."

It is not enough for the same reason as fetishism is not enough —because there is a larger Whole of which one's own country is only a small part. To give to an isolated part of the universe that reverence which properly belongs only to the Whole (or in the words of religion, to God) is idolatry; and idolatry is not only philosophically absurd, it is also disastrous in practice. The worship of a part as though it were the Whole provokes strife with the worshippers of other isolated parts. Each system of idolatry encourages its adherents to hate the adherents of all other systems.

In the case of patriotism we see that an idolatrous love of one's country is always accompanied by dislike and contempt of other people's countries. Where the nation is regarded as being in some sort a God, men feel that they have an excuse for indulging in pride and vanity in regard to themselves and their own people, and

70

scorn and dislike in regard to the members of other nations. Hellenes and Barbarians, Chosen People and Gentiles, Aryans and Non-Aryans, Proletarians and Bourgeois, God's Englishmen and "The Lesser Breeds without the Law"—the words expressing self-praise and contempt for others have varied from age to age and from country to country; but the disgraceful sentiments of idolatrous patriotism have always been the same.

To get rid of patriotism altogether is neither possible nor even desirable. Every human individual is born into one particular society and brought up to speak one particular language. His habits of thought and feelings are shaped in the moulds of one particular national tradition. It is inevitable that he should feel a special devotion for the community of which he is a member. Moreover, the fact that he is in specially close contact with his fellow-citizens imposes upon him special duties towards them— just as the even closer contact with parents, wife, children imposes upon him special duties towards his family. There is, then, a form of patriotism which is not only natural, but also right. Patriotism is wrong only when the country is deified and men's love for it becomes associated with pride and vanity on the one hand and contempt, suspicion and hatred on the other. The tree is known by its fruits, and a patriotism whose fruits are boasting and lying, swindling and stealing, threatening, bullying and, finally, wholesale murder, cannot conceivably be a good thing.

Circumstances cause us to feel a special love for and loyalty towards our country and impose, at the same time, special moral duties towards it. Among those duties is the duty to do all in one's power to preserve one's country from acting in ways which one knows to be wrong. It is a duty which, if we love our country, we shall undertake the more willingly; for nothing is more painful than to see a person one loves disgrace himself. The active pacifist is a better patriot than those imperialists and militarists who want their country to behave as a robber, a bully and a murderer. (See *Moral Equivalent of War; Nationalistic Religion.*)

The Peace Pledge Union

The Peace Pledge Union dates back to the day when Canon Sheppard invited any man who felt as he did to send him a postcard stating that he renounced war and would never again take part in another one. The invitation was given through the following letter which appeared in the Press on 16th October, 1934:—

The main reason for this letter, primarily addressed to men, is the fresh urgency of the present international situation, and the almost universally acknowledged lunacy of the manner in which nations are pursuing peace.

The situation is far graver than we allow ourselves to acknowledge, and the risks we are running by our present methods far graver than those which a more enlightened policy would involve.

Up to now the Peace Movement has received its main support from women, but it seems high time now that men should throw their weight into the scales against War.

I represent no Church and no peace organization of any description, but merely, I suggest, the mentality to which the average man has recently arrived without, as it seems, the knowledge of his accredited leaders in Church and State, or, for that matter, without their assistance.

It seems essential to discover whether or not it be true, as we are told, that the majority of thoughtful men in this country are now convinced that war of every kind or for any cause, is not only a denial of Christianity, but a crime against humanity, which is no longer to be permitted by civilized people.

Have we reached that state of belief?

I believe that we have, but I am certain that the time has come when we must know if that is a false or true statement.

The idea behind this letter is not to form any fresh organization, nor to call pacifists together to abuse those who conscientiously are not able to agree with them, but to attempt to discover how strong the will to peace has grown.

For myself, I believe that a vast number of male citizens who do not belong to any peace society and even dislike some of the methods of those who do, are only waiting an opportunity to declare once and for all that they have done with wars of every kind.

Many persons are avowing their determination to use violence, not only between nations, but within the nations.

An ever-increasing dependence on excessive force is evident in the movements known as Communism and Fascism.

It is time that those men who have not hitherto acted in any public way, but who wish the repudiation of methods of violence, should come into the open.

Would those of my sex who, so far, have been silent, but are of this mind, send a post-card to me within the next fortnight, addressed to:—

East Lodge,
Ashley Park,
Walton-on-Thames,

to say if they are willing to be called together in the near future to vote in support of a resolution as uncompromising as the following:—

"We renounce War and never again, directly or indirectly, will we support or sanction another."

If the response to this letter be as large as conceivably it may be, a notice will be sent at the earliest possible moment with full particulars of the day and date on which the demonstration will be made.

The response was immediate and overwhelming. Cards began to come in at once, and there has been a constant stream of them ever since. By the end of the first twelve months the number of pledged members had reached a total of some 80,000, and by the beginning of 1937 it had grown to nearer 130,000.

So "Dick Sheppard's Army" was enlisted and the first demonstration which the original letter had promised was held at the Albert Hall in June, 1935, when over 7,000 men of all ages (many of them ex-Service men), most professions, and very different circumstances gathered from all parts of the country to register their determination to have nothing more to do with war.

It was not long, however, before the question arose as to what effective use could be made of this answer to his personal appeal. He saw that it was no longer possible to regard it as a kind of private venture. By reason of its numerical and moral strength it has become a national movement. Canon Sheppard therefore invited some leading men and women to join him as sponsors, and it became the Peace Pledge Movement under the guidance of these sponsors, who today consist of Harold Bing, Vera Brittain, H. Runham Brown, General Crozier, James Hudson, Aldous Huxley, Storm Jameson, George Lansbury, Rose Macaulay, Stuart Morris, Philip Mumford, Lord Ponsonby, Charles Raven, Bertrand Russell, Siegfried Sassoon, H. R. L. Sheppard, Donald Soper, Arthur Wragg, Alex Wood and Wilfred Wellock.

So far the Movement had been confined to men, but the problems of Peace were obviously as much the concern of women as of men, and so the decision was taken to ask for the signatures of women.

Once more there was an immediate response, although the Press did not give the same publicity to this new phase as to the earlier letter. At first the women's pledge differed slightly from the men's, but henceforward there will be one common pledge— the simple renunciation of the war method in all circumstances. Both men and women are admitted on the same basis with the one reservation that it is intended to keep such a balance between the two sides of the Movement, that the number of women signatories will not be allowed to exceed the number of men signatories. So the Peace Pledge Union—for such is its name today—covers the whole country and represents one of the biggest movements in our national life.

A start was made by taking temporary offices in Trafalgar Square. Today, headquarters are housed in offices at 96, Regent Street, and Max Plowman has become General Secretary. Mr. John Barclay is acting as Group Organizer and it is hoped that area secretaries will be appointed in due course.

A word must be said about General Crozier, to whose care was entrusted the keeping of the records at the Recruiting Headquarters in his charge at Walton-on-Thames, where originally all the Pledge Cards were filed. With the acquisition of permanent headquarters in London, however, this department has been transferred to Regent Street.

In the meantime, the Union is busy with the organization of

local groups. All over the country signatories have been asked to meet at some hall, easy of access, in order that they might get to know one another, and be put wise as to the aims of the Movement.

In many cases a Regional Committee links up the contiguous groups, and groups are dividing themselves into teams of ten to twenty members. It is within these groups and teams that the real work of the Peace Pledge Union must be done.

It is sometimes said that Pacifism is a mere negation; but if it begins with the refusal to take part in war, it does not and cannot end there. We have an obligation to work out the lines of constructive peace. To that end, Aldous Huxley wrote the first official pamphlet of the Movement, "What are you going to do about it?" explaining its aims and basis. Gerald Heard has written a second which deals more with organization. Other pamphlets and leaflets have been written and are in preparation. There is ample material for the groups who are continuing courses of corporate study on the general aims of the Peace Movement or on any particular subject which may appeal to them; e.g. the Colonial problem, the New World Conference, etc. Groups also provide the opportunity for the exchange of views among their members, who can thus face up to individual difficulties and become equipped to answer attacks in the Press, etc. Members must be ready also to be missionaries and embark on propaganda through open-air and other meetings. Indeed, every individual member of a group can find some job that he or she can do; and all should be doing something. The Union now has its official paper in *Peace News*, which is published weekly. It is hoped that every member will become a regular subscriber and endeavour to secure an ever-increasing circulation.

Other ventures are worthy of note. The Union opened a shop in Ludgate Hill. Every day a large number of inquiries were dealt with, and for two different periods midday meetings were held in the basement. These were attended by a growing number

75

of those whose work brought them to the City. The Union also opened an office in Brussels during the International Peace Congress in 1936. There its representatives were able to make contact with many Continental pacifists. The Union held a special meeting at the conclusion of the Congress, at which the aims, program and methods were explained to a gathering consisting, in the main, of British and American delegates. A most useful conference was also held with leaders of Continental Pacifist Organizations. Some twenty groups were represented, and there was a discussion on possible ways of co-ordination with special reference to a proposal to inaugurate an International Pacifist Movement.

At the beginning of 1937 the P.P.U. carried out an intensive campaign, in the course of which many of the large cities and towns in East England, Scotland and Wales were visited by a team of speakers who addressed large and enthusiastic meetings.

Later in the year an event of real significance to the peace movement occurred when the No More War Movement decided to abandon its separate identity and become merged in the P.P.U. To facilitate this, two of the No More War Movement representatives were added to the sponsors and an undertaking was given that as soon as an opportunity arose the whole movement should be given as democratic and representative a shape as possible. The actual constitution of the P.P.U. is being worked out and it is hoped that before long it will be finally approved and adopted.

It should be added that the P.P.U. is affiliated with the War Resisters' International, fuller particulars of which will be found elsewhere in this encyclopædia.

The policy of the P.P.U. arises out of the basis of membership which is the renunciation of the war method. It is specially concerned with the present race in armaments and is taking every opportunity to protest at the British Armament proposals. Particularly it is asking that the public shall refuse to participate in the Anti Air Raid Precautions on the ground that they are inadequate, and calculated to develop a war mentality and prepare the way for the conscription of the Civil population. Further it is concerned by the fact that the attempt to cure unemployment by rearmament means that many a man who has a conscientious objection to making arms is being offered war-work as the only method of ending a long period of enforced idleness.

It is recognized that it is not sufficient merely to say "No" to War. Pacifism must have a constructive policy and there is a moral obligation on the Union to work out such a positive program. The P.P.U. would press for the immediate calling of a new World Conference at which the representatives of all nations (rather than governments) should be invited to sit on terms of absolute equality around the "family" table in order that their needs and grievances might be frankly discussed. If we are to avoid war we must be prepared to discuss all the causes of possible war in a spirit of understanding and sympathy. All cards must be laid on the table, and those who "have" must recognize their responsibility towards those who "have not." The P.P.U. would also press for a reconstructed League of all the Nations, with such a court of equity as would make possible an extension of the mandate system, and from the Covenant of which the territorial clauses of the Treaty of Versailles should be dissociated and the penal clauses eliminated. For the P.P.U. cannot support sanctions.

Its verdict against war is absolute and it repudiates the war method as much when used in Self-Defence or in support of the League and Collective Security as in actual aggression. It is prepared to press for a general refusal to supply the financial and material sources necessary for war-making to both parties to a dispute as a logical extension of the determination of its members not to take part in war. For, above all, the P.P.U. stands for the method of non-violent resistance. It is not just content to do nothing. It aims at so working out the technique of non-violent resistance that it will set free the new spirit and create the new attitude in the world. It is not a specifically Christian movement nor is there any credal or denominational test of membership. But it does see Pacifism in terms of a Faith. As it denies the right of material force and power to usurp the position of ultimate authority, so it seeks to appeal to spiritual and moral power. It is a fellowship of men and women who are prepared to study constructive peace-making, become enthusiastic missionaries in the cause, and accept such discipline as would be necessary if we are all going to repudiate in all relationships the destructive method of violence and prove the redeeming power of Love.

We are living in critical days. It is not enough to desire peace or to talk peace. We must make personal decisions and live peace.

Any one, therefore, to whom this appears as a paramount issue, will find within the P.P.U. the ground on which he or she can meet with other pacifists, the encouragement of belonging to a great and growing movement, the fellowship within which is included the training of spirit, mind and body, essential if we are to rid the world of war. Peace cannot be made by Treaties, Pacts or Systems of Collective Security. It can only come when we create the conditions within which Peace is inevitable. The P.P.U. denies that war is inevitable—that it is anything but a sin, and it aims at creating those conditions which will make peace inevitable. It is therefore anxious to include within its membership and training everyone who is ready wholly to renounce war and to live instead for peace.

Peace Treaties

It is often said that war begets war. But it would be more correct to say that the Peace Treaties signed at the conclusion of a war almost invariably sow seeds of future conflicts. Of the Great War it has been quite fairly asserted that while we won the war we lost the peace. It is a good, although an extreme, instance showing how victors in their hour of triumph cannot act justly. They are thinking of the immediate past, not of the future; and punishment is the idea that is uppermost in their minds. The vanquished had been incessantly described while the war lasted as a criminal nation which was solely responsible for the war. Although this charge was, as time passed, qualified, mitigated, and finally no longer asserted, it was at the moment of triumph the dominant justification for punishment. Moreover, the people in the triumphant nations, wounded and suffering and still enflamed against the enemy, could be counted on to support the infliction of severe punishment. The atmosphere thus created was irresistible. Consequently purely punitive articles were inserted in the Treaties of Versailles and St. Germain, with the enthusiastic consent of the Allied and Associated Powers.

The payment of a fantastic indemnity was imposed on Germany, singled out as the chief culprit, unilateral disarmament was enforced on her, she was deprived of all her colonies, and her frontiers as well as those of her allies were adjusted according to strategic considerations to cramp and weaken their national life. In four years Germany had been beaten to her knees. In the subsequent twenty years every effort had to be made to set her on her feet again. This process was too slow, although the victorious governments gradually realized that the creation of a danger spot of resentment and of a spirit of revenge, the natural result of their punishment, must dislocate the economic life of all nations and be a menace to world peace. So, as we now find, the Treaties are being scrapped bit by bit and the follies of Versailles and St. Germain are being retracted, lest the imposition of any of the penal clauses should lead to another war.

This example is fresh in our minds. Others could be quoted. Twenty-five years after the signature of the Treaty of Vienna (at the conclusion of the Napoleonic wars) only one clause delineating the frontiers of Switzerland remained in force.

79

Police Methods

War is often justified on the ground that when it is "in support of Law" (which means in practice when it is being waged by one's own country) it is no more than police action. (This was the view expressed by the Archbishop of York when arguing against pacifism.) Let us consider the differences between the police and the military:

(1) The police are generally unarmed. Their prime task is the prevention of crime and the forestalling of public disturbances.

(2) When a crime has been committed, or when trouble has broken out, the function of the police is to arrest the person or persons who are guilty. They have no power of inflicting punishment and they are not permitted to use more force than is necessary to secure the arrest of the guilty party.

Armies are radically different from police forces.

(1) They are armed, and the more efficient their arms become, the more indiscriminate becomes the destruction which they inflict.

(2) The force which they are empowered to use is not limited. Their function is not to restrain the guilty; it is to destroy all things and people within their range. When the police wish to arrest a criminal, they do not burn up a town in which he is living and kill or torture all its inhabitants. But this precisely is what an army does, particularly an army using modern weapons.

(3) States arrogate to themselves the right, not only to judge other states, but also, by means of their armies, to punish them. The principle is wholly repugnant to law; moreover, the process of punishing a guilty nation entails the destruction of countless innocent individuals. An army with tanks and bombing squadrons is not and cannot be a police force. Nor can its essentially evil and destructive functions be moralized by calling it a League army, an instrument of collective security, etc. Police operate with the universal consent of the community which employs them. Armies operate at the order of one among the nations or the few nations which are allied together.

(See *Force*; *International Police Force*; *Sanctions*.)

Political Implications of Pacifism

The ultimate realities of the human world are individual men and women. Physically, all human beings belong to a single species and a spiritual unity underlies all their divergencies of native ability and acquired habit. These are the facts of experience upon which the pacifist bases his philosophy. His fundamental ethical principles spring from these facts and may be formulated thus: Human personality must be respected. Individuals, in the words of Kant, must always be regarded as ends in themselves, not as means. It is the duty of every man to do all in his power to realize in practice that fundamental human unity which is obscured by the organized greed and the organized hatred of our nationalisms, our religions and our economic systems.

The political implications of pacifism may be briefly summed up as follows:

(1) Democratic institutions. Pacifism is incompatible with any form of tyranny. Conversely war and preparation for war on the modern scale are incompatible with personal liberty and democratic institutions. In the world of today an enslaved country under a tyrant is an efficient war-machine; a democratically organized country is not. We are faced with the choice between preparation for war, accompanied by slavery, on the one hand, and pacifism, accompanied by personal liberty and democratic institutions, on the other.

(2) Decentralization. Democratic principles cannot be effectively put into practice except in a community where authority has been as far as possible decentralized. Another important point: it is hard in a decentralized state for any one man to impose his will on the whole community. Social reform aims at taking away the opportunities for evil. In a decentralized state the ambitious man is not "led into temptation"; in other words, he is given few opportunities for indulging his ruling passions at the expense of others. It is of the utmost importance that the amount of power that can be wielded by any one individual should be strictly limited, and one of the great merits of decentralization is that it

automatically does this. To place limitations on personal wealth and the private ownership of the means of production is desirable for the same reason.

(3) Local and professional self-government. Decentralization must be accompanied by self-government, not only in municipal matters but also in industry and the professions. Industrial organizations are, too often, miniature dictatorships. Respect for human personality demands that there should be decentralization into self-governing groups in all the trades and professions. In many cases, as Dubreuil has shown in his interesting book, *A Chacun sa Chance,* decentralization into self-governing groups leads, not only to more satisfactory human relations, but also to greater efficiency.

(4) Improvement of social services and extension of educational facilities. It is unnecessary to elaborate this point.

(5) Disarmament, unilateral if necessary. Liquidation of empire, either by liberations of subject peoples or by transference of control, under a genuine mandate system to international authority.

(6) Removal of barriers to international trade.

(See *Economic Implications of Pacifism.*)

Prestige and National Honour

Prestige is the diplomatic name for vanity. In individuals, vanity is regarded as stupid and contemptible. In nations it is regarded as something admirable. Owing to our double system of morality, we condemn the man whose actions are motivated by vanity; but the nation which goes to war for the sake of its prestige (in other words, for the sake of national vanity) is regarded as reasonable and even noble.

Whenever questions of national honour and prestige are being discussed, it is good to remember the following points:

(1) The nation is not a person and is therefore incapable of

82

having the feelings which politicians and journalists like to attribute to it. The nation consists of a collection of individual men and women. To say that the nation has feelings and a will apart from the feelings and wills of individuals composing it, is false.

(2) The ruling classes find that they can consolidate their power by representing the nation as a kind of superhuman person with feelings and a will of its own. As representatives of this superhuman person, they partake of its divinity and they are able, by means of propaganda, to persuade the masses that what they, the rulers, want to do is what the divine, national person wants to do.

(3) The ruling classes are much more preoccupied with questions of national prestige than the masses. The reasons for this are of various kinds. (a) Being rulers, they tend to associate themselves with the nation they control. Its successes are their successes; its failures are their failures. National prestige is largely the personal prestige of the nation's diplomats, ministers, civil servants and the like. (b) National prestige is in many cases associated with colonial possessions. Colonial possessions offer a particularly attractive field for the speculative investor. Colonies may not be profitable to the community which owns them; often, indeed, they are a burden on the taxpayers of the colonizing country. In many cases, however, they are extremely profitable to a small class of financiers, who find that they can get very high yields for their money in colonial enterprises. Another class which profits by the existence of colonies is the class from which administrators are drawn. These people get a secure income out of their country's colonial possessions and, more important, an opportunity to exercise power in a way which would be impossible at home. Not unnaturally, the members of these two classes are keen imperialists, and feel that any threat to a colonial possession is a threat to the nation's honour and prestige. Newspapers are owned and edited by members of these two classes. Newspaper opinion

is therefore intensely preoccupied with questions of national honour and prestige. But newspaper opinion is not the opinion of the masses. To ordinary working men and women it would be a matter of almost complete indifference if the Japanese, for example, were to seize Hong-Kong. They would not feel that national honour was compromised and they would not feel that it was worth while, for the sake of prestige, to send their sons to go and murder and be murdered in a far-eastern battle. If they knew how Hong-Kong had been acquired, they would feel even less concern about the keeping up of British prestige. Hong-Kong was ceded to us at the end of the war which we fought in order to compel the Chinese Government to take the opium which we were growing in India. The Chinese Government regarded opium as a curse and tried to stop the trade. The British Government compelled the Chinese to take opium by force of arms. When the war was over, Hong-Kong was seized as an indemnity. National honour, it must be admitted, is a very curious commodity.

Propaganda

On the outbreak of war it is as necessary to inflame public opinion into a state of indignation and hatred of her enemy as it is to supply the fighting forces with munitions. The case against the enemy must be stated with complete bias and a suitable amount of exaggeration. Any arguments in support of the enemy's case must be suppressed. As early as possible atrocities perpetrated by the enemy must be circulated and the enemy's cruel treatment of prisoners described in order to prevent desertions. In the official circular issued during the Great War, when an endeavour was made to collect the necessary material, it was written: "Essential not literal truth and correctness are necessary. Inherent probability being respected, the thing imagined may be as serviceable as the thing seen." Lies, therefore, are circulated

84

by each government to stir up resentment in their people. In a country which has not conscription they have to be more lurid and more frequent than in conscripted nations. Faked photographs are useful and studios for the photography of hideous mutilations can be set up. A good catch-phrase is of special value. In the Great War the Kaiser's supposed reference to the British expeditionary force as "the contemptible little army" helped recruiting more than any other effort that was made. It was only discovered after the war was over that he never said anything of the kind and was not even at the place where he was supposed to have made this statement. No invention about the enemy published independently by the press is ever checked. But any attempt to plead for peace or to say a good word for the enemy may be ruthlessly punished.

It will thus be seen that there was unlimited use, not only of physical violence, but also of fraud. Lies are as necessary in war as shells or planes. Meanwhile militarists assure us that war is the school of virtue. (Consult *Falsehood in Wartime*, by Lord Ponsonby.)

Where the intervals of peace are used for the preparation of fresh wars, propaganda also plays an important part. It is a significant fact that it is precisely in those countries where military preparations are carried on most intensively that truth is most carefully distorted and suppressed. In the liberal countries there is no official peace-time censorship, such as exists in the totalitarian states. But this does not mean, unhappily, that there is no suppression or distortion of truth in the press of these countries. Newspapers are now run almost exclusively for profit. The result is that nothing must be printed that may dry up the sources of profit. Anything which might frighten away advertisers is kept out of the papers. Nor must we forget the power of the socially irresponsible rich men who own newspapers. These men dictate policy to their editors according to the whim of the moment or their own pecuniary interests. Private, plutocratic censorship takes the place in liberal countries of the official state censorship of totalitarian countries. Luckily, the whims and the financial interests of the plutocrats are not identical. What one suppresses, another allows to appear. More truth gets through in the liberal than in the totalitarian countries. Still, the system in both is thoroughly vicious. (Consult Hamilton Fyfe's *Press Parade*.)

Racialism

Racialism is the belief that certain human groups, commonly and often erroneously called races, have in respect of all their members innate mental or moral differences from other groups.

Where these groups are races in the scientific sense, where, that is to say, there are well-defined physical differences between one group and another, it is possible that these physical differences have mental or moral counterparts. It may be, for example, that the physiological causes which produce red hair and an aquiline nose are linked with qualities of the inner man different from those linked with black hair and a snub nose. But while this may be the case, the attempts which have hitherto been made to prove it cover far too narrow a field of investigation for their results to be accepted with any confidence.

Racialism, however, as it is popularly understood, has little to do with race as scientifically defined. The Jews are regarded as a race, yet they are a community of the most diverse physical types, united only by a common religion and to some extent a similar environment. The "Latin races" consist of people of various types, united only by the fact that their ancestors were thoroughly conquered by the Romans. The "British race" is descended from a score of immigrant waves, offshoots of larger groups which remained outside.

It is impossible to suppose that such groups possess innate qualities except by completely ignoring the effect of environment upon character.

86

Revolution

Left Wing pacifists denounce the violence of capitalists, but consider that any violence used by themselves or their friends in defence of a socialist community against foreign aggressors, or, within a capitalist community, against the ruling classes is fully justified. Let us consider these two contingencies.

(1) In modern air warfare there is no defence except counter-attack, directed against the centres of population. If a socialist state is attacked, its airmen must go and drop fire and poison on the enemy's cities. It is extremely unlikely that they will ever kill a member of the enemy's capitalist government, for the good reason that governments always take extremely good care to remove themselves to places of safety. The people who will bear the brunt of the socialist airmen's attack will be workers and their wives and children. Thus, the proletarian state will be "defended" by the wholesale slaughter of proletarians.

Another point: a socialist state which is to wage war successfully against its enemies must be at least as well organized, for military purposes, as they are. But high military efficiency cannot be achieved except by resorting to policies which are essentially fascist and imperialistic in character. Military efficiency demands extreme concentration of power, a high degree of centralization, the training of the masses in passive obedience to their superiors, the imposition of some form of conscription or slavery to the state, and the creation of a local idolatry with the nation or a semi-deified tyrant as the object of worship. The defence of Socialism against Fascism by military means entails the transformation of the socialist community into a fascist community. Even before war has broken out, the process of military preparation will have transformed the liberty, the justice, the democracy for whose sake violence is to be used, into slavery, hierarchical privilege and tyranny. During the war and after it, the state of things will of course be much worse than before. There is only one method of defence which will not transform socialism into its opposite, and that is the method of non-violent resistance. A socialist community of men and women educated to be free and self-reliant, and trained in the methods of non-violence as intensively as they are now being trained in the methods of violence could allow a foreign army to invade its territory and still put up a defence of socialism that would have a good chance of being successful. Military defence, on the contrary, has no chance whatsoever of being successful. Even if the socialists win the war they will long since have ceased to be socialists. Nor will they be able, after victory, to return to their principles. Surrounded by defeated enemies, all thirsting for revenge, they will have to go on preparing for future wars.

(2) Tanks, planes, gases and thermite have made nonsense of the old revolutionary tactics. The days of the barricade are over. No violent revolutionary movement can hope to be successful unless it disposes of modern armaments and the services of technicians. Where both sides have modern weapons, revolution becomes a civil war (as in Spain), and there is massacre and destruction on an enormous scale.

Social revolution is a movement for humanity and against all that is base and inhuman. A social revolution that is prepared to slaughter and destroy is a contradiction in terms; a bloody revolution is not a change for the better, it is a repetition of all that is worst and least human in the existing order. Moreover, if the revolution is to slaughter efficiently, it must be organized on a military basis, that is, it must become a fascist dictatorship. Karl Marx called violence "The midwife of a new order of society." The facts do not bear this out. Violence begets violence and is therefore the perpetuator of the old order. Barthélemy de Ligt has summed up the whole matter in a single phrase: the more violence, the less revolution.

Advantages of non-violent resistance. (1) In the modern world the masses are not in a position to use violence as effectively as the ruling classes. It is by the use of non-violent tactics, including the refusal to work, to pay taxes, to buy certain classes of goods that the masses can resist oppression most effectively. (2) Violence on the modern scale destroys vast numbers of lives and vast amounts of accumulated wealth (buildings, railways, machinery, etc.). The casualties among non-violent resisters may be high; but it is unlikely, as history shows, that they will be as high as in a violent struggle. Where non-violent resistance is used, there is no destruction of accumulated wealth. (3) The use of violence leads to a definite lowering of moral standards, a definite dehumanization of individuals participating in the slaughter and destruction. The use of non-violence leads, as was clearly demonstrated in South Africa, in Corea, in India, to a raising of the human level among all concerned.

Objections to the use of non-violent tactics:

(1) "They are not effective." Answer: If sufficient numbers, sufficiently well trained, employ non-violent methods, they are effective. The non-violent opposition of the Hungarians to Austrian oppression (1861–7), the non-violent resistance put up by the Indians in Natal against the oppression of the South African government (1907–13), the non-violent refusal of the Finns to submit to conscription (1902), the non-violent action of English workmen protesting against the Government's military campaign against Bolshevik Russia—these were all fully successful. The Hungarians were given all they demanded; the Finns were not conscribed; the iniquitous legislation against the Hindus was repealed; and the British Government was forced to abandon its military activities against Russia.

(2) "It would take a very long time to carry through a revolution by non-violent means." Answer: It will probably take even longer to carry it through by violence. Indeed, there is good reason to believe that a genuine revolution can never be carried out violently. The French revolution used violence and resulted in a temporary military dictatorship and the permanent imposition upon all Frenchmen of military slavery, or conscription. The Russian revolution used violence; and today, Russia is a military dictatorship. It looks as though genuine revolution, that is, the

89

change from the inhuman to the human, could not be effected by means of violence.

(3) "The cases already cited prove how difficult it is to induce people to use non-violent methods." Answer: Every people is conditioned by its history. Long oppressed by the Tsars, living in a badly organized society which, in 1917, had been reduced to anarchy, the Russians were probably foredoomed by their history to make use of violence in their revolution. This is not true of the peoples of the Western democracies. Thanks to the Quakers and other sects of Protestant Christians, the English have long been familiar with pacifist ideas. They have not, in recent times, had to suffer very violent oppression, while habits of humanitarianism are well established in English society. The organization of non-violent action in favour of a genuine social revolution would not be very difficult in England. The same is true of such countries as Holland, Denmark, Norway, Sweden, and to a lesser extent of Belgium and France. (See *Civil War; Force; Non-Violence*.)

Sanctions

The moral problem of Sanctions is the moral problem of war. Economic sanctions cannot remain merely economic; applied with vigour, they can only lead to war. Sanctionists try to conceal this fact by calling their brand of war by high-sounding names. We must not be deceived by words. "Collective security" means, in the circumstance of today, a system of opposed alliances. And "international police force" is merely a composite army furnished by a group of allied powers. As for "military sanctions"—they are plain war; and war is always war, whatever you may choose to call it.

Once war has broken out, nations will take sides or remain neutral according to their national interests, not as any international covenant dictates. Speaking at Leamington (November 20, 1936) Mr. Eden stated that "our armaments may be used in bringing help to a victim of aggression in any case where, in our judgment, it would be proper under the provisions of the Covenant to do so. I use the word 'may' deliberately since in such an instance there is no automatic obligation to take military action. It is, moreover, right that this should be so, for nations cannot be expected to incur automatic military obligations save for areas where their vital interests are concerned." This means that, in practice, a League war against an aggressor would be simply a war between two groups of allied powers, with other neutral powers looking on. Sanctionists believe that the mere display of a great military force would be enough to deter would-be aggressors. The greater your force, the slighter the probability that you will have to use it; therefore, they argue, re-arm for the sake of peace. The facts of history do not bear out this contention. Threats do not frighten the determined nor do the desperate shrink before a display of overwhelming force. Moreover, in the contemporary world, there is no reason to suppose that the force mustered against an aggressor will be overwhelming. The "League" and the "aggressor" will be too well-matched sets of allied powers.

"Military sanctions" are to be applied in order to bring about a just settlement of disputes. But the prospects of achieving a just settlement at the end of a League war are no better than at the end of an ordinary war. Passions run so high during war, that it is morally certain that the final settlement will be unjust and that another war will break out as soon as the conquered feel strong enough to take their revenge.

Not only would sanctions fail to produce the results they are meant to produce; they cannot even be applied. The neighbours of aggressor states will always be deterred from applying even economic sanctions by the thought that they will be the first to suffer reprisals. Countries will fight only when their vital interests are involved. Upholding the League Covenant is not regarded by any nation as a vital interest. Those who refuse to enforce sanctions against an aggressor have themselves infringed the Covenant. Who is going to enforce sanctions against *them*?

Morality and practical common sense are at one in demanding that Article XVI should be omitted from the Covenant and that the League should concentrate on active co-operative work for removing the causes of war. The attempt to cure war, once it has broken out, by means of Sanctions (that is, more war) is fore-doomed to failure.

(See *International Police Force; League of Nations, The.*)

Secret Treaties

When war is declared the nation is likely to have the support of declared allies, but it will also wish to enlist the support of other nations. It therefore becomes necessary to decide on division of the spoils in the event of victory. The history of the Great War provides numerous examples of Secret Treaties concluded in these circumstances. Between 1915 and 1917 secret engagements were entered into between this country and France, Italy, Japan, Roumania, Russia, Serbia and Montenegro, covering a very large field of possible conquests which might be expected.

To mention only two of the more important stipulations: By the secret Treaty of London, signed in April 1915, Italy was to receive the Trentino and the Tyrol as far as the Brenner, Trieste and Istria, all the Dalmatian coast except Fiume, full ownership of Vallona and a protectorate over the rest of Albania, a "just share" of Turkey and "equitable compensation" in Africa. A few weeks earlier Russia had been promised Constantinople, several Mediterranean islands and bits of Thrace and Asia Minor.

The text of these Treaties was discovered in the archives of the Russian Foreign Office and published by the Russian Government after the revolution. They illustrate very clearly the fact that, once war has broken out, all considerations of justice disappear. Nothing matters any more except victory and, to secure victory, governments are prepared to make the most cynically immoral arrangements with anyone whose aid can be bought.

(See *Secret Treaties*, by F. Seymour Cocks [Union of Democratic Control]. Temperley, *History of the Peace Conference*, Vols. 5 and 6.)

Shelley

In 1819 a meeting in favour of parliamentary reform, held in the Peterloo Fields at Manchester, was broken up by a cavalry charge. Six persons were killed and many injured. When the news reached Shelley, who was living in Italy at the time, "it roused in him," says Mrs. Shelley, "violent emotions of indignation and compassion." The great truth that the many, if accordant and resolute, could control the few, as was shown a few days later, made him long to teach his injured countrymen how to resist. Inspired by these feelings, he wrote *The Mask of Anarchy*. The method of resistance inculcated by Shelley in *The Mask of Anarchy* is the method of non-violence.

> Stand ye calm and resolute,
> Like a forest, close and mute,
> With folded arms and looks that are
> Weapons of unvanquished war. . . .
>
> And if then the tyrants dare,
> Let them ride among you there,
> Slash, and stab, and maim and hew—
> What they like, that let them do.
>
> With folded arms and steady eyes,
> And little fear, and less surprise,
> Look upon them as they slay
> Till their rage has passed away.
>
> Then they will return with shame
> To the place from which they came,
> And the blood thus shed will speak
> In hot blushes on their cheek.

Every woman in the land
Will point at them as they stand—
They will hardly dare to greet
Their acquaintance in the street.

And that slaughter to the Nation
Shall steam up like inspiration,
Eloquent, oracular,
A volcano heard afar.

Rise like Lions after slumber
In unvanquishable number—
Shake your chains to earth like dew
Which in sleep had fallen on you—
Ye are many—they are few.

War Resisters' International

The Peace Pledge Union is affiliated to the War Resisters' Inter.
national and has now become the British Section. But there are
forty-nine other sections in twenty-four different countries—some
of them large national movements, others quite small. Some are
legal and work openly with much publicity, others are illegal and
have to work underground. The International extends into sixty-
eight countries in all of which it has its members and correspondents.

The Declaration adopted at the first meeting of the International
in 1921 and confirmed at each successive Conference since, is:
"War is a crime against humanity. We therefore are determined
not to support any kind of war and to strive for the removal of all
causes of war." To this Declaration each member subscribes.

A very remarkable Statement of Principles was drawn up at the
first meeting fifteen years ago and finally adopted at the First
International Conference in 1925. This statement is so comprehensive that no change has been desired and no addition made to it.
Were this statement re-written today—1937—reference might be

made to war to defend democracy or war for an ideal, but our Statement of Principles leaves us in no doubt. The War Resisters' International, while often impelled to sympathy with one side in a conflict more than with the other, recognizes that the resort to armed violence, or any form of warfare, is damaging most of all to the "good cause."

STATEMENT OF PRINCIPLES

WAR IS A CRIME AGAINST HUMANITY.

It is a crime against life, and uses human personalities for political and economic ends.

WE, THEREFORE,

actuated by an intense love of mankind,

ARE DETERMINED NOT TO SUPPORT

either directly by service of any kind in the army, navy, or air forces, or indirectly by making or consciously handling munitions or other war material, subscribing to war loans or using our labour for the purpose of setting others free for war service.

ANY KIND OF WAR,

aggressive or defensive, remembering that modern wars are invariably alleged by Governments to be defensive.

Wars would seem to fall under three heads:

(a) *Wars to defend the State* to which we nominally belong and wherein our home is situated. To refuse to take up arms for this end is difficult:

　　1. Because the State will use all its coercive powers to make us do so.

　　2. Because our inborn love for home has been deliberately identified with love of the State in which it is situated.

(b) *Wars to preserve the existing order of society* with its security for the privileged few. That we would never take up arms for this purpose goes without saying.

(c) *Wars on behalf of the oppressed proletariat,* whether for its liberation or defence. To refuse to take up arms for this purpose is most difficult:

　　1. Because of the proletarian régime, and, even more, the enraged masses, in time of revolution would regard as a traitor any one who refused to support the New Order by force.

2. Because our instinctive love for the suffering and the oppressed would tempt us to use violence on their behalf.

However, we are convinced that violence cannot really *preserve order, defend* our home, or *liberate* the proletariat. In fact, experience has shown that in all wars, order, security, and liberty disappear, and that, so far from benefiting by them, the proletariat always suffer most.

We hold, however, that consistent pacifists have no right to take up a merely negative position, but *must recognize*

AND STRIVE FOR THE REMOVAL OF ALL THE CAUSES OF WAR.

We recognize as causes of war not only the instinct of egoism and greed, which is found in every human heart, but also all agencies which create hatred and antagonism between groups of people. Among such, we would regard the following as the more important today:

1. Differences between *races*, leading by artificial aggravation to envy and hatred.

2. Differences between *religions*, leading to mutual intolerance and contempt.

3. Differences between the *classes*, the possessing and the non-possessing, leading to civil war, which will continue so long as the present system of production exists, and private profit rather than social need is the outstanding motive of society.

4. Differences between *nations*, due largely to the present system of production, leading to world wars and such economic chaos as we see today, which eventualities, we are convinced, could be prevented by the adoption of a system of world economy which had for its end the well-being of the entire human race.

5. Finally, we see an important cause of war in the prevalent misconception of the State. The State exists for man, not man for the State. The recognition of the sanctity of human personality must become the basic principle of human society. Furthermore, the State is not a sovereign self-contained entity, as every nation is a part of the great family of mankind. We feel, therefore, that consistent pacifists have no right to take up a merely negative position, but must devote themselves to abolishing classes, barriers between the peoples, and to creating a world-wide brotherhood founded on mutual service.

War Resistance is not an end in itself, it is a way of life to achieve an end. The goal, in the expression of the Socialist is, Liberty, Equality, Fraternity; in that of the Christian it is, Truth, Beauty, Love, a world where all can and will desire to co-operate for the common good.

THE COST TO THE INTERNATIONAL

There are 493 war resisters in the prisons of Europe alone, young men who have resolutely resisted the conscription laws of their country and who face loss of liberty, ostracism, poverty and often death. Many thousands have passed through prison, many have died in prison or after release. You are not asked to pity them, you will need all your pity for the soldier boys blindly led to the shambles. The man in prison you can respect, look up to him as your leader in the struggle.

THE WORK OF THE INTERNATIONAL

The International is guided by a Council which is elected for three years at the Triennial Conference which meets in a different country each time. The paid staff number three, the voluntary staff thirty-six. The budget is a little over £1,450 per annum and is raised by voluntary contributions.

The War Resisters' International has become a clearing house of ideas as well as a practical centre for the transfer of letters between countries where there is not even a postal convention providing for direct mail or where censors are too difficult to avoid. The International acts as a banker, holding contra accounts to overcome the restrictions on transfer of currency. It serves the Movement in innumerable ways.

Sometimes it does big jobs, sending its representatives to International Labour Movements, Conferences and even to Governments.

The International has to speak in many tongues. Fourteen languages are normally used and for this the services of twenty-eight voluntary translators have been enlisted who work regularly for the movement.

The War Resisters' International publishes its quarterly bulletin, *The War Resister,* in French, German, English and Esperanto, together with much other literature. Every publication goes into Russia in the Russian language. Several publications in Spanish are at the disposal of Spanish comrades both in Spain and South

America. Literature in Italian finds its way into Italy, while re-prints appear in a dozen other languages.

THE SECTIONS OF THE INTERNATIONAL

No adequate idea of the Sections and their work can be given here. Many are illegal, their work has to be carried on with great care and our members take very considerable personal risks. The International often has to take over all records and not only keep direct contact with the leaders of sections, but with thousands of individual members. This work cannot be reported here.

In more democratic countries the movement has grown rapidly in recent years. In Denmark, for instance, where the membership has been doubled each year for several years—4,000 members in a little population of only one million is considerable. The U.S.A. has 10,000 members in one Section and many thousands in an-other. In Canada, 2,000 have signed the Peace Pledge Union's Declaration and the International has had to take over direct contact pending the formation of the Canadian Peace Pledge Union.

Space is quite inadequate to convey the immensity of this world-wide family, living a way of life, forerunners of a Revolution that will one day make of the world a garden where all shall co-operate for the good of all.

Women in Modern War, Position of

Between 1914 and 1918 the part played by women in carrying on the war was considerable. In France, for example, towards the end of the war, 1,500,000 women were employed in the war indus-tries alone. In England the number of women employed in industry at large was about three millions. Of these, a considerable propor-tion worked in munition factories. Most of the rest took the place of men who were thus released for military service.

In the last war, women gave their services voluntarily. In the next, they will almost certainly be subject to conscription. In the words of a French military writer. Colonel Émile Mayer, "It is the function of the military authority to exploit its human materials [*sic*] as best it can, in the interests of national defence, without regard to the age of the individuals." Again, in time of national crisis, every citizen "is at the disposal of the State, whatever his or her sex." In any future war there will be, not merely military conscription, but also industrial, intellectual and moral conscription: and the whole population, women, children and the aged, as well as men, will be subjected to this State-imposed slavery. War is no longer an affair conducted by a small body of professionals; it has become totalitarian. Women are as intimately concerned in it as men.

Index

Appendix A

An Additional Note on the Peace Pledge Union (1984)

Dick Sheppard died suddenly on 31 October, 1937, but the movement which he had hitherto run in a very personal way was strong enough to develop its own momentum and ways of working. Since 1939 the governing body of the PPU has been an elected Council, the role of sponsors being purely honorific.

In 1939 also Dick Sheppard House, 6 Endsleigh Street, London WC1, was purchased out of the memorial fund for Dick Sheppard as the permanent headquarters of the PPU.

Although *Peace News* still continues as a pacifist paper (now published fortnightly) its formal links with the PPU were severed by mutual agreement in 1960. The PPU now has a monthly journal *The Pacifist*. The bookshop venture was eventually permanently established as Housmans Bookshop, but since 1960 also that has been run independently.

The reference to the "proposal to inaugurate an International Pacifist Movement" reads very oddly, because such a role has been fulfilled since its inception by the War Resisters International. It is known that the Brussels Congress of 1936 presented problems for the PPU in that the majority of continental participants were not pacifist in the sense of wholly renouncing war, and it is likely that the body envisaged was an international of organisations concerned with peace rather than wholly pacifist. This continental use of the word 'pacifist' still causes some confusion.

The Second World War naturally tested the allegiance of PPU members to their pledges, and there were some who fell away at this time (including four of the sponsors mentioned—Storm Jameson, Rose Macaulay, Philip Mumford and

Bertrand Russell) but many new people joined during the War. Numbers of members refused military service and other forms of directed labor, even at the cost of imprisonment.

The policy of the PPU continues to arise out of the pledge as the basis of membership, although there is no longer any concern whether women might outnumber men as members. The personal renunciation of war is seen as the responsibility of everyone, regardless of sex, age, class, religion or nationality, and the co-operation of everyone is needed in bringing about the ultimate abolition of war.

The emphasis indicated by Huxley on the calling of world conferences no longer applies to the PPU. It is now generally accepted that such a policy, though sincerely advocated, was extremely naive. Indeed, the only visible product of so-called disarmament conferences since the 1930s has been an ever more rapidly increasing escalation of the arms race with more and more states joining in. The PPU has been increasingly influenced by Gandhian concepts of personal responsibility and small group action, as well as the more recent experience of Martin Luther King, Jr.

Again, the 1930s distinction between the so-called 'have' nations of Britain, France of Belgium as against the 'have-not' nations of Germany, Italy and Japan (cf. the Encyclopaedia entry of "Haves and Have-Nots") now appears not merely ridiculous but immoral, when the real division, then even more than now, has been between the rich northern countries of the First and Second Worlds and the poor southern countries of the Third World.

The PPU's attitude towards sanctions has also changed. Whilst any form of military sanctions is necessarily opposed, economic sanctions have on certain occasions been supported by the PPU. Any form of trading in arms is naturally inconsistent with renunciation of war, whilst it has been felt appropriate to respond to the call of liberation movements in South Africa to boycott South African goods and banks with investments in that country.

Despite all these developments in detail, Huxley's final paragraphs on the PPU, commencing, "For above all the PPU stands for nonviolent resistance" still very much represent the present position of the PPU. Some wording would be changed in such a statement today, but the basic content of that passage still represents, after nearly half a century, the spirit and raison d'etre of the Peace Pledge Union.

This is perhaps demonstrated in two major current concerns of the PPU. In the Campaign against Militarism it is sought to expose, question and change all the aspects in our society which make the killing of children, women and men acceptable. The Peace Education Project produces a range of materials and speakers for use in schools and other places of learning whereby the very ideas of education for peace which Huxley discusses elsewhere in the *Encyclopaedia* may be brought to fruition.

Appendix B

An Additional Note on the War Resisters' International (1984)

The number of Sections and the number of countries in which the WRI operates have fluctuated considerably over the years since 1937. Despite the Second World War and the Nazi occupation of most of Europe, individuals continued to oppose militarism in many places, even though some were executed and others suffered in concentration camps. The WRI was also active in relief work for refugees from the Spanish Civil War and Jewish refugees from Germany and Austria.

Since the War, Sections have been re-formed and become active in western Europe (including Spain), but there are no Sections in the eastern bloc. Informal contacts are, however, maintained with some individuals, and at the time of the Soviet invasion of Czechoslovakia in 1968 the WRI organized small demonstrations by groups of westerners in Moscow, Warsaw, Budapest and Sofia.

One of the major tasks of the WRI remains coordination of resistance to military service in the majority of countries throughout the world. WRI supports equally the "absolutists" or total resisters, those who deny the right of the state to compel people to perform any form of service, as well as conscientious objectors who are prepared to perform alternative civilian service. Each year 1st December is commemorated as Prisoners for Peace Day, when greeting cards are sent to those imprisoned for refusing military service and demonstrations are held in many countries.

WRI is recognised by the United Nations as a non-governmental organisation, and from time to time gives evidence to UN Committees as well as to other bodies such as the Council of Europe and the European Parliament.

After a period in Brussels during the 1970s, the Headquarters of the WRI returned to London and are now established at 55 Dawes Street, London SE17. The journal of the WRI is now the *WRI Newsletter,* published six times a year in English, but attempts are being made for additional publication in French and German.

William Hetherington,
Chairperson, Peace Pledge Union

PART TWO

Handbook of Nonviolence
by Robert A. Seeley

American Friends Service Committee: Founded in 1917, the American Friends Service Committee is an international service organization of the Religious Society of Friends (Quakers). It believes in the dignity and worth of every person and is committed to nonviolent social change. Its programs include peace education, social and technical assistance to people in developing countries, and organizing within the U.S. to end racism, sexism, and poverty. It has ten regional offices in the United States. It is not a membership organization.

Animals and War: Among the most uncomplaining and uncomprehending victims of war are animals. In earlier times most of these were direct victims of combat—ten thousand dead horses at the Battle of Waterloo, hundreds or thousands of others dead in nearly every major battle involving cavalry. Romantic pictures of the cavalry do not show the sufferings of the horses.

Even as late as World War II horses were used as transport animals, and many died under fire. Although its armored combat (Panzer) units were the most destructive the world had yet seen, the German Army of 1939–45 was largely horse-powered. Horse cavalry was last used in Poland in 1939, with disastrous results for both Polish soldiers and the horses they rode and on portions of the Russian front in World War II.

Today the bulk of animal victims of war are either indirect casualties of fighting, as in Vietnam, or animals used in laboratory tests of new weapons. Modern warfare, which destroys the natural environment at previously unheard-of rates, kills both wildlife and domestic animals indiscriminately, just as it does civilians. (Discussion of the specific damage to Vietnam will be found in the article on the INDOCHINA WAR.)

Animals used in military experiments range from rats and mice used to test nerve gas, to monkeys used to test the effect of laser weapons on the eyeball. (The weapon in question melted the animals' eyes in their sockets.) Under one Pentagon program, anesthetized animals are deliberately wounded to give military doctors practical training in treating modern wounds. Public outcry forced the Pentagon to stop using dogs for such training; the animals of choice are now goats and sheep.

Military attempts to use animals for actual combat have included the obvious—e.g., attack dogs—and the bizarre. Probably the strangest of these efforts was the navy's program to train dolphins as living bombs. Navy scientists found that it was impossible to train dolphins to injure human beings unless they were very young—under two years old. The navy eventually abandoned the project.

It is ironic that while the navy found it impossible to train dolphins to be killers, many specialists in animal behavior argue that war is the result of natural and inevitable human aggressiveness. The most prominent among these theorists, Konrad Lorenz, suggests that aggression is a kind of instinctive force in humans and other animals which from time to time must be released, and is released in war. Though Lorenz himself supports efforts to end war his theory, carried to its logical conclusion, can be used to justify virtually any military preparation or abuse.

Authorities disagree on whether animals engage in combat similar to human combat. Jane Goodall, studying chimpanzees in the wild, found that these apes sometimes fight much like human warriors. This behavior occurred only over a brief period, however, and does not appear to be typical of chimpanzee behavior.

Even if they are correct, theories of animal combat do not explain human warfare. While aggressive responses to attack are normal among human beings, they are not the same as military responses. Military forces spend millions of dollars training soldiers—not merely to follow orders, but to be aggressive in certain ways and at certain times. Military training is designed not only to channel and control aggressiveness, but to instill it.

Much of modern combat, in fact, involves little or no aggression. Artillery bombardment, the most destructive kind of ground combat, requires such technical skill that soldiers operating the guns are trained to go about their jobs as matter-of-factly as possible lest by hasty firing they miss a target and expose themselves to danger. The same is true of air combat: piloting an aircraft requires absolute self-discipline and control.

The more traditional infantry battle, in which opponents may actually see each other, may be said to release aggression. But even in such combat the soldier who completely loses control may well die as a result. An instinctive, uncontrolled aggression would actually be a handicap for a combat soldier, though infantry combat can cause a kind of "blood madness" in some instances.

It is unlikely that animal studies will explain the causes of human warfare. At best they can only confirm what is obvious: that humans and other animals have the potential for aggressive and violent behavior. This fact, amply documented though it is, in no way justifies or explains the grotesque human institution that is warfare. Animal studies can give insights into human behavior, including war, but a full theory of the causes of war must include the many specifically human factors that make human warfare so much more destructive than combat between animals. Nor do animal studies show that war as practiced by humankind—with its high-technology weapons, mass destruction, and brutal calculus of combat losses—is inevitable.

(See also: CHAIN OF COMMAND, COMBAT, CONVENTIONAL WAR, MILITARY TRAINING, WOMEN AND WAR)

Antipersonnel Weapons: The distinction between antipersonnel weapons and ordinary weapons is, like that between strategic and tactical nuclear weapons, somewhat artificial. Military weapons, be they swords, bullets, explosive shells, or nuclear bombs, kill and maim people. Thus all such weapons are in some sense antipersonnel (or anti-*person*) weapons.

Nonetheless it is true that among explosive and incendiary weapons some are designed to destroy targets, such as gun emplacements and tanks, and some to kill and maim people (enemy personnel). Since gun emplacements and other targets are generally defended or operated by people, the moral distinction between these two types of weapon is not clear. The assumptions underlying the two types of weapon design, however, explain the particularly gruesome effects of antipersonnel devices.

Since the 1982 Israeli invasion of Lebanon, the most notorious antipersonnel weapon has probably been the cluster bomb. When detonated, this device releases several hundred small "bomblets" which scatter over an area of several hundred square yards. These smaller bombs detonate in turn and can kill or maim anyone unlucky enough to be within range. In Lebanon, as in other places where cluster bombs and similar devices have been used, the victims of the explosions were more likely to be civilians than soldiers. Their wounds, if they were not killed outright, were particularly frightful because of the effects of flying bomb fragments and multiple explosions around them. Many victims were children.

Those familiar with the war in Indochina found the effects of the cluster bomb shocking but not particularly surprising. Similar weapons had been routinely used in Vietnam with similar effects on similar groups of people. In addition to antipersonnel devices like the fragmentation bomb, the most famous antipersonnel weapon used in Vietnam was napalm, a highly inflammable chemical compound which clings to human flesh as it burns.

During the Indochina War, the United States showed particular ingenuity in designing antipersonnel weapons—so much so that it still leads the world in this dubious category. Vietnam became a kind of testing ground for fiendish new devices. The results were predictable. Most of the casualties in Vietnam, by some estimates up to 95 percent, were civilians.

One type of American fragmentation bomb illustrates particularly well the thinking underlying these devices generally.

114

When detonated this device released transparent but potentially lethal plastic pellets. Surgery to remove these pellets was extremely difficult and time-consuming; a single operation tied down enemy medical facilities for hours. To civilian observers this seemed a side-effect of such weapons, but it was in fact the desired military effect. The "side-effects," in military terms, were the effects on the wounded.

The December 1979 Soviet invasion of Afghanistan led to a protracted and bloody counterinsurgency war which, by late-1985, showed no signs of abating. As in all such wars, antipersonnel weapons, including fragmentation bombs, were used extensively. Although official secrecy has concealed their extent, civilian casualties in the Afghan War have unquestionably been high.

Military planners have their own term for the civilian casualties and the suffering which inevitably accompany the use of antipersonnel weapons. Horrible wounds and the deaths of children are called collateral damage. (In nuclear planning, collateral damage in an attack on a missile base can include millions of dead.) It would be more accurate and honest to say outright that antipersonnel weapons are designed to inflict indiscriminate suffering.

At least that is what modern versions of such weapons do. Weapon designers may intend them to kill soldiers only but the actual effect, as shown over and over, is to kill and wound far more civilians than soldiers. Wars today are fought in populated areas, not on battlefields far removed from the city. Weapons today are not only more destructive than older weapons, they destroy in particularly terrifying ways. And their targets, for the most part, are third parties who often have no idea what the fighting is about or who is fighting whom.

(See also: CONVENTIONAL WAR, GUERRILLA WARFARE, INDOCHINA WAR, MIDDLE EAST, "SMART" WEAPONS)

Apartheid: *Apartheid* is the system of legal separation of the races practiced in South Africa. South African law recognizes three categories of people: whites, "coloreds" (people of Asian and mixed racial background), and blacks (people of pure African descent). These three groups are required to use separate public facilities, live in separate areas, and—in the case of whites and coloreds—vote for separate Parliaments. Blacks, who do not have full citizenship, have neither representation in Parliament nor the right to vote.

The *apartheid* system is supported by an elaborate apparatus of state repression, including internal passports for blacks (the so-called passbooks, without which blacks cannot travel in white areas), state censorship, espionage against dissenting groups, and the creation of homelands for blacks. These homelands, which constitute a small percentage of South African territory, are said by the government to provide adequate living space for the black population. In fact, they give the government a means of controlling the movement of blacks and maintaining white hegemony.

South Africa has about four million whites; its black population is approximately 25 million. *Apartheid* maintains the power of the white minority. Reforms such as the legalization of racially mixed marriages—much hailed by apologists for South Africa when it became law in 1984—do not change the fundamental relations between the races. In South Africa whites have political power and blacks do not.

International revulsion at South Africa's policies led to widespread protest. Arms sales to the South African government are forbidden by a United Nations resolution, and South Africa has generally been regarded as a pariah among nations. Efforts to bring an end to foreign investment in the South African economy (divestment) became particularly significant in the early 1980s. In the United States, divestment became the focus of a widespread and well-organized student movement. Two anti-*apartheid* activists, Chief Albert Luthuli and Bishop Desmond Tutu, have been awarded the Nobel Peace Prize.

In 1984–85, internal protests against *apartheid* led to the deaths of over five hundred blacks at the hands of South African police. The government declared a state of emergency in which its already near-dictatorial powers were increased substantially to include preventive detention, military censorship, and similar measures. The new powers did not stop the protests.

The U.S. government under President Reagan held to its previously announced policy of constructive engagement, attempting to influence South Africa by persuasion rather than nonviolent pressures such as economic sanctions. Constructive engagement was, in effect, a rationale for doing nothing to end *apartheid,* for it was clear that mere persuasion without the use of political and economic pressure had no chance of moving the Botha government.

Apartheid is enforced not only by the police, but also by the South African Defense Force (SADF), one of the most heavily armed and proficient counterinsurgency armies in the world. Although there were many calls for armed struggle from both inside and outside South Africa, the likelihood of success for violent revolution in South Africa, the likelihood of success for violent revolution in South Africa was questionable. The SADF had fought African nationalist guerrillas to a standstill in the territory of Namibia and had repeatedly demonstrated that it was loyal to the government, ruthless in its methods, and militarily powerful. Though largely deprived of arms from the international market, the SADF did not lack for firepower. The South African arms industry had become one of the largest in the world.

For those outside South Africa, the only methods likely to be effective were nonviolent ones. Support for armed struggle which was perforce largely rhetorical, was of far less use than divestment and economic sanctions. This was particularly true in the United States and in England, whose government also opposed economic sanctions. Both had large investments in South Africa. Sanctions by either or both governments would have put enormous pressure on the South African government to end *apartheid.*

All the same, change is coming to South Africa. Whether it will come by violence or by nonviolent means is not clear, but further bloodshed seems likely. The black population is unlikely to stop its protests against a system that reduces its members to nonpersons. For the government seems unlikely to modify its policies. Increasingly violent conflict—the result, at bottom, of *apartheid*'s inherent violence—seems the most probable and tragic result.

(See also: GUERRILLA WARFARE)

Area Bombing Campaign: "Strategic bombing" is a military euphemism for aerial attacks on an opponent's territory using tons of high explosive or nuclear weapons. Though the practice can be traced back as far as the eighteenth century, it reached its peak of destructiveness in the various bombing campaigns of World War II. The largest of these were the Allied area bombing campaigns against Germany and Japan.

The first use of area bombing tactics in World War II was by the Germans, who bombed civilian targets in Warsaw in 1939. But it is of little real importance who started the bombing. Both sides bombed enemy territory and deliberately killed thousands of civilians.

German bombing efforts were on a very small scale compared to those of the Allies. The Luftwaffe had been designed primarily to support the German army's blitzkrieg tactics, and had few heavy bombers compared to Britain's Royal Air Force. The RAF had concentrated on building heavy bombers between the wars because mass bombing was central to its strategic doctrine. Thus when the British army was driven out of continental Europe in 1940 the Air Lords claimed that bombing alone could defeat Germany.

At first the British bombers flew by day. This was necessary because accurate bombing was impossible by night, and RAF doctrine at the time called for destruction of military targets such as factories, harbors, and rail yards. The unescorted bombers met heavy German resistance and suffered heavy losses. This continued throughout the war. In the end Britain's losses among its aircrews were 53,573.[1]

In an effort to cut its losses and yet continue the bombing, the RAF ordered its bombers to fly by night. Since night bombing was inaccurate with the instruments available at the time, the bombers no longer sought military targets but bombed "areas"—cities—instead. The Air Lords' rationale was that bombardment of cities would hinder German industry and so terrorize German civilians that national morale would break and the Nazis would be forced to surrender. One RAF ideologue, Lord Cherwell, composed an extraordinary memorandum which claimed that the aim of the air war was to "de-house" the German population.[2]

German industry in fact remained productive until mid-1944 when the bombing campaign began to have some effect on it. Even then, and when the war ended, German factories were producing one to two thousand aircraft per month.[3] German morale did not break until the very end when the war had been irretrievably lost on the ground. By 1945 the Luftwaffe and other German air defenses had lost much of their effectiveness, and Allied bombers (now including Americans) ranged far and wide over Germany. Some 7.5 million Germans were made homeless.[4] Total German casualties are unknown, but were probably over six hundred thousand. The most famous and controversial bombing mission was the destruction of Dresden. (See separate article on DRESDEN.) The attack on Hamburg created the first firestorm ever seen in warfare—a massive wall of flame which roasted people to death in their bomb shelters.

The American Army Air Corps (now called the Air Force) wreaked similar havoc on Japanese cities. Tokyo was virtually leveled in a night of firebombing. Eight million Japanese were made homeless.[5] The campaign against Japan reached its nadir with the destruction by nuclear weapons of Hiroshima and Nagasaki.

At the time, the strategic bombing campaign was controversial in the United States and England. Its critics ranged from the military philosopher B. H. Liddell Hart to the pacifist and writer Vera Brittain. Later critics have suggested that the campaign served little military purpose since Germany had exhausted herself in the Russian campaigns and could have been defeated by conventional land warfare.

There is little doubt that the area bombing campaign went on far beyond the point where it served any significant military purpose, and for the basest of reasons. The British and

American air commanders were seeking their share of post-war military spending and approbation.[6] The height of the campaign came in 1945 when Allied armies were already moving toward Berlin and the military issue was all but decided. Ninety percent of the bombs dropped on Japan were dropped during the last five months of the war.[7] It is unlikely that military necessity required such bombing of an all but defeated enemy.

The legacy of the area bombing campaign is still with us. The campaign is the direct ancestor of today's practice of aiming nuclear missiles at enemy cities. While not the first direct attack on civilians in the history of warfare, area bombing was the largest and most destructive up to its time. Despite its questionable military effectiveness, it established air power (for which read bombing of civilians) as a major element of United States strategy. Thus American bombers dropped more high explosive on North Vietnam than had been dropped in the whole of World War II. This latter-day air war had little military effect but its consequences for civilians were devastating. Area bombing ended with the first use of nuclear weapons in combat, thus opening the nuclear age in warfare.

Worst of all, the area bombing campaign made massive direct attacks on civilians by military forces not only strategically respectable but, in the minds of U.S. planners, morally respectable. It did this despite its faintly unsavory reputation at the time, despite its great destructiveness for little purpose, and despite pictures of bombed cities and burned children.

The willingness of World War II strategists to think in terms of destroying entire cities has now become a willingness to think of destroying an entire nation at a stroke. Planners in countries possessing nuclear weapons calmly prepare for a holocaust much worse and more final than Hitler could have imagined. This is the ultimate legacy of the area bombing campaign.

(See also: DRESDEN, HIROSHIMA AND NAGASAKI, INDO-CHINA WAR, NUCLEAR STRATEGY, NUCLEAR WEAPONS AND WAR)

1. Max Hastings, *Bomber Command* (New York: The Dial Press, 1979), p. 11.
2. *Ibid.*, pp. 127–132.

3. Peter Calvocoressi and Guy Wint, *Total War: The Story of World War II* (New York: Pantheon Books, 1972), p. 503.

4. Lee Kennett, *A History of Strategic Bombing* (New York: Charles Scribner's Sons, 1982), p. 182.

5. *Ibid.*

6. Hastings, *op. cit.*, gives many instances of such maneuvering for postwar position. See also Gregg Herken, *The Winning Weapon: The Atomic Bomb in the Cold War 1945–1950* (New York: Alfred A. Knopf, 1980) for an extensive discussion of the significance of the atomic bomb and the Hiroshima and Nagasaki bombings in postwar superpower struggles.

7. Kennett, *op. cit.*, p. 182.

Arms Control and Disarmament: It is easy to confuse arms control and disarmament. Disarmament means dismantling national armed forces (or at a minimum, national nuclear forces) down to a mutually agreed level, either in mutually acceptable stages or as quickly as technically feasible. Arms control means mutual agreement to stop building new arms or to stop building as many new arms as before. It can also mean agreement to limit the numbers of arms held by each side, or to set upper limits on certain categories of arms. A disarmament agreement would lead to a reduction in the size of national arsenals; an arms control agreement would not necessarily do so, and in practice has not done so.

In recent years both the U.S. and Soviet governments have stopped discussing disarmament. Public debate has instead focused on arms control. The result has been to rule disarmament nearly out of public consideration while allowing the superpowers to reach mutual agreements which permit the arms race to continue. A recent survey of arms control agreements since World War II found that all such agreements contained significant loopholes and omissions which permitted arms development and research to continue. These agreements have, on the whole, done nothing to reduce national arsenals. Some have facilitated expansion of those arsenals.[1]

Arms control negotiations have in fact become another way of waging diplomatic and political warfare. The typical pattern today goes like this: One side proposes a radical step which it knows the other will find unacceptable. The other

121

side rejects the proposal. The first side then points an accusing finger and bemoans its opponent's "lack of seriousness" about arms control.

A recent example shows the process at work. As an "alternative" to the highly dangerous deployment of Pershing II and cruise missiles in Europe, President Reagan proposed that the Soviet Union abandon its SS-4, SS-5, and SS-20 missiles. In exchange the U.S. would forego its new deployments. The Soviets, who view their SS-20s as a necessary counter to U.S. missiles already in place, found Mr. Reagan's proposal unacceptable, as experts in these matters had predicted. The Soviets then made a counterproposal which was equally bogus.[2] Mr. Reagan thereupon declared, loudly and repeatedly, that the Soviets were not "serious" about arms control.

In the sense that the Soviet Union is unlikely to give the U.S. a perceived advantage in arms, this is true enough. It is also true of the U.S., however. For both sides, controlling arms—and thereby making human survival more likely—is secondary to pursuing national interest. Thus arms control negotiations break down, lead to defective agreements, or simply drag on interminably, not because arms control is impossible, but because stopping the arms race is incompatible with the traditional pursuit of national advantage through diplomacy.

These are serious flaws. Yet arms control negotiations are clearly better than no negotiations if the only alternative is failure to communicate at all.

The choice, however, is not between negotiations as they are now conducted and an unstoppable race to oblivion. At least three proposals show promise of breaking the arms control deadlock.

Though it is a kind of arms control proposal, the nuclear freeze proposal would be a first step toward mutual disarmament. Because it favors the interest of neither side, it could permit both to move toward disarmament. There is a real danger, however, that the proposal will be seen as an end in itself by a U.S. government which sees arms control as simply another way of winning the Cold War. (Further discussion of this dilemma will be found in the article on the NUCLEAR FREEZE MOVEMENT.)

A second proposal, with less popular support than the nuclear freeze, is for the U.S. to begin a series of "unilateral initiatives," which would be designed to increase trust between the major powers and to encourage responses from the Soviet Union. For example, the U.S. could have canceled or delayed deployment of the Pershing II and cruise missiles with no actual loss in security yet with potential benefit to the effort to end the arms race.

A third proposal, more radical than the first two, is for the United States to dismantle its military establishment without waiting for a Soviet response, and adopt a policy of nonviolent civilian defense. Though unlikely to gain enough popular support to force its adoption, this proposal is worth further study. (Nonviolent defense of the U.S. is discussed under NONVIOLENCE.) Nonviolent defense is under serious study among Europeans seeking an alternative to the NATO-Warsaw Pact military confrontation.

A final arms control proposal is of some importance because it has become popular in Congress as an alternative to the arms race. This is the so-called build-down proposal, under which each side would agree to destroy two or even three old nuclear weapons for every new weapon deployed. The flaws in such a proposal are obvious. It does nothing about nuclear weapons development, thus permitting the refinement of nuclear technology to proceed as fast as the superpowers wish. It would force each side to jettison weapons which, in many cases, were already scheduled for destruction. And it sets no limits on the destructiveness or size of weapons, nor on the numbers of new weapons deployed. Build-down would, in short, not be arms control at all. It would simply disguise the continuation of the arms race, while giving the impression that all was well.[3]

(See also: COLD WAR, DETERRENCE, NONVIOLENCE, NUCLEAR FREE ZONES, NUCLEAR FREEZE MOVEMENTS, NUCLEAR STRATEGY, NUCLEAR WEAPONS AND WAR)

1. Paul Walker, *Seizing the Initiative: First Steps to Disarmament* (Philadelphia and Nyack, NY: American Friends Service Committee and Fellowship of Reconciliation, 1983).
2. See Lawrence Freedman, "Negotiations on Nuclear Forces," *Bulletin of the Atomic Scientists*, Vol. 39, No. 10 (December, 1983), pp. 22–28.

3. Christopher Paine, "Breakdown on the Build-down," *Bulletin of the Atomic Scientists*, Vol. 39, No. 10 (December, 1983), pp. 4–6.

Battlefield: The term "battlefield" is frequently used when speaking of military matters. For example, a particular weapon is said to have good battlefield characteristics, or certain small nuclear weapons are considered battlefield weapons.

Traditionally the word battlefield has implied a place where armies met and fought, relatively isolated from civilians and in a limited space. Today that use of the term is obsolete. Now a battlefield may encompass an entire European country, and combat is in no way isolated from the civilian population.

As it happens this particular abuse of language serves a political purpose. By speaking of battlefields, politicians and military officers arguing for more weapons and money can conjure up visions of traditional military glory and somehow give the impression that combat, death, and destruction of property *all happen somewhere else.* This is easy for many in the United States to believe because since the Civil War there has been no combat whatever on U.S. soil. Wars have always happened "over there."

The use of obsolete terms like battlefield is a cruel deception, however. With modern missiles and air transport, battles no longer happen "over there," nor would they in an all-out war. They would not be traditional battles at all, but rather impersonal death falling from the sky.

Even in ground combat, battlefield now means little or nothing. Civilians in the path of a modern army die and are maimed, whatever the objectives or ideology of the army, because of the uncontrollable destructiveness of modern weapons.

(See also: CONVENTIONAL WAR, GUERRILLA WARFARE, NUCLEAR WEAPONS AND WAR, UNITED STATES)

Berrigan, Daniel and Philip: Daniel and Philip Berrigan first became well-known to the public as the result of a nonviolent raid on a local draft board in Catonsville, Md., in early 1968. The Berrigans and seven other companions, later to be known as the Catonsville 9, entered the local board office and poured blood on draft files. They were arrested. Their trial, a significant event in the history of the Catholic Left, was portrayed in Daniel's play, *The Trial of the Catonsville 9.*

The Berrigans had been active in the peace movement for many years before Catonsville. At the time both were Roman Catholic priests. Philip left the priesthood in the early 1970s. Daniel, who is a major poet in addition to his peace actions, remains in the priesthood.

Since the Catonsville action, the Berrigans have remained significant figures in the nonviolent peace movement. Their style of direct action, which was exemplified by Catonsville, is symbolic and personal. It includes civil disobedience as an essential part. Thus in the late 1970s, the Berrigans were involved in symbolic missile destruction at a defense plant in Southeastern Pennsylvania (the Plowshares 8 action), in which they entered the plant illegally and attempted to dismantle the missiles with hammers. They were arrested, and their trial became the subject of the film, *In King of Prussia.* The Plowshares action led to a series of similar actions by different groups throughout the United States in the late 1970s and early 1980s.

Bishops' Pastoral Letter: In May 1983, the American Conference of Bishops issued a major statement on nuclear war to its congregations in the United States. Titled "The Challenge of Peace: God's Promise and Our Response," and popularly known as the Bishops' Pastoral, the statement did not represent an authoritative teaching of the church as a whole. It did, however, draw on statements by the Pope and Vatican Council II, including Pope John XXIII's encyclical, *Pacem in Terris,* which spoke for the whole church. The

Pastoral has been highly influential not only within the Roman Catholic church but in the Protestant religious community.[1]

The Pastoral represents a systematic attempt to apply the traditional Just War Theory to nuclear weapons and war. It does not address the application of Just War standards to modern conventional warfare. The bishops reach three central conclusions:

- The use of nuclear weapons under any circumstances violates the Just War criteria;
- Just War criteria also preclude the intention to use such weapons;
- Possession of nuclear weapons as a temporary deterrent to aggression is acceptable, provided that such possession occurs in the context of serious efforts to achieve disarmament.

The bishops also deal extensively with the conditions required for peace, with the relation of peace and justice, and with the implications of the letter's analysis for individual conscience. The letter calls upon Catholics, including those in the military, to consider whether they may rightly take part in preparations for nuclear war. It also praises conscientious objectors and those who have committed themselves to nonviolence.[2]

Within the U.S. military, which has a large Catholic population, the Pastoral was perceived as a major threat to the implementation of U.S. nuclear policies. An April, 1985, article in *Military Law Review* outlined the dilemmas faced by Catholics in the military and by the command structure as a result of the Pastoral's teaching.[3]

There are difficulties with the Pastoral's reasoning. In deterrence theory, possession of nuclear weapons implies the threat to use them. This in turn implies the intent to use them in certain circumstances—i.e., in retaliation for an attack. Thus the bishops' call for possession of nuclear weapons without intent to use them undermines deterrence which, as a temporary state, they find acceptable. Supporters of deterrence find this reasoning unsatisfying. The problem, however, is not that the bishops undercut deterrence theory. Their rejection of the nuclear threat is one of the Pastoral's strengths. Still, they have not followed their reasoning through to its logical conclusion: the complete *rejection* of deterrence. This weakens the Pastoral and diminishes its moral force.

Such criticism, though, is far less important than recognition of the Pastoral's positive value. The bishops suggest that possession of nuclear weapons can be justified only if the nation possessing them is genuinely seeking peace—and not by words alone, but by actions. This is quite different from standard deterrence theory, which posits a continuous state of conflict held in check solely by the threat of nuclear holocaust.

The Bishops' Pastoral was part of a growing peace and justice movement within the Roman Catholic church in the late 1970s and early 1980s. In addition to older Catholic groups like the Catholic Worker, the Catholic Peace Fellowship and Pax Christi, the Catholic peace movement grew to include nonviolent resistance to U.S. policy in Central America, the establishment of Peace and Justice offices in many dioceses, and symbolic acts like those of the Plowshares movement, whose members entered factories that manufactured nuclear missiles and engaged in symbolic destruction of the missiles until arrested. The Pastoral, whatever its faults, gave voice to many of these concerns while serving as a vehicle for grassroots peace education.

(See also: DETERRENCE, JUST WAR THEORY, NUCLEAR STRATEGY, NUCLEAR WEAPONS AND WAR)

1. For one collection of Protestant responses, see Dean C. Curry, ed., *Evangelicals and the Bishops' Pastoral Letter* (Grand Rapids, Mich.: Wm. B. Eerdmans Pub. Co., 1984).
2. For discussion of the Pastoral and conscientious objection, see Gerard A. Vanderhaar, "Bishops' Pastoral Praises War Resistance," *CCCO News Notes*, Vol. 35, No. 3 (Autumn, 1983), p. 10.
3. Capt. Mary Eileen E. McGrath, "Nuclear Weapons: A Crisis of Conscience," *Military Law Review*, Vol. 107 (Winter, 1985), p. 191.

Brazil, Nonviolence in: Brazil is the largest country in South America. It is rich in natural resources which, with careful development, could make it one of the most prosperous nations on earth. Instead, it is a country of appalling injustice. The richest 1 percent of the population controls 18 percent of the nation's wealth, while the poorest 50 percent controls only 14 percent of the wealth. Around twenty-five million Brazilian children are malnourished; fifteen million have been abandoned.[1] Brazilian police routinely torture not only dissenters but ordinary people suspected of nonpolitical crimes. Multinational corporations are gradually purchasing large tracts of land and, through intermediaries with private police forces, driving the rural population from their homes. Thirty-seven million Brazilians have been evicted from their land.

The movement to counter the violence of the Brazilian government and the multinational corporations began with small strikes and other nonviolent actions in the late 1950s and early 1960s. It has grown to become the largest nonviolent movement in the world. In 1968 the Catholic church in Brazil, which had previously acted as a conservative or even reactionary social force, joined the nonviolent movement. This break with tradition in a largely Catholic society gave the movement a power not seen since Gandhi's liberation of India and King's nonviolent civil rights campaigns in the early 1960s.

Along with nonviolent tactics like strikes and civil disobedience—which in Brazil involve very great risks—the Brazilian movement has developed approximately eighty thousand "base communities" *(communidades de base),* an innovation which has spread to other nonviolent movements in Latin America. "Small, interlocking groups of peasants and workers, the communities are the building blocks of a new, nonviolent society—religious groups that also are people's councils, linking Catholicism with civic action, education with freedom and solidarity with Christ. That association of piety, learning and civic action is revolutionary in a country where the only previous solidarity came from oppression. In many parts of Brazil the community has become the first link in a potentially powerful chain connecting urban and rural unions, slum associations and universities, Protestant and Catholic churches."[2]

The issues confronting the Brazilian nonviolent movement

include the expropriation of land by multinational corporations, wages and working conditions in Brazilian industry, militarism and disarmament, the status of women, racism, and the movement for liberation in Central America. Because local conditions and issues differ sharply, it is impossible to generalize about nonviolent methods in Brazil. One of the best-known nonviolent campaigns occurred in Alagamar, a rural area. There, the peasant movement has tried to prevent expropriation of their land by lawsuits, nonviolent occupation of the house of a judge who had jailed some of the movement's members, and even replanting fields which had been ravaged by a landowner's hired thugs. In other areas, other methods have been used.

Like other nonviolent movements in Latin America, the Brazilian movement's success or failure will be significantly affected by United States policy. The United States supports the repressive Brazilian regime. U.S.-based multinational corporations are among those driving Brazilian peasants from their land. Thus nonviolence in Brazil must be supplemented by nonviolent action in the U.S.

A recent and encouraging development has been the effort, coordinated in the U.S. by the American Friends Service Committee and other groups, to link the various Latin American nonviolent movements with nonviolent movements in the U.S. Such linkages may in the long run help to transform Latin American society in general and Brazilian society in particular. But the main source of change in Brazil will be the Brazilian people themselves, whose movement, if successful, will rival King's and Gandhi's for courage and historical significance.

(See also: CAMARA, DOM HELDER; CENTRAL AMERICA; GANDHI MOHANDAS K.; KING, MARTIN LUTHER, JR.; NON-VIOLENCE)

1. Penny Lernoux, "The Church in Brazil," *Maryknoll*, Vol. 75, No. 9 (September, 1981), p. 10.
2. *Ibid.*, p. 13.

Caldicott, Helen, M.D.: Helen Caldicott, M.D., is an Australian pediatrician well-known for her work in the anti-nuclear movement. She is a founding member and President Emeritus of Physicians for Social Responsibility, a former member of the faculty of Harvard Medical School, and founder of Women's Action for Nuclear Disarmament (WAND). In the early 1980s, Helen Caldicott was one of the most sought-after lecturers on the arms race. She believes, as she wrote in her book, *Missile Envy*, that "rapid nuclear disarmament is the ultimate issue of preventive medicine."

Works by and about Helen Caldicott include *Missile Envy—The Arms Race and Nuclear War* (William Morrow, 1984) and *If You Love This Planet*, a documentary film.

Camara, Dom Helder: The first Brazilian church official to speak out against the injustice of Brazilian society was the Archbishop of Recife, Dom Helder Camara. In 1967 Dom Helder publicly criticized Brazil's military dictatorship. At the time few had the courage to mention, let alone question, the government's use of mass arrest and torture.

Dom Helder quickly became known as the Red Bishop of Brazil. He was harassed by Brazilian authorities and vilified by Brazilian media. The Brazilian church considered him a dangerous radical.

By the end of the 1960s, however, the church in Brazil had begun to take public stands against government policies—first against torture and other human rights violations, and later against the economic and political injustice of Brazilian society. Camara's stand had been vindicated.

The Brazilian church's work has been costly. Since the late 1960s, fifty bishops have "suffered arrest, torture, defamation and death threats. . . . 26 priests have been expelled from Brazil, 185 arrested and 4 murdered."[1] But the nonviolent movement in Brazil has become the largest in the world. Its prophet is Dom Helder Camara. Of Dom Helder, Pope John

Paul said when he visited Brazil in 1980, "Dom Helder is the brother of the poor and *my* brother."

(See also: BRAZIL, NONVIOLENCE IN)

1. Penny Lernoux, "The Church in Brazil," *Maryknoll*, Vol. 75, No. 9 (September, 1981), p. 6.

Central America: The isthmus connecting Mexico and Colombia is divided into seven nations: Guatemala, Belize, El Salvador, Honduras, Nicaragua, Costa Rica, and Panama. These countries have been a major focus of U.S. foreign policy and military intervention since the early nineteenth century.

The U.S. provided financial and military aid to Guatemala, El Salvador, Honduras, and Panama for many years. Costa Rica, which has no formal army, receives only economic aid. The U.S. has sent "advisers" to train troops in El Salvador. It has conducted massive joint military "exercises" with Honduras—maneuvers which though styled as training in fact posed a direct threat to the government of Nicaragua, President Reagan's bête noire in the region. Central American officers are educated at U.S. military schools. And the United States has pressured the government of Costa Rica to increase its self-defense efforts.

All this is done in the name of defeating "Communist intervention," by which the U.S. government means the widespread guerrilla warfare on the isthmus. U.S. policymakers argue that the various Central American wars result from Soviet and Cuban (and now Nicaraguan) intervention and that failure to defeat the guerrillas would have "geopolitical consequences."

The evidence, however, supports a contrary conclusion: the primary interventionist power in Central America is not Cuba or the Soviet Union, but the United States. To the list of interventions cited above could be added many earlier instances, including military aid, covert warfare directed by the

131

U.S. Central Intelligence Agency, and direct military intervention like that in Nicaragua in 1914.

It is worth recalling that the Somoza regime, which was overthrown by revolution in 1979, was originally established with the help of U.S. Marines and the U.S. government. The Somoza family during their tenure maintained one of the most repugnant governments in the world. They repressed dissent using violence and torture, controlled much of Nicaragua's economy, and left their country in such a state that the rebuilding process, even without harassment by the United States, will take years.

Beginning in 1982 the United States engaged in a covert or proxy war against the revolutionary government of Nicaragua. The CIA recruited and funded a guerrilla army consisting of veterans of Somoza's National Guard and others, who wished to end the Sandinista government. This war was technically unlawful under the so-called Boland Amendment—then in force—which forbade any CIA or other U.S. actions designed to overthrow the Nicaraguan government. Thus the CIA-recruited army, called the *contra*, was said by the Reagan administration to be countering weapons shipments to guerrillas in El Salvador.

In El Salvador, U.S. military and economic aid supported a government whose many violations of basic human rights led to a congressionally-mandated requirement that the president certify "progress" in human rights whenever funding for El Salvador was to be renewed.

U.S. funds also support a highly repressive government in Guatemala. There, government-sponsored death squads have made life a nightmare of random killings and disappearances.

In mid-1983 the President appointed a Commission on Central America chaired by Dr. Henry Kissinger. The commission's report recommended increased economic aid and strict human rights requirements. These steps in themselves would be desirable. But the report persisted in the basic U.S. error regarding Central America. It argued that developments in the region are significant and must be addressed by U.S. policy because of their effect on the "struggle against communism."

Despite frantic administration efforts to "prove" the existence of Soviet and Cuban influence in Central America, however, the evidence is that the revolutions there were indigenous and had little to do with Cold War maneuvering. Thus the Kissinger commission report perpetuated an American perception which had little or no foundation in fact.

Detailed discussion of Central America and proposals for peace in the region is impossible in a short article. The primary difficulties in the region, or at least the primary reasons for U.S. intervention, are clear from the record. Central American economies have, by and large, been dominated by U.S. corporations: in Honduras, until recently, the United Fruit Company, for instance. U.S. intervention there predates the Russian Revolution and has little to do with stopping communism and much to do with safeguarding these economic interests.

At the same time, with the exception of Costa Rica, the Central American countries have been ruled by elites who control most of the resources and cooperate with U.S. economic interests while the vast majority of their countries' people live in poverty. It is hardly surprising that, insofar as they are not resigned to their lot, these people wish to rid themselves of governments which are oppressive as well as U.S. economic dominance which helps to keep them poor.

The American government's failure to understand that revolutionary aspirations in Central America are both genuine and indigenous to the region has led to its current tragic policy. Its efforts to protect U.S. interests in the region have led to the war against Nicaragua, whose revolution, if successful, may provide a model for other Central American countries.

Whether the Nicaraguan revolution can succeed is impossible to predict. The history of violent revolutions is discouraging; most such revolutions have led to dictatorships and little real change for the majority of people. But it is clear that *any* effort for social change can succeed only with great difficulty under the kind of pressure generated by U.S.-sponsored violence. The U.S. government complained that the Nicaraguan government has repressed newspapers and has not held free elections. This was perfectly true, and deplorable. But the responsibility for these developments rests, at least in part, with the United States. The *contras* have made establishment of democracy and economic development difficult indeed for the Sandinista government.

American efforts to repress change are, like many such efforts, shortsighted. The Central American countries have much to gain from friendship with the United States. This has been true of the Nicaraguan government, which has tried to establish trade with the U.S., and it would be true of any other revolutionary government. There is no good reason why the U.S. could not trade with Central America without making it a source of cheap goods and without the exploitation that has characterized previous U.S.-Central American relations. By seeking to maintain its privileges, however, the U.S. damages the chance for such long-term relations. It is unlikely that American-sponsored military repression can succeed indefinitely in the region.

Nonviolent efforts for change in Central America must, in the light of this, be directed not only at change there, but at change in U.S. policy. The United States supports much of the violence of the Central American governments and stopping such support is crucial. This means change not only in policy but in basic attitudes. As long as the U.S. continues to regard Central America as "our backyard" (Mr. Reagan's phrase), the people of the region will continue to suffer war, disappearances, death squads, and economic oppression.

(See also: NONVIOLENT INTERVENTION, SANCTUARY, UNITED STATES)

Chain of Command: The structure of modern military forces varies little from one country to another. Individual soldiers are grouped into small units; several of these units form a larger unit; several of these larger units form a still larger unit; and so on. In the U.S. Army, individuals form a platoon, platoons a company, companies a battalion, battalions a regiment, regiments a division, divisions a corps, and corps an army. Each of these units is commanded by an officer, with officers of higher rank commanding the larger units. This method of organization is called the chain of command.

The purpose of all this dividing is to make the military into a series of interchangeable parts and to facilitate military administration. Although commanders gain all credit for winning battles, it is actually impossible to conduct a military operation from the top. The overall command sets general strategy, determines objectives, and gives general orders; but the smaller units must implement these orders.

At the same time when a unit has had too many of its members killed or wounded to be effective in battle, it can be replaced with a similar unit. Or the unit can be supplied with replacements—i.e., fresh people—who are considered for military purposes to be interchangeable parts.

The military structure has three effects, one intended and the others unintended. The intended effect is to build group cohesion so that soldiers will obey orders because they are part of a group. In combat soldiers regularly take risks and commit acts which would be nearly unthinkable in civilian life. Mild-mannered, gentle people will kill—often with abandon. Frightened young soldiers (and virtually all soldiers are young and frightened) will charge into the teeth of opposing fire, moving forward even when those around them are already dead. The conflict between what soldiers do in combat and their natural impulses can in fact be so severe that some never completely recover. Group cohesion and training help to make combat possible for the young men caught up in it. In theory, too, they provide officers with control over the course of a military operation.

The chain of command also has two unintended but highly dangerous effects. One of these is isolation. Commanders are not only physically far from the action, they also possess absolute authority. Those lower in the chain of command hesitate to tell the truth to those above for fear of punishment—in army slang, the "cover-your-ass" syndrome. Thus a general who devises a foolish plan of attack, as Montgomery did at the Battle of Arnhem (1944), may be shielded from information which contradicts his wishes. The results can be disastrous in both human and military terms.

A second and more pernicious effect of the chain of command is the ingrained military habit of depersonalization. Commanders seldom see the soldiers they command. They think not of people, but of "replacements"; not of soldiers dying and suffering agony from their wounds, but of "losses." Without such a habit of mind, most commanders could not easily direct military operations. Command perceptions are built into the command structure; they act as a shield against the reality of suffering and death which is combat.

Commanders also, and quite naturally, see all problems in military terms. They think, as they are trained to do, in terms of "enemies" who are simply units to be "neutralized" or "knocked out." As a guide for policy, such thinking has time and again led countries into war. It becomes more dangerous still when adopted by civilians in government who should be dealing with political complexities, not military simplifications. This is the danger in thinking of Central America as an arena for military combat between "freedom" and "communism."

Commanders are trained to see the situation in these simple terms. But it is folly to believe that they are seeing reality. Basing political judgments on military perceptions can lead only to endless war and suffering.

(See also: CENTRAL AMERICA, COMBAT, MILITARY TRAINING)

Children and War: Children suffer both directly and indirectly from war. Their agonies are the more terrible because often they do not understand what is happening to them and have no idea what actions, if any, they can take to escape from the chaos and bloodshed around them.

Physically, war is one of the most destructive situations a child can face. The so-called collateral effects of modern warfare include deaths and wounding of civilians, many of them children. Worse, modern strategy often dictates deliberate attacks on civilians. Thus in Vietnam children were frequently killed, wounded, or uprooted as the result of deliberately planned military operations. Tens of thousands of children died at Hiroshima and Nagasaki. One-third of the Nazis' Jewish victims were children. And on and on—the examples could be multiplied by hundreds or thousands.

Even after the end of actual fighting, it is not uncommon for children to become physical casualties. War leaves behind it a vast detritus of shells, land mines, unexploded bombs, and other lethal apparatus. Much of this deadly trash is cleared from the battlefield when the fighting is over, but much remains. Children, who frequently have no idea what a shell is let alone that it may be dangerous, often play with these instruments of death with predictable and tragic results.

Those children who are not direct casualties of the fighting may become indirect casualties. Starvation tactics such as blockades and sieges hit children particularly hard because children are still growing. The dislocations and disruptions of normal services, such as public health, have frequently led to major epidemics like the so-called Spanish influenza after World War I.

The psychological effects of combat have been extensively studied with regard to soldiers, but less with regard to civilians generally and children in particular. It is clear, however, that combat is the kind of trauma from which a child recovers only with difficulty, if at all. Where children need security and predictability in their worlds, combat is insecure and unpredictable. Things happen at random: wounds, explosions, the death of a parent. The child's home becomes unsafe, and he or she must move, often with no idea of a destination and no hope of real safety. The child becomes part of a refugee migration, of little concern to the authorities in most cases except insofar as he or she clogs the roads and impedes military movements. Little wonder that photographs of the children of war invariably show them wide-eyed, haggard, and terrified.

The indirect effects of war on children are less obvious, but they are very real. Military budgets not only in the United States but in every country have become large at the expense of public welfare, food, and development programs. In the Third World, where much of the population lives at or near starvation level, weapons expenditures often far outstrip any conceivable military purpose. Thus the starving children of

Chad are "protected" by American Redeye ground-to-air missiles, each of which costs enough to feed several villages for years on end.

Starvation in the United States is far less widespread than it is in the Third World but it exists, and it exists in part because the money to alleviate it or eliminate it is spent on weapons. The federal Aid to Families with Dependent Children Program, among other programs to benefit children, was cut $1.2 billion by the Reagan administration. In the meantime Congress appropriated $6.64 billion for development of the MX missile, a dangerous first-strike weapon whose only possible use is the destruction of millions of children. Again the examples could be multiplied into the hundreds.

Children in the U.S. today suffer psychological effects from the prospect of nuclear war which are only now being studied in detail. By the age of four or five some children begin to show fear about the future; by adolescence many feel that they have no future. The writer Jonathan Schell argues that the prospect of human extinction undercuts nearly every human endeavor—art, literature, music, science, politics—and leads to the sense that it is pointless.[1] These effects are also evident among older children, many of whom suffer from depression and despair.

Even the prospect of extinction, however, has not defeated many children. Some, such as the Children's Campaign for Nuclear Disarmament, are seeking an end to the insanity which their elders, without consulting them, have planned. Children, more than any other group, have the right to question war and all that it means. To an adult, war may be a matter of balancing costs against benefits in the amoral way of the nuclear strategists. To a child this can never be so.

(See also: ANTIPERSONNEL WEAPONS, AREA BOMBING CAMPAIGN, GUERRILLA WARFARE, INDOCHINA WAR, NUCLEAR WEAPONS AND WAR, WAR AND THE ENVIRONMENT, WOMEN AND WAR)

1. Jonathan Schell, *The Fate of the Earth* (New York: Alfred A. Knopf, 1982), Part II.

Civil Defense: Government programs which are supposed to protect the citizenry from death in a nuclear war have existed in one form or another since the bombing of Hiroshima and Nagasaki. They have included evacuation plans for major cities, bomb shelters, and actual air raid drills.

During the middle and late 1950s many cities in the United States required participation in local air raid drills. Pacifists and others who regarded civil defense as a dangerous waste of time and money frequently refused to take part—by sitting in a city park when the sirens sounded, for instance—and many were arrested. At least 122 people, and probably far more, were arrested and charged with refusal to participate in air raid drills.[1]

Nuclear weapons are so destructive that protection against them is at best a forlorn hope. Those at the center of the blast would be incinerated no matter how protected. As the experience of Hamburg and Dresden showed, those unfortunates who took shelter might be roasted to death in the firestorm which is likely to follow a major nuclear explosion. Attempts to evacuate major cities would lead to traffic jams of unimaginable size. If evacuation took place during a time of rising international tension, the evacuation itself could make war more likely. Survivors of a nuclear war would find a world in which medical services, food, water, and so on, had become suddenly unavailable. Most would likely die a lingering and terrible death.

All of these arguments against the civil defense program are known and well-documented. Yet the Reagan administration, far from abandoning the program, has proposed to spend $4.2 billion on it.[2] T. K. Jones, undersecretary of the air force, has suggested (apparently in all seriousness) that "everybody's going to make it if there are enough shovels to go around." Jones' model shelter, however, might prove difficult to build: "Dig a hole, cover it with a couple of doors and then throw three feet of dirt on top. It's the dirt that does it." (1982) It is not entirely clear who throws the dirt on top.

This sort of idiotic pronouncement would be easy to dismiss as mere lunacy were it not taken seriously at high levels of the government. The Federal Emergency Management Agency (FEMA) has projected U.S. recovery from a nuclear attack within a few years. This projection contains so many false assumptions—that a nuclear attack would have no long-term effects, that nuclear war would be over after the first exchange of missiles, and that no nuclear explosion would hit a U.S. nuclear power plant, for example—that it qualifies as wish fulfillment rather than serious policymaking.[3]

The government's revived civil defense program has included such "practical" steps as printing millions of post office change-of-address forms so that those evacuated can get their mail; requiring all federal agencies to draw up plans for surviving with the bureaucracy intact; and approaching city governments to ask them to draw up similar plans. City governments, however, are more sophisticated now than they were in the 1950s. Many have refused to draw up the requested plans, passed resolutions condemning nuclear war and civil defense, and—as did Cambridge, Massachusetts—tried to educate their citizens about the effects of nuclear war.

Civil defense is an easy target for satire, but nevertheless defense preparations remain dangerous. In the 1950s displays of bomb shelters at county fairs, air raid drills, and similar efforts, however foolish, helped to maintain hysteria about war with the Soviet Union. They also gave the illusion that nuclear war was possible without the end of civilization.

The public is under no such illusion today. Opinion polls show that in this matter Americans have far more common sense than their government. The danger today is that the government may come to believe its own pronouncements. Mr. Reagan and his advisers apparently believed civil defense proponents like Jones or Colin S. Grey, a prominent nuclear strategist and administration adviser, who argue that with civil defense the nation would "lose" only ten million in an all-out nuclear war. That such thinking could be taken seriously shows clearly how out of touch the government was with reality and with the people who, in theory, give it power.

Military planners make much of Soviet civil defense planning; they argue that it can "tip the strategic balance," whatever that means when both sides can destroy the world ten times over. Soviet planners may, they say, be tempted to start a nuclear war because they think their nation could survive it intact.

This argument has little to do with Soviet reality and much to do with getting the civil defense budget through Congress. The Soviet civil defense program is no more likely to be effective than FEMA's program. It is poorly drawn, administered by military officers who have failed at more prestigious commands, and—like the American plans—full of ludicrous assumptions. Just one will suffice. The Soviet Union has few automobiles. This has obliged the planners to arrange for "crisis relocations" on foot, and evacuees are expected to carry their food supplies on their backs.[4]

Only in the bizarre world of nuclear strategy could such plans be taken seriously for a moment.

(See also: AREA BOMBING CAMPAIGN, DRESDEN, HIROSHIMA AND NAGASAKI, NUCLEAR STRATEGY, NUCLEAR WEAPONS AND WAR)

1. Figures compiled from various issues of *CCCO News Notes*.
2. Center for Defense Information, "President Reagan's Civil Defense Program," *Defense Monitor*, Vol. XI, No. 5 (1982), p. 5.
3. *Ibid.*, contains a full discussion of the FEMA program.
4. A full discussion of the Soviet program will be found in Andrew Cockburn, *The Threat: Inside the Soviet Military Machine* (New York: Random House, 1983), ch. 14.

Civil Disobedience: The practice of civil disobedience, or refusal on principle to obey an unjust law, has ancient roots. The Bible gives many examples of men and women who chose to obey God rather than the sovereign, and Greek philosopher Socrates chose death rather than end his teaching as directed by the Athenian authorities.

In modern times civil disobedience has been an important part of the American tradition and of the worldwide nonviolent tradition. Many earlier actions in the American Revolution were nonviolent, planned violations of British laws which the colonists considered unjust. The antislavery movement, the Underground Railroad, much of the early labor movement, and the modern movements for social change all relied heavily on civil disobedience as part of their witness.

The most famous and influential theorist of civil disobedience was Henry David Thoreau. His essay "On the Duty of Civil Disobedience" (1849), influenced Gandhi, Martin Luther King, Jr., and, in various ways, thousands of others ranging from peace movement leaders to students who have read it as a class assignment. Thoreau refused to pay a Massachusetts poll tax and spent a night in jail. He argued that the tax supported slavery and the aggressive U.S. war against Mexico, both of which he opposed. "It is not desirable," he said, "to cultivate a respect for the law, so much as for the right. . . . Law never made men a whit more just; and, by means of their respect for it, even the well-disposed are daily made the agents of injustice." This argument, which holds that the demands of conscience are higher than the demands of the law, is central to all civil disobedience.

Civil disobedience on the individual level tries to lead by example. The man or woman who refuses to obey a "Keep Out" sign at a nuclear facility often hopes that others will follow or will oppose nuclear power or nuclear war in their own ways. It is common now for such individual actions to be part of a larger legal action. While the majority of the demonstrators remain behind police lines, in such actions, those who have chosen civil disobedience cross the lines.

On a small scale, such action is still a kind of leading-by-example. One of its goals is to influence public opinion to change the unjust law or abolish the unjust policy. Civil disobedients usually cooperate with arrest, court procedures, and imprisonment as a way of affirming basic social values. (Gandhi in fact taught his followers to be model prisoners.) Civil disobedience at this level seeks change indirectly.

Larger civil disobedience campaigns, like many of Gandhi's actions, can bring change more directly and quickly than individual witness. Governments operate only with the consent of the governed. If that consent is withdrawn on a very large scale the government cannot enforce the law. Thus the civil rights movement of the early 1960s was successful with mass civil disobedience—lunch counter sit-ins, for instance—because these actions made segregation laws impossible to enforce, while at the same time influencing public opinion throughout the country.

The classic instances of civil disobedience, and the most

142

successful, are nonviolent. Civil disobedience is not, however, an inherently nonviolent tactic. If poorly planned and undisciplined, civil disobedience can lead to confrontation with police and military forces assigned to keep order in a demonstration. Since the authorities, particularly military forces, are trained in responding violently, confrontation between demonstrators and the law often leads to violent repression. Demonstrators who have had no training in nonviolent tactics can, and frequently do, respond to violence with violence.

This creates, or can create, a difficult situation for organizers of a demonstration. Even though the demonstration itself and the planned civil disobedience may be nonviolent, television news—which emphasizes the "visual"—is eager to seize on any instance of violence. For television, nonviolence is too tame: it involves no tear gas, no firing of shots, and not a single thrown rock or piece of garbage. In cases where the demonstrators are nonviolent, the television cameras will often focus on the violence of the police. The public thus gets the impression that the demonstrators were also violent.

Because influencing public opinion is such an important part of civil disobedience and social change movements generally, organizers of actions have long recognized this media bias as a major problem. They have coped with it through careful planning and thorough training in nonviolent discipline, by scheduling civil disobedience separately from the larger, legal demonstration, and in other ways depending on local conditions.

Even with biased news coverage, however, civil disobedience remains an important component of any nonviolent campaign. The central argument that conscience is superior to law underlies much other war resistance. Nonviolent civil disobedience would also be essential to any plan for nonviolent civilian defense.

(See also: GANDHI MOHANDAS K., GOLDEN RULE AND PHOENIX, KING, MARTIN LUTHER, JR., NAZIS AND NONVIOLENCE, NONVIOLENCE, THOREAU, HENRY DAVID, WAR RESISTANCE)

Cold War: The conflict between the United States and the Soviet Union, though described in ideological terms by the rulers of those countries, is actually a struggle for economic, political, and military power. That ideology has relatively little to do with this struggle is evident from the behavior of the two nations. The United States habitually supports repressive dictatorships in the name of democracy and liberty. And in the name of socialist revolution, the Soviet Union has in practice supported governments whose credentials are more antisocialist than socialist. One example was the U.S.S.R.'s support for the ultra right-wing Argentine government in the Falklands (Malvinas) War—an impossibility if Soviet policy were made on purely socialist grounds. Thus the rhetoric which portrays the Cold War as democracy vs. communism, or socialism vs. imperialism, while it has some basis in fact, cloaks a more basic struggle between the two powers.

During the 1950s and early 1960s in the United States this struggle for mastery was called the Cold War. Though metaphorical this language could be taken literally without straining the truth. No shots were fired in any fighting directly between the two powers, yet each side sought military dominance over the other by sheer weight of nuclear and conventional arms. The U.S. intervened militarily in countries such as Korea and Vietnam, while the Soviet Union aided U.S. opponents in those countries. And both countries sought influence around the world by the use of economic and military aid. NATO and the Warsaw Pact are products of the early post-World War II power struggle.

It is commonly suggested that the Cold War was replaced in the mid-1970s by a new relationship between the superpowers, called "detente." In the sense that the two nations talked with each other and sought mutually beneficial arms control agreements, this is true. Detente was an improvement over the obvious tensions of the 1950s and early 1960s. Its tangible results, however, were of far less importance than the change in atmosphere which it represented. During the period of detente both sides continued to arm themselves and both continued their power struggle, though with less overt hostility. Detente, which was seen by the press as a sharp turn

144

away from the Cold War, was in fact only a first step toward peace.

The costs of the Cold War and of the revived "new" Cold War are immense for both sides. The Soviet Union, which suffers from inefficiency and technological underdevelopment, has channeled a crippling amount of its resources and scientific knowledge into war preparations. It has remained a police state, is closed to many outsiders and suspicious of all of them, and is thus unable to become a fully accepted member of the world community. Whether an end to the Cold War would result in improvements in the Soviet way of life is impossible to tell, though as long as the Cold War persists Soviet despotism may only become harsher.

For the United States the costs of the Cold War have, in some respects, been even more severe than for the Soviet Union. Russia, which has no tradition of democracy, was a dictatorship long before the Cold War. But in the U.S. the Cold War has distorted economic priorities, diminished personal and political liberty, and corrupted political discourse so thoroughly that much political debate resembles Orwell's "newsspeak"—the renaming of the MX missile, a giant strategic nuclear weapon, from MX to "Peacekeeper," for example.

It is also unlikely that in the absence of the Cold War the U.S. would have had a law such as the now defunct Smith Act, which outlawed organizations that "advocate the overthrow" of the U.S. government by force. Most Americans did not think of the act's primary target, the Communist party, as a political party at all, but as a foreign agent or spy, a conspiracy to be stamped out. In fact, however, the Smith Act outlawed political groups, thereby setting a dangerous precedent. Many countries suppress political parties on the grounds that they advocate the overthrow of the government. Among them are some of the most appalling dictatorships in the world.

The destructiveness of the 1950s Communist-hunters, such as Senator Joseph McCarthy and the House Un-American Activities Committee, are well-known and, outside of far right-wing circles, generally deplored today. Still, the revived Cold War has suggested a dangerous revival of such witch-hunting. Ultra-right wing publicists, for example, have suggested that the nuclear freeze movement is actually a tool of Moscow. The evidence for this was undocumented and inaccurate.

(The economic costs of the Cold War are discussed in the article on the MILITARY-INDUSTRIAL COMPLEX.)

The new Cold War was not solely a product of the Reagan administration. During the mid- to late 1970s press reports by the hundreds told of a Soviet arms buildup whose size was often exaggerated. Right-wing critics of the Nixon, Ford and Carter administrations spoke and wrote repeatedly of a "growing Soviet military superiority" and of a completely fictitious U.S. "unilateral disarmament." By repeated mention this mixture of outright lies, exaggerations, and half-truths came to seem like the truth, until it became very difficult for politicians to suggest that the U.S. and the Soviet Union could and must learn to live together.

Unlike the 1950s, though, the current spate of Cold War rhetoric has met substantial opposition. The peace movement, which was small in the 1950s, has grown until it could bring a million people to a demonstration in New York on June 12, 1982. Thus the revival of the Cold War is not a sign that all is lost. It may instead be the death throes of an era that is ending.

(See also: MILITARY-INDUSTRIAL COMPLEX, NATO AND WARSAW PACT, NUCLEAR FREEZE MOVEMENT, NUCLEAR WEAPONS AND WAR, SOVIET UNION, UNITED STATES)

1. Frank Donner, "The Campaign to Smear the Nuclear Freeze Movement," *The Nation*, Vol. 235, No. 15 (November 6, 1982), p. 462.

Combat: The moral objections to war, and thus to combat, are clear even to many generals. What is far less clear is the solution to the mystery of combat: Why are soldiers willing to fight in the first place? Why, against their own interests, against their instinct for self-preservation, and against a great body of moral and religious teaching, do people go on fighting?

This issue is crucial not only for armies, which teach people how to fight, but for pacifists and others who seek to abolish war. Is combat a "natural" state? Do people fight out of blood-lust or out of some deeply buried destructive instinct? Do they die for their country, their comrades, or for no reason at all?

The study of combat is not in itself the study of the causes of war. Causes of war are many: diplomatic blunders, lust for money and power, ideological conflicts, to name a few. War as an institution is more than combat.

Nor is the study of combat the study of warfare. Warfare is concerned with military strategies, weapons, and tactics; with how wars are fought, in other words, not with why people fight or what it is like to fight.

Combat is the actual fighting which is at the heart of war. It is a lethal contest between two military forces, each organized in its own way for efficient killing. It can be a fight between two units of ten soldiers each or a vast offensive over a fifty-mile front. Combat has changed in intensity and duration over the years; battles have grown longer and more destructive. This growth in destructiveness has only deepened the mystery. If a soldier's "will to combat" was difficult to understand during the age of musketry, what are we to say of it in the age of battlefield nuclear weapons, nerve gas, and "smart" weapons?

Types of Combat

It is important to distinguish among the various types of combat. Each type has its own distinctive features, and the various factors cited under "Theories of Combat," below, will influence combatants differently, or not at all, depending on the type of fighting and the kinds of military forces engaged. The major types of combat today may be listed as follows:

Infantry Combat: Fighting between bodies of foot soldiers is the traditional form of combat. Infantry seldom operate without mechanized or air support.

Mechanized Combat: Battle between groups of tanks. This kind of fighting does not usually occur in pure form,

147

even in so-called tank battles. Most such battles also involve infantry and aircraft. Modern infantry is also mechanized: it is transported to the battle zone by ground vehicle or helicopter instead of marching there on foot.

Air Combat: Battle between aircraft. This includes fighting between small fighter aircraft and bombing attacks.

Artillery Combat: Though generally used in support of infantry, artillery (long-range guns and rockets) frequently engages in duels with opposing artillery.

Naval Combat: Battle between ships, including submarines. This is traditionally the purest form of combat because ships, unlike bodies of soldiers, cannot suddenly panic and run away. Modern naval combat usually includes air combat and artillery battles.

It is evident even from this deliberately simplified list that some forms of combat involve closer contact with opposing forces than others. Thus infantry combat is often called close combat. Theories of combat have most often tried to explain close combat rather than the more impersonal forms of battle.

It is clear also that combat's destructiveness varies almost directly with its impersonality. The most impersonal forms of combat, aerial bombardment and missile attack, are also the most destructive. In ground combat, artillery, which is highly impersonal in its operation, is also responsible for most of the destruction. (It accounted for more deaths in the two world wars than any other type of weaponry.)

Theories of Combat

Politicians, philosophers, psychologists, historians, and other students of war have tried to explain combat in various ways. None of the explanations advanced is completely satisfactory, but taken together they can provide the beginning of a theory of combat. They also provide hope that war, far from being inevitable, can be abolished.

Patriotism or Political Commitment: Politicians are prone to argue that soldiers fight primarily for a cause: "to

148

preserve freedom," "for the fatherland," and so on. Soldiers know this is nonsense. A soldier may enlist out of patriotism, but as George Orwell put it, "a soldier anywhere near the front line is usually too hungry, or frightened, or cold, or, above all, too tired to bother about the political origins of the war."[1] An exception might be made for guerrilla warfare, particularly guerrilla resistance in an occupied country, but even highly patriotic soldiers are unlikely to fight for long unless other factors sustain them.

Outside of actual battle, patriotism has a strong appeal—particularly in wartime. Thus although soldiers seldom fight for patriotism once in combat, their love of country enables the politicians who decide for war to raise a military force even when their citizens would be better off not fighting. (Patriotism is, of course, only one among many factors which motivate recruits to join the military.)

Hatred of the Enemy: At the center of the mystery of combat lies a paradox: Combat is unutterably destructive, yet soldiers may not have any personal hatred for their opponents. Soldiers will often say, quite truthfully, that they respect their opponents and wish they did not have to fight them.

This does not mean that combat is nonviolent, that soldiers do not try to kill each other, or that soldiers never hate each other. On the contrary. Armies frequently use racial hatreds to build fighting spirit, as in Vietnam where to the U.S. military every Vietnamese was a "gook." As fighting drags on soldiers may come to hate each other even if they did not at the beginning. (An astonishing example of this process occurred during World War I. Christmas of 1914 was a time of fraternization between opposing troops on the western front. But such friendly contact between German and English or French troops never occurred again during the war, and probably could not have done so because of the bitterness engendered by the fighting.)

Personal hatred, however, is not essential to combat. British troops in the Falklands (Malvinas) War did not hate the Argentine troops; rather they pitied them because they were young conscripts. Yet British arms killed over seven hundred Argentines in brief but intense fighting.

149

Depersonalization: Far more important to combat is the process of turning one's opponent into a nonperson. This is evident both in military terminology—where a person on the opposing side is simply "the enemy," and a group of people wearing opposing uniforms become simply a "target"—and in military practices such as wearing uniforms. Soldiers become nonpersons not only for their opponents but for their own commanders. Thus commanders speak not of "people killed and wounded," but of "losses" or "casualties." Such impersonal terminology is actually essential to military operations. It enables commanders to plan attacks, and so on, in which they know that a certain number of the people under their command will be killed and wounded. At the same time, insofar as soldiers on the ground think of their opponents as people, they are less able to kill. The military habit of referring to opponents by a kind of collective singular—e.g., "Jerry" for German soldiers; "Charlie" for Vietnamese guerrillas—arises from the need to depersonalize the opponent.

Instinctive Aggression and Territoriality: Konrad Lorenz, a prominent student of animal behavior, and Robert Ardrey, a gifted playwright and amateur anthropologist, among others, suggest that aggression in human beings is instinctive, as is protection of territory. This view goes beyond the evidence, and it does not explain the peculiar kind of violence which occurs in combat. Modern combat, particularly artillery and other long-range combat, can involve little or no overt aggression. Soldiers and sailors operating artillery are most concerned with aiming and firing their guns, usually in a well-rehearsed and calm manner. They may never see their opponents. If aggression is a drive which is released in combat, what is such impersonal destructiveness as this? Surely it is combat, even though it is calm and calculated. There is little that is instinctive about an artillery duel.

Defense of territory, or "positions," is so common in battle that it is easy to confuse such tactics with animal defense of territory. They are not the same. A defensive position is selected for military and tactical reasons, not because of instinct. It may, unlike the territories of many animals, shift as

150

battle causes it to shift. Opposing troops attack positions because their superiors order them to do so, generally for tactical reasons (because a hill commands a wide view of the combat zone, say). This is not territoriality in the biological sense.

Nor is defense of the nation a kind of territoriality. The nation is a large and abstract conception. So, as discussed above, is its defense. Soldiers in combat rarely fight for the nation. This fact alone undercuts the theory of defense of territory.

It is true that in close combat something like blood-lust is released among soldiers. Thus it is reasonable to suggest that combat can draw upon reserves of human aggression; military forces depend on such reserves. But blood-lust does not start wars. Decisions of politicians start wars. Nor does blood-lust make the decision for combat. Superior officers decide on combat in a certain place at a certain time, and they give the orders to fight. Only after the fighting has begun can the violence of combat become almost an end in itself.

Drugs and Fatigue: Studies of combat have recognized, though not emphasized, the crucial role of psychological and physical numbness in sustaining soldiers through battle. In Vietnam combat soldiers regularly fought under the influence of narcotics. In the trenches of World War I, the British army supplied its troops with strong navy rum before an attack. It is likely that drugs and alcohol have made combat bearable for soldiers in most armies at most times. It is certain that combat soldiers drink heavily or, as in Vietnam, use narcotics extensively when they are away from the battle zone.

Fighting soldiers are also, quite simply, tired. While this is not always the case, just as not all soldiers enter combat intoxicated, sheer fatigue can prevent a soldier from realizing the insanity of the battle going on around him, causing him to go on because he is too tired to think of the consequences of doing what he is told.

Illusion of Immortality: Young combat soldiers commonly believe that even though combat is deadly they themselves will not be hurt. There is no clear explanation of this phenomenon, but it is noticeable not only in combat soldiers but also in people who engage in other dangerous occupations.

Paradoxically, the opposite belief—fatalism—often sustains a soldier through combat. Soldiers may even simultaneously believe that they will not be hurt and that if a bullet "has their name written on it," there is nothing they can do and so they may as well go on fighting.

Training: Military training, which is discussed in a separate article, is designed to build a soldier's aggressiveness while at the same time submerging him or her in a group. It also trains soldiers in violent responses until they are automatic. This explains in part why tired or drugged soldiers can continue to fight.

Male Bonding: Studies by the U.S. military following World War II showed that soldiers fight not because they are naturally aggressive but because they are part of a small group which holds them to a certain code of honor. Combat is so terrifying that without group support soldiers would probably find it impossible to bear. Their "buddies" become essential life-support systems, and thus there follows the willingness to fight "for one's buddies." The need for small group support and the need to repay the group with courage under fire may themselves be partially a product of the combat situation.

Fear: Combat is frightening. It is unpredictable, lethal, chaotic, noisy, dirty, and smelly. The fear which battle creates, however, may actually force soldiers to stand and fight. On the one hand, a soldier who runs loses his life-support system, the respect of his group; on the other hand, running in combat can actually be dangerous. Thus one half of the "fight or flight" response—a physical and psychological reaction common to animals and human beings under stress—is for all practical purposes closed to a combat soldier. (Desertion, which is common in wartime, is more likely to occur before or after a battle than during it. This was particularly true in Vietnam where desertion was extremely difficult at the best of times.)

The result is that soldiers, under the pressure of the combat situation itself, fight as they probably would not if flight were readily available. When flight does occur, it is likely to be a group phenomenon. Military training and discipline seek to overcome the tendency to flee by making fighting automatic and by punishing flight. It is no accident that most armies have punished desertion in wartime more severely than almost any other crime—often with execution. This practice results from the attempt to close off the possibility of flight, thus forcing soldiers to fight.

Combat is not inevitable. Even the brief survey above shows that the decision for combat is a conscious human decision (not an unconscious drive) which results from policy and strategic considerations over which individual soldiers have little control. Military combat is hedged about with myriad devices to force soldiers to do battle: military training, group bonding, punishment of deserters, even distribution of rum. It is unlikely that such devices would be necessary if war were instinctive. Thus the combat situation is a conscious human construction for which soldiers are consciously prepared both mentally and physically.

To say that combat is not inevitable is not to say that abolishing war will be easy, however. Clearly it is not and will not be. But if combat were instinctive, the struggle against war would be hopeless indeed. Though it does not show how combat can be ended, the analysis above does give hope that humanity can put an end to war and learn to live in peace.

(See also: BATTLEFIELD, CHAIN OF COMMAND, CONVENTIONAL WAR, LAWS OF WAR, MILITARY TRAINING, WOMEN AND WAR)

1. George Orwell, "Looking Back on the Spanish War," in *A Collection of Essays by George Orwell* (New York: Harcourt, Brace, Jovanovich, 1953), p. 189.

Communism: In the name of countering communism, the U.S. has supported venal dictatorships in countries around the world. It has stifled domestic dissent, as in the era of Senator Joseph McCarthy and the Hollywood blacklist. It has spent hundreds of billions of dollars on military hardware and personnel. None of this has availed. Communism as political and economic thought has not gone away; as ideology it has retained its attraction for Third World revolutionaries; as a system of government and economics, embodied in the various so-called Socialist states, it has not, despite extreme difficulties, collapsed.

None of this is very surprising. Communism is first of all an idea, and it is futile to counter ideas with armies. The attractions of Marxist thought are many, in part because Marx provided more penetrating insights into the human condition than most other economic thinkers. The ideology of class warfare which lies at the center of Marxist thought blends well with Third World liberation struggles, that are usually challenging a government and a class system supported by the Western capitalist states.

Marxist thought takes as its starting point the conflicts of interest among the various social classes. This assumption, which is well-supported by facts, leads Marxists to conclude that economic and social class, and class interest, are the most important determinants of human behavior. They also conclude that capitalism, or private ownership of the means of production, based as it is on exploitation of the working class by the owning class, contains inherent contradictions which will eventually lead to working class revolution.

As it happens the specific predictions which Marxists made in the nineteenth century turned out to be largely false. Marx himself thought that the revolution would occur first in one of the more developed countries of Europe. In fact the revolution (or *a* revolution dominated by Marxists) occurred in Russia, which Marx regarded as unready for socialism. The failure of Marxist predictions demonstrates that, though styled as "scientific," Marxism is as yet no more scientific than are other economic theories.

As a tool of social analysis, however, Marxism is not only useful, it is almost universally used. The business executive from Indiana, the marketing expert from New York, even the

154

President of the United States, all frequently speak in terms of economic and class interests and analyze issues in this way. They do not support social or economic revolution but they are nonetheless followers of Marx in the same way that many educated people are followers of Freud: his thought has affected their way of seeing the world.

The flaws in Communist theory are many. Not only is it one-sided, it fails to take into account human biology, psychology, and culture. Marxism's worst defect, however, is its failure to address what happens after the revolution. Marx himself spoke of this only in vague terms, and his difficult (and occasionally imprecise) writing style has led to varying interpretations. The aftermath of revolutions made in Marx's name has been totalitarian and in some cases appallingly violent. One thinks of the Russian Revolution, the atrocities of Pol Pot in Kampuchea (Cambodia), and the various authoritarian governments of Eastern Europe.

Marx predicted the end of the state when it was no longer needed to enforce class interests; the end of war when the international working class had seized power; and just distribution of economic goods. None of these has occurred. Governments like that of the Soviet Union have not withered, but grown more powerful. "Socialist" states have, as in the case of Vietnam and Kampuchea, fought each other in bitter combat. And within the Soviet Union itself, there is an elite of party and government officials, intellectuals, and artists who can obtain goods more easily and in greater quantity than the general public.[1]

These developments were, if not entirely inevitable, predictable. Seizing power by violence requires military-style organization, ruthlessness, and in most cases secret and conspiratorial methods. Revolutionaries who use such methods cannot suddenly change the habits developed over the course of years. Thus Lenin, who insisted on strict party discipline and government by an elite when out of power, continued to insist on these things when in power.[2] Revolutionaries easily acquire a habit of violence and elitism; they do not easily lose it.

Despite its flaws, Marxist ideology speaks to deep-seated resentments among Third World peoples, particularly intellectuals. The reason for this is not hard to see. Western interests, generally those of major Western companies, have dominated many Third World countries, sometimes for hundreds of years.[3] Thus for many years Honduras was practically an outpost of the United Fruit Company. Little wonder that Third World revolutionaries, who are generally ardent nationalists, turn to Marxism for an understanding of their nations' predicament. Marxism provides them not only with an analysis but with a prescription for action.

Many U.S. politicians often attribute Third World revolutions to a monolithic "Communist conspiracy." Diplomatic breaks between China and the Soviet Union and the wars among Socialist states show that there is no such conspiracy. The attraction of Marxist ideology is rooted in the injustice to be found in nearly all Third World countries. It is folly to counter such ideology with military force. That can only increase the injustice, making peaceful change ever more difficult to achieve.

Using force against the Marxist idea is also, in the nuclear age, foolhardy. Whatever our differences from Marxist-ruled countries, we must learn to live with them lest all die. Nuclear weapons have no ideology.

(See also: COLD WAR, SOVIET UNION, STALIN/UNITED STATES)

1. See, among others, Hedrick Smith, *The Russians* (New York: Ballantine Books, 1976), ch. 1.
2. A fascinating portrait of Lenin will be found in Harrison Salisbury, *Black Night, White Snow: Russia's Revolutions 1905–1917* (Garden City, N.Y.: Doubleday, 1978).
3. For a full discussion of multinational corporations in the modern world, see Richard J. Barnet and Ronald E. Muller, *Global Reach: The Power of the Multinational Corporations* (New York: Simon & Schuster/Touchstone, 1974).

Conscientious Objection: Conscientious objection is both a legal provision in conscription laws and military regulations, and a moral stance against war. The legal definition varies from country to country. Most countries that have conscription do not recognize any right of conscientious objection at all.

156

As a moral position conscientious objection can be more universally defined. A conscientious objector (CO) is a person who cannot take part in all war, or some wars, or some part of war (for instance, maintaining nuclear weapons) because he or she believes it would be wrong to do so.

Most Western countries allow legal alternatives only for men and women who object to all war. An exception is Great Britain, which exempts objectors to particular wars and even did so during World War II.[1] These countries generally recognize moral and religious objectors and deny exemption to "political" objectors. The line between a moral and a political objector, however, is seldom entirely clear. Conscientious objectors are usually assigned to duty as unarmed soldiers (noncombatants) or to a period of civilian work in lieu of military duty.

In the United States the Military Selective Service Act (draft law) provides exemption from military duty for persons who object on religious or moral grounds to all war. Military regulations allow such objectors to receive discharge or transfer to noncombatant status if they develop objections to war after enlistment.

The tradition of recognizing conscientious objection in some form goes back to the Civil War conscription laws. Both the Union and the Confederacy made provisions for CO's, though these provisions—like the draft laws themselves—were unevenly applied. The World War I Selective Draft Act provided for objectors who belonged to a recognized pacifist church. This provision was probably unconstitutional and certainly unenforceable; it was modified by executive order early in 1918 to include all religious objectors. However, all objectors were required to serve in the military as noncombatants, and those who refused such service faced military court-martial. Some World War I objectors were still in military prison when President Roosevelt amnestied all World War I resisters in 1933.

The 1940 Selective Training and Service Act for the first time provided civilian alternative service for CO's. Objectors were placed in work camps called Civilian Public Service (CPS). There they performed duties ranging from fighting forest fires to serving as human guinea pigs for medical experi-

157

ments. Both Congress and the church groups which had administered CPS were dissatisfied with the arrangement and when alternative service was reinstated in 1951 CPS was abandoned. Instead the Selective Service System assigned objectors to employers on a case-by-case basis. In theory, pay and benefits for CO's were the same as those for any other worker. In practice Selective Service accepted primarily low-paying, menial jobs as alternative service, which draft officials tended to consider a form of punishment.[2]

Inductions under the U.S. draft ended in 1973. Military regulations, however, still provide for discharge or transfer to noncombatant service for conscientious objectors. Like civilian objectors, military objectors must show that they object to all war on religious or moral grounds. Processing of conscientious objector claims in the military is extremely complex and time-consuming. It involves a detailed series of questions, three required interviews, and a final decision at military branch headquarters.[3]

United States law is among the more liberal with respect to CO's. In countries such as Greece and Spain recognition of conscientious objectors has become a major issue for the peace movement. In other countries, particularly the Scandinavian countries, virtually any type of objection can lead to exemption. Few countries, however, allow for conscientious objector discharges from the military. The majority of countries have no provision at all for CO's. A 1982 United Nations report found that of seventy-nine countries surveyed only twenty-three allowed exemption for conscientious objectors.[4]

Conscientious objection usually becomes an issue for the public and for individuals when a country has conscription. This is not always the case, as witness the hundreds regularly discharged each year from the U.S. military on grounds of conscience. In South Africa, where white male conscription is universal, conscientious objection to fighting for apartheid has become a major issue and has led to hundreds of desertions from the South African Defense Force. In 1979 the United Nations passed a resolution calling on member states to receive South African deserters as refugees. This resolution, which was the first of its kind in UN history, was a major step toward developing a right in international law to refuse military service. Its practical effect, however, has been questionable because many countries were already granting refugee status to South African deserters.[5]

Conscientious objection is primarily an individual position. Its political implications, particularly those of legally recognized conscientious objection, have been a matter of some dispute within the peace movement. During the Indochina War some peace activists argued that lawful conscientious objection actually helped the draft system to work, thus prolonging the war. Since the number of recognized CO's (thirty-five thousand) was small compared to the numbers subject to the draft (roughly ten million), it is not clear whether legal provision for CO's could have had such an effect.

The argument has some merit in a quite different sense, though. Conscientious objection alone probably could not stop a war. There is little doubt that if the number of conscientious objectors seeking legal redress became large enough to affect military manpower supplies, the government would try to narrow the availability of CO status. This actually happened in West Germany. In 1980 objectors were permitted simply to opt out of the draft by sending in a postcard declaring their objections. In the few months that this provision was in effect hundreds of thousands of people sent in the required postcard. A German court, under heavy political pressure, finally threw out the provision.[6]

Like war resisters generally, conscientious objectors are not effective in frustrating military recruitment. Nonetheless they have been influential out of all proportion to their numbers. During the Indochina War conscientious objection became a part of the public consciousness, and individual objectors were able to raise questions about the war and U.S. policy as they could not have done if they themselves had not taken a stand. This was true both of legally recognized objectors and of those, such as objectors to the Vietnam War only, whose positions required them to break the law.

Equally important, the large numbers of conscientious objector applications sent to the Selective Service System in the early 1970s did in fact contribute to the breakdown of conscription. Along with hundreds of thousands of appeals and applications for other deferments, these applications became a form of collective—yet perfectly legal—war resistance, effective in a way that individuals acting alone could not have been. The breakdown of the draft in the early 1970s remains one of the most astonishing achievements in the history of the American peace movement.

(See also: CIVIL DISOBEDIENCE, CONSCRIPTION, JUST WAR THEORY, NUCLEAR PACIFISM, WAR RESISTANCE)

1. On selective objection in Great Britain, and the history generally of CO's there, see Denis Hayes, *Challenge of Conscience* (London: George Allen & Unwin, 1949).

2. A thorough history of pacifism generally in the U.S., and of conscientious objection, is Peter Brock, *History of Pacifism in the United States from the Colonial Era to the First World War* (Princeton, N.J.: Princeton University Press, 1968), and its sequel, *Twentieth Century Pacifism* (New York: Van Nostrand, Reinhold, 1970).

3. For a thorough discussion of in-service conscientious objection, see Robert A. Seeley, ed., *Advice for Conscientious Objectors in the Armed Forces* (Philadelphia: Central Committee for Conscientious Objectors, 1984).

4. United Nations Economic and Social Council, "Question of Conscientious Objection to Military Service," June 15, 1982.

5. Gordon Browne, "The UN Accepts Conscientious Objection," *CCCO News Notes*, Vol. 31, No. 3 (Fall, 1979).

6. I am grateful to War Resisters International for supplying this information.

7. A more complete discussion of conscientious objection under the draft law is contained in Robert A. Seeley, *Handbook for Conscientious Objectors* (Philadelphia: Central Committee for Conscientious Objectors, 1982).

Conscription: Conscription, or the draft, is the practice of forcing young men (and sometimes young women) to perform military duty when called by the government. It probably goes back in some form to ancient times. In its modern form it originated with Napoleon Bonaparte who used conscript armies to expand the French empire. Conscript armies fought both world wars (on both sides), the Indochina War, and the Korean War. Today conscripts fight on one or both sides in virtually every war.

There was no conscription in the United States until the Civil War. Draft laws in both the Confederacy and the Union proved so unpopular that they were quickly abandoned when hostilities ended. The World War I draft law and the 1940 Selective Service Act which provided manpower for World War II were also allowed to expire. In 1948, however, following reports of Soviet troop movements on the Turkish border, Congress passed the modern Selective Service Act. Though the authority to induct people into the military expired in 1973, the Military Selective Service Act (so named in 1971) remains in force, and 18-year-old men have been required to register for the draft since July 1980.

From a military point of view conscription solves three problems: expanding the military quickly; replacing losses (soldiers killed and wounded); and pursuing an unpopular war. At the same time, the availability of conscript soldiers has often tempted generals to expend human lives recklessly. Thus Napoleon boasted that he could afford to lose twenty-five thousand men a month, an unheard-of casualty rate at that time. World War I, in which incompetent generals callously sent waves of conscripts to die under machine-gun fire, resulted in ten million military dead.

It is unlikely that the Indochina War could have been fought at all without the draft. Despite massive resistance, the draft provided replacements throughout the U.S. ground war in Vietnam when voluntary recruitment would have been impossible. A government which does not have the power to conscript cannot, as the U.S. did in Vietnam, carry out a war which has no popular support.

The 1979 Soviet invasion of Afghanistan and the war which followed would also have been impossible without conscription. Most Soviet combat troops, including some of those in elite units, are conscripts. The Soviet-installed Afghan government also relies on conscription to fill the ranks of its army.

Liberal draft advocates argue that conscription is fairer than voluntary recruitment and that a U.S. president who can call upon a conscript army will be less likely to use nuclear weapons in a major war. Both these arguments fly in the face of reality. Studies by Michael Useem and others have shown that the composition of the U.S. military was little different under conscription than it has been in the ten years since voluntary recruitment alone has been used.[1] And no president or military commander is likely to commit half a million Americans to death or maiming—as would happen in the first few weeks of a major land war—if he or she believes that nuclear weapons provide a quick solution with few American casualties. Faced with a choice between nuclear bombardment and American casualties in 1945, President Truman opted to destroy Hiroshima and Nagasaki. That is the only historical evidence available. It gives little comfort to the liberal draft advocates.[2]

In addition to its inherent dangers, conscription is a particularly objectionable addition to the powers of the state. It violates a conscript's privacy completely, forcing him or her to give up not merely money or liberty but life itself. Its enforcement requires a bureaucracy whose business it is to inquire into family matters, conscientious beliefs, and physical and mental ailments. Draft registration, seemingly a mild form of conscription, is now enforced by nationwide computer checks, using lists of licensed drivers in an effort to detect non-registrants.

None of this should be surprising. Conscription is inherently coercive and it has been a prime tool of dictators. In Hitler's Germany it was universal: the penalty for violation was death. In the Soviet Union it is universal. Draft advocates cite the use of conscription in countries such as Holland, where conscription coexists with a healthy democracy. But even in a strong democracy, conscription can lead—as it did in the U.S.—to the use of troops for military intervention without popular consent.

(See also: CONSCIENTIOUS OBJECTION, CONVENTIONAL WAR, INDOCHINA WAR, NATO AND WARSAW PACT, NUCLEAR WEAPONS AND WAR, WAR RESISTANCE)

1. See Michael Useem, "The Draft, Social Class, and Recruitment," *CCCO News Notes*, Vol. 34, No. 2 (summer 1982).
2. For a fuller discussion of liberal draft supporters and the arguments against their position, see Robert A. Seeley, "Drafting the Liberals," *CCCO News Notes*, Vol. 34, No. 4 (winter 1983).

Conventional War: Nuclear weapons have not been used in combat since the bombings of Hiroshima and Nagasaki in 1945. Since then some twenty-five million people[1] have died in wars fought without nuclear weapons. In the twentieth century war deaths have been upwards of eighty-five million and may approach one hundred million. Entire populations have been reduced to bands of refugees barely able to survive, and untold amounts of property have been destroyed.

Public concern has understandably focused on the danger of nuclear war. But these appalling figures show that more traditional forms of warfare have also become destructive beyond humanity's worst nightmares. The change is not merely in quantity of destruction; it is also a change in the quality and intensity of the carnage. Military technology changes so rapidly that when compared with modern weapons, the weapons of the two world wars might as well be spears or bows and arrows.

Modern armies differ from older armies in five significant ways:

Size: Although some military operations—the U.S. invasion of Grenada, for example—may use small numbers of troops, modern armies in general are far larger than pre-twentieth–century armies. Military losses in World War I were ten million—a previously unheard-of number of casualties. The U.S. military today considers 2.1 million soldiers, sailors and airmen a minimum number needed for its mission. Other armies, such as the Soviet (four million) are even larger. In any major land war between the superpowers the numbers of troops engaged would be in the hundreds of thousands. U.S. Defense Department projections for such a war call for four hundred thousand "replacements" after six weeks of fighting, implying four hundred thousand killed and wounded.[2]

Mobility: Armored vehicles (tanks and troop transporters), helicopters, strike aircraft, transport aircraft, all have served to widen the area of destruction which a modern army can cause. It is likely that in an all-out conventional war in Europe all of Germany would become a battlefield, even if nuclear weapons were not used.

The army's latest tactical doctrine, called the AirLand Battle, includes such a result as part of the plan: "Depth is the heart of the AirLand Battle concept. We must use the entire depth of the battlefield to attack the enemy and prevent him from concentrating his forces at his point of choice. The deep battle will delay, disrupt, or destroy the enemy's uncommitted forces—those not in contact with our troops—and isolate his committed forces so they can be defeated."[3]

This new mobility has changed the pace of modern warfare. It would deepen the plight of refugees who would for the most part have nowhere to go. It would mean that destruction of property, including irreplaceable buildings, works of art, and libraries, would be nearly complete within the combat zone. Armies, with their increased firepower, would range over the whole contested area leveling it as they went.

Firepower: The destructive power of modern conventional weapons would have been inconceivable even twenty years ago. This increase in firepower represents not merely greater explosive power but a different and more devastating *kind* of power. A shell, bomb, or rocket may contain a large number of explosive "bomblets" or miniature mines which would be spread over the battle zone on impact—sometimes covering an area 300 by 1,000 meters with deadly explosive. Antitank shells are filled with fragments of depleted uranium which reacts with iron to melt the tank's armor and turn the inside into an inferno. Cluster bombs may contain as many as seven hundred bomblets which can destroy tank armor and which, on striking earth, jump to waist height before exploding. These developments and more make the modern battle zone far more lethal than any previous battle zone in history.[4]

Accuracy of Weapons: In earlier wars, even including the Indochina War, the weapons used had a good deal less than 50 percent chance of hitting their targets. Guided by human skill exercised under trying conditions, and subject to all manner of mishap, older weapons missed far more often than they hit. Not so modern weapons. A World War II antitank weapon might find its target in 10 percent of cases. The modern equivalent would find its target in 90 percent of cases.

This new and frightening accuracy results from modern guidance systems which are built into missiles small enough in some cases to be fired from hand-held weapons. The Exocet missile used by Argentina in the Falklands (Malvinas) War can be guided to its target from a distance of forty nautical miles. It flies just above water level, correcting its course as required to reach its target. Ships without special defense systems are helpless against Exocet attack.

Modern guidance systems may include small internal computers, heat-seeking devices which target jet and internal combustion engines, laser guidance systems, and so on. (These guidance systems and their effects are discussed in more detail in the article on "SMART" WEAPONS.)

Tactics: Direct attacks on the civilian population, though forbidden by the laws of war, have today become standard military operating procedure. The area bombing campaign in World War II established aerial bombardment of cities as a major component of land warfare. Counterinsurgency warfare is war against the entire population. In an all-out conventional war civilian casualties would almost certainly outnumber military casualties—as they have in every war in this century save World War I.

All of these developments make it foolhardy and wicked to discuss conventional war as though it were an acceptable or humane alternative to nuclear war. There is no doubt that all-out nuclear war would have greater and more lasting effects than all-out conventional war. But the horrors of conventional warfare are greater now than they have ever been. The military historian John Keegan puts the point well:

. . . it is a delusion to hope that reliance on conventional weapons will spare mankind the physical and psychological consequences of international ineptitude and ill-will. Both the great wars of this century were almost unmitigated disasters for the people on whose territories they were fought. The ingenuity and productiveness of the industrial nations ensure that any conventional war into which they might stumble in the future, even if they were able to keep their fingers off the nuclear trigger, would be yet more unbearable.[5]

Modern conventional war is not merely more destructive than earlier war. It is far more dangerous because of the advent of nuclear weapons. A high intensity conventional war could easily inflict the same level of damage on the area where it was fought as would a low intensity nuclear war.[6] This overlap between the destructiveness of nuclear and conventional weapons is the most disturbing of modern trends. It erodes the traditional distinction between nuclear and conventional war. As conventional weapons have grown larger and more indiscriminate, nuclear weapons have become smaller, until today a large conventional bomb may have more explosive power than a small battlefield nuclear weapon such as a nuclear land mine.

At the same time the United States and the Soviet Union have come to rely so heavily on nuclear weapons that any confrontation between them could result in nuclear exchange. There is no doubt, for example, that "small" nuclear weapons, which are deployed there by the thousands, would come into use very quickly in any all-out European war. From nuclear land mines to nuclear attacks against the enemy's homeland is a short step, and more likely under the pressures of combat to seem both necessary and desirable. This would be especially true as the armies engaged suffered casualties at a (likely) faster rate than in any war in history. (A further discussion of war as it would affect Europe will be found under NATO AND WARSAW PACT.)

There has been no all-out conventional war. But none of the discussion here is based on speculation. Military planners envision the effects of intense land war by projecting from the known effects of modern weapons. Some of these effects have been observed in tests. Many more of them—far too many—have been observed in actual combat. In the Middle East, the Israeli military and the forces of its opponents are both armed with modern weapons, including heat-seeking missiles, cluster bombs, and other weapons which would be used in all-out conventional war. Modern weapons are being used in El Salvador and, because of the arms trade (in which the U.S. is the world's top supplier), in most of the other wars which at any given moment are taking place around the world.[7] The Exocet missile proved its deadliness in the Falklands (Malvinas) War; in that same war undetectable plastic land mines showed that modern conventional war can leave large areas of land unfit for human habitation, probably permanently. Nerve gas, which brings instantaneous and hideously painful death, and which would probably be used in all-out war, has been tested extensively on laboratory animals.

A European land war is, for many reasons, unlikely to have any result but nuclear holocaust. Thus the main effect of conventional military technology has been to make "little" wars more deadly. This state of affairs, in which new weapons are developed for an intense war and then used against guerrillas and the civilian population, is likely to continue. It is clear that the only long-term remedy for the threat of nuclear war is not more conventional weapons, but the abolition of war itself.

(See also: ANTIPERSONNEL WEAPONS, BATTLEFIELD, GUERRILLA WARFARE, INDOCHINA WAR, MIDDLE EAST, NATO AND WARSAW PACT, NUCLEAR WEAPONS AND WAR, RAPID DEPLOYMENT FORCE, "SMART" WEAPONS, SOVIET UNION, UNITED STATES, WAR AND THE ENVIRONMENT)

1. I am grateful to Michael T. Klare of the Institute for Policy Studies for this estimate.

2. Projection from various Pentagon "mobilization scenarios" for land war in Europe. See, e.g., *America's Volunteers* (December 31, 1978), a Department of Defense study of military recruitment and the draft.

3. Lt. Col. Jonathan P. Tomes, "A Primer on the AirLand Battle," *The Army Lawyer*, Department of the Army Pamphlet 27-50-132, December, 1983, p. 7.

4. See John Keegan, "The Specter of Conventional War," *Harper's*, July, 1983, pp. 8–14; and Michael T. Klare, "The Conventional Weapons Fallacy," *The Nation*, April 9, 1983, pp. 438–444.

5. Keegan, p. 14.

6. Cf. Klare, pp. 443–444, and Klare, "Leaping the Firebreak," *The Progressive*, Vol. 47, No. 9 (September, 1983), pp. 31–33.

7. The Center for Defense Information, a nonprofit education and resource center, estimates that there are 40 wars at present (1983). See "A World at War," *Defense Monitor*, Vol. XII, No. 1 (1983 issue #1).

Czech Resistance, 1968:

In August 1968 the armies of five Warsaw Pact nations invaded Czechoslovakia. Called a "military exercise" for public consumption,[1] the invasion was an attempt to crush the liberal Czech government of Alexander Dubcek. Czech officials, realizing that their armed forces were outnumbered, offered no military resistance. Dubcek and other Czech leaders were kidnapped by the Soviet KGB.

Then, without preparation or training, the Czech population began a campaign of nonviolent resistance to the invaders. The Czech resistance prevented the installation of a collaborationist government for eight months. In the end the resistance broke down because of a disruption in its nonviolent discipline.[2]

Tactics used by the Czech resistance included clandestine radio broadcasts, brief general strikes, work slowdowns, and courageous resistance by officials of the Dubcek government. Though the Soviets prevailed militarily within three days, they were forced to negotiate with the Czech leaders, reaching a compromise (the Moscow Protocol) which left most of the reform leaders in their positions of power. Only eight months later, when riots at the Aeroflot offices in Prague provided an excuse to remove the reform leaders, did the Soviet invasion accomplish its objectives.

Though ultimately defeated, the Czech resistance provides a remarkable example of the potential of nonviolent resistance. It was a spontaneous development, organized under the worst possible conditions—in the teeth of an invasion no less—and carried out with no prior training. A military force organized as quickly and with as little training would have been destroyed utterly within hours, and even the well-prepared Czech armed forces quickly realized that they could not hold out for more than three or four days.

The achievements of the Czech resistance resulted from maintaining nonviolent discipline, attacking the invaders at their most vulnerable point—supply lines—and encouraging the breakdown of Soviet morale. Soviet morale could hardly fail to break down during an invasion that failed to gain total control within a period that started as days, and then became weeks, and eventually months.

At the same time Soviet soldiers, trained to respond only to violence, had no resources for responding to mass nonviolence. They were invading a country where life was obviously better than in their own. This last factor is cited by Soviet emigrés who participated in the invasion and found that after a week they wished only to go home or, in many cases, to remain in Czechoslovakia permanently.

As new research reveals, critics of nonviolence could easily argue that the mobilization for the invasion was confused, the chain of command incompetent, and the Soviet soldiers themselves poorly trained.[3] This is true; but the main point remains. Not only Soviet soldiers, but well-trained and well-led Eastern European soldiers, took part in the invasion. These soldiers could not prevail over the Czech resistance. Nor, though perhaps for different reasons, was their morale better than that of the Soviet troops. The Czech resistance against an army of five hundred thousand is, considered in any light, a remarkable achievement.

1. *Pravda* accounts read by author in Leningrad, August, 1968.
2. This account of the Czech resistance is based on that reprinted in Murray Polner, ed., *The Disarmament Catalogue* (New York: Pilgrim Press, 1982), p. 171.
3. Cf. the eyewitness account of the Czech invasion in Victor Suvorov, *The Liberators: My Life in the Soviet Army* (New York & London: W. W. Norton, 1981), pp. 153–192.

Day, Dorothy: The life of Dorothy Day (1897–1980) was one of the supreme examples of radical Christianity translated into action. In her youth a Marxist and member of the International Workers of the World, she converted to Catholicism in the 1930s. In 1933, with Peter Maurin (d. 1949), she founded the Catholic Worker Movement, whose consistent pacifism and effort to root out poverty and injustice became an example to the rest of the Catholic church and to other Christians. The worker movement is best-known for its hospitality houses in cities around the United States. At a Catholic worker house those in need could receive food and shelter without charge or question.

In a society built on images and celebrity, Day's integrity stood out and made her work a potent force for change. She was not content merely to ladle soup for the poor; she spoke out against the institutions which cause and perpetuate injustice. During World War II she maintained her pacifist witness while working to end fascism and lobbying for repeal of quotas on Jewish immigration. In 1939, she helped found the Committee of Catholics to Fight Anti-Semitism. During the 1950s she was active in the movement for a nuclear test ban and in other peace witness; during the 1960s she demonstrated repeatedly against the Indochina War. Amid all this activity, the hospitality houses and the basic principles of the Catholic Worker Movement remained at the center of her life.

Dorothy Day received few honors during her lifetime, and

she refused most of those. She did not participate in the circles of power and influence but continued the quiet work to which she had committed her life. When she died, the historian David O'Brien called her "the most significant, interesting, and influential person in the history of American Catholicism."[1]

1: Quoted in Robert Ellsberg, "By Little and By Little," *Shalom News* (Shalom Catholic Worker House Newsletter, Kansas City, Ks.), September, 1983. See, too, William D. Miller, *Dorothy Day: A Biography* (New York: Harper & Row, 1982) and Robert Ellsberg, ed., *By Little And By Little: The Selected Writings of Dorothy Day* (New York: Knopf, 1983).

Deterrence: The rationale for United States nuclear weapons policy since 1945 has been the doctrine of deterrence. This theory holds that potential adversaries, primarily the Soviet Union, will attack the United States and its allies with nuclear weapons unless the U.S. threatens them with damage so great in retaliation that an attack would not be worth the cost. Soviet strategic theory also follows a form of the doctrine. Both sides believe that only their nuclear arsenals prevent the other side from launching its missiles.

The doctrine of deterrence is based on a paradox which undercuts it almost completely. On the one hand, it assumes that potential adversaries are mad: that they would, if only they could, destroy more people and property at a stroke than all previous wars. On the other hand, it assumes that these same adversaries are calculating and rational: that they will carefully balance costs against benefits and decide not to launch the attack because they would lose too much as a result.

In fact despite the mythology surrounding diplomacy and foreign policy, nations do not calculate costs and benefits this closely. Nor are national leaders, with a few well-known exceptions, insane. To find a national leader who combines insanity with utter, cold rationality is highly unlikely.

Even more telling is the actual experience of history. In the mid-1940s the United States possessed a monopoly on nuclear weapons. If deterrence were the only reason that nations do

170

not launch their nuclear weapons, one would have expected the U.S. to annihilate the Soviet Union. Advocates of "preventive war," such as Gen. Curtis LeMay, actually argued for such a course. Yet the U.S. did not launch its weapons.

Nations simply do not behave in the manner assumed by deterrence theory. Each side in the arms race bases its decisions on political considerations, national pride, and even (in the case of the U.S.) whether it is an election year. The threat of destruction, far from cowing either side into submission, is far more likely to lead to the deployment of new weapons in the effort to seek advantage. This has happened many times, the most recent being the U.S. deployment of the Pershing II and cruise missiles in Europe. The Soviet response was not to become more tractable but to announce that its missiles would be deployed closer to the U.S. coastline to counter the Pershing II and cruise. Deterrence in this case did not stop the Soviet Union from menacing the U.S. It had quite the opposite effect.

Such growth in mutual insecurity will always be the case under deterrence because both sides are constantly maneuvering for advantage or for some kind of winning formula. The result is an upward spiral in the level of armaments which are said to be necessary for deterrence.

In effect deterrence has become the public rationale for the nuclear arms race. To suggest that there is some difference in deterrent value between eight thousand and ten thousand missiles makes little sense when even a tenth of these missiles could kill the entire human race. The arms race does not increase deterrence. It increases the insecurity of one's adversary. But since one's own security depends absolutely on the adversary's belief that one has no advantage and will not launch his missiles, increasing the other side's insecurity is a very dangerous business indeed. Confronted with what seems like a decisive inferiority, a nation may decide to launch its missiles out of sheer terror at what it suspects the other side may do.

This undesirable and insane state of affairs is regarded as normal by most political commentators. Despite the hundreds of wars since 1945, they continue to say that deterrence prevents war. They continue to suggest that we have our weapons because the Soviets are seeking our destruction—conveniently ignoring our willingness to threaten the death of hundreds of millions of Soviet citizens. They continue to affirm the doctrine of deterrence even as it daily makes the world a more dangerous place in which to live.

Proponents of deterrence argue that adherence to the theory has prevented war. The proof of their argument, they say, is the fact that there has been no nuclear war since 1945. That is perfectly true. But history is not encouraging on the question of whether armaments prevent war. A study by the *Canadian Army Journal* (1960) found that of 1,587 arms races between 600 B.C. and 1960, all but ten ended in war.[1]

It is foolish to imagine that the current arms race will defy history and bring lasting peace. So statesmen imagined in the years before 1914, when nations armed themselves as never before. That arms race did nothing to prevent world War I. It made the war worse when it did come. Ten million soldiers paid with their lives for the nations' reliance on deterrence. In the next war, the dead will not be soldiers only. All may die—men, women, children, civilians and soldiers alike.

Deterrence provides neither peace nor security. It is an illusion which, in the end, must fail. To suggest otherwise is to ignore the clear evidence of history and common sense.

(See also: AREA BOMBING CAMPAIGN, CONVENTIONAL WAR, NUCLEAR STRATEGY, NUCLEAR WEAPONS AND WAR)

1: Quoted in Sidney Lens, "Deterrence Hardly Deters," *The New York Times*, December 25, 1983.

Dolci, Danilo: Best known as a nonviolent organizer and worker among the very poor in Sicily, Danilo Dolci became a committed pacifist during World War II when, after evading duty in Mussolini's army, he was arrested for antifascist activities, escaped, and spent the remainder of the war living underground. After the war he renounced his career as an architect and went to Sicily, an area whose poverty had sickened him in his childhood. There he has worked ever since as a political organizer and educator.

The heart of Dolci's work has been the formation of small groups of people known as *autoanalisi popolare* (popular self-analysis). These groups, which are similar to the "base communities" in Brazil, meet, study the roots of their problems, and seek to develop ways to change and improve their lives. Among actions inspired by Dolci's work have been the construction of a badly-needed dam and a "strike in reverse" in which unemployed and underemployed workers constructed a road which the government had refused to repair. For this latter action, Dolci and six trade unionists were beaten and imprisoned. Much of Dolci's more recent work has focused on the education of children.

Dolci's commitment to nonviolence is not a mere choice of tactics. He declared himself as a conscientious objector during World War II, even though there was no provision for such status. "If we decide to survive," he says, "perhaps not out of love but out of fear, we will be compelled to build a new culture, a new morality, and a new organization. And these will have to be nonviolent."[1] Dolci's own work has helped point the way to the new, nonviolent order of which he speaks.

(See also: BRAZIL, NONVIOLENCE IN, CIVIL DISOBEDIENCE, NONVIOLENCE)

1. Discussion with seminar participants at Resource Center for Nonviolence, Santa Cruz, Ca. Quoted in Scott Kennedy and Steven Belling, "A Teacher Who Listens: Danilo Dolci," *Win;* Vol. 18, No. 16 (September 1, 1982), p. 7.

Draft: (see also: conscription, conscientious and war resistance)

Dresden: The Allied strategic bombing campaign against Germany (1940–45) reached one of its low points with the raid on Dresden on the night of February 13, 1945.[1] An ancient and well-loved German city, Dresden had no military importance. Its population had been swollen by an influx of refugees, many of them fleeing from previous Allied bombing raids. The bombing took place during a children's carnival.

A full night of firebombing led to a firestorm similar to the one that occurred in Hamburg and the one which was later to occur in Hiroshima. Thousands of small fires coalesced into one large fire which generated heat so intense that those unfortunates who had taken shelter were roasted to death. Few buildings were left standing or unburnt.

Casualties in the Dresden bombing will never be accurately known. Lee Kennett's *History of Strategic Bombing,* the most authoritative general work on the subject, cites estimates ranging from twenty-five thousand to half a million.[2] David Irving puts the number of dead at 130,000.[3]

Reaction to the Dresden bombing in Britain was immediate and critical. Though labeled a "military target" for public consumption, Dresden had in fact been a city which produced watches and china figurines. It was a popular tourist destination between the wars and was known to many Britons. The British public was therefore skeptical about the rationale for the bombing raid. Winston Churchill himself decided that it was time to review "the question of bombing German cities simply for the sake of increasing terror, though under other pretexts."[4]

The Dresden bombing remained a source of embarrassment to some British politicians until some time after the end of World War II. Not so for the leaders of the Royal Air Force's Bomber Command. Although the Dresden bombing brought strategic bombing into public disrepute, Air Marshall Sir Arthur Harris defended the campaign vigorously. He suggested that the objections to Dresden were merely emotional. They were, he said, "connected with German bands and Dresden shepherdesses."[5]

(SEE ALSO: AREA BOMBING CAMPAIGN, HIROSHIMA AND NAGASAKI, NUCLEAR WEAPONS AND WAR)

1. A complete but somewhat dated account of the raid is David Irving, *The Destruction of Dresden* (New York: Holt, Rinehart & Winston, 1963).

2. Lee Kennett, *A History of Strategic Bombing* (New York: Charles Scribner's Sons, 1982), p. 161.

3. Irving, *op. cit.*, Appendix contains an extensive discussion of Dresden casualties.

4. Kennett, *op. cit.*, p. 188.

5. *Ibid.*, p. 188.

European Peace Movement: It is a mistake to speak of the European peace movement, as if there were a centrally-organized and led entity by that name. Each European country, including many in Eastern Europe, has its own independent peace movement which addresses the issues and concerns peculiar to that country. In Britain, which has an independent nuclear deterrent, the issues differ from those in West Germany—and so with other countries.

At the same time peace activists in the various countries maintain communication, cooperation on joint projects, and share common concerns. Thus it is fair to say that there is an international peace movement in Europe, though it has not yet become and probably never will become a single entity.

The European peace movement achieved its greatest growth and influence in response to the 1979 NATO decision to deploy Pershing II missiles in Germany and cruise missiles in England. Some NATO governments, such as that of Britain, inadvertently helped the growth of the peace movement by their attempts to justify the decision and reassure their populations. In Britain a government civil defense manual called "Protect and Survive," which recommended bomb shelters built out of sandbags piled on a table, quickly became a laughingstock and convinced the public that its leaders were not to be trusted on such life-and-death matters as nuclear war.

By 1983 the peace movement in Europe had become a kind of third party to inter-government discussions of nuclear policy. In Germany, the Green Party, running on a strong peace platform, had become a political force to be reckoned

175

with. In England, the Women's Encampment at Greenham Common Air Base (where cruise missiles were to be deployed) attracted major publicity and raised awkward questions for the government—including the issue of who controlled the missiles (the U.S. does). Neither the Green Party nor the Greenham Common action, nor the many mass demonstrations in major European cities, have stopped the NATO deployment. They have, however, made it more difficult, thereby making the governments of the various countries answerable as never before for their nuclear policies.

Critics of the European peace movement, primarily Americans, suggest that its goal is a neutral Europe and that this would bring Europe into the Soviet sphere of influence. The first argument is perfectly true. European writers such as E. P. Thompson have said repeatedly that the only safe policy for Europe is disengagement from the Cold War. It does not therefore follow, except in the twisted logic of the Cold War, that Europe would become a Soviet satellite. The Europeans who have taken to the streets are as much opposed to Soviet nuclear policy as to NATO nuclear policy. Soviet efforts to manipulate the peace movement in Europe have been unsuccessful for precisely this reason.

A neutral, or nuclear-free, Europe is desirable not only for Europeans but for humankind generally. Although, for many reasons, all-out war in Europe is unlikely, current policies on both sides would make such a war lead, quickly and almost unstoppably, to nuclear holocaust. Europe is the most heavily armed area of the world, a continent in which a tank brigade on maneuvers might inadvertently touch off war should it lose its way. It is evident that any level of disarmament in Europe would decrease the threat of war there, and thus the threat of nuclear war generally. A nuclear-free Europe would be a major step toward preventing nuclear war.

An interesting development has been the growth of the nongovernment peace movements in the Eastern European countries. Each of those countries has a government-sponsored peace movement, which serves largely as a forum for blaming all tensions on the West. Independent peace movements in East Germany and other Warsaw Pact countries have

176

begun to challenge the official line. Though small by comparison with the official peace movements, they are an important development deserving of support.

(See also: CONVENTIONAL WAR, NATO AND WARSAW PACT, NUCLEAR WEAPONS AND WAR)

Fellowship of Reconciliation: Founded in 1914, the Fellowship of Reconciliation is an international, interreligious organization dedicated to the achievement of peace and justice. Its headquarters in the U.S. is in Nyack, N.Y., and it has chapters throughout the U.S. The International Fellowship of Reconciliation is headquartered in Alkamaar, Holland, and has chapters in many countries in Europe, Asia, Africa, and South America. It provides information and advocates citizen action on disarmament, the draft, nonintervention and human rights. FOR publishes the monthly *Fellowship*.

Friends: See American Friends Service Committee

Gandhi, Mohandas K.: The thirty-year struggle to free India from British colonial rule was led by Mohandas K. Gandhi, a British-trained barrister with no official standing. Gandhi's career had begun in South Africa where after organizing an Asian ambulance corps in the Boer War he led a nonviolent campaign to improve the status of Asians in South Africa.

When he returned to his home in India Gandhi organized a campaign of civil disobedience, boycotts, and other nonviolent tactics. Gandhi's campaign sought the end of British rule in India and in 1947 it achieved this objective. In 1948

Gandhi was assassinated by a Moslem who saw the non-violent campaign as a step toward the subjugation of Moslem by Hindu.

Gandhi's philosophy of nonviolence was rooted in Hinduism. Its central concept was *satyagraha* (roughly, soul force), or the power of one mind to influence another without the use of physical force. "Nonviolence to be a potent force must begin with the mind," Gandhi said. "Nonviolence of the mere body without cooperation of the mind is nonviolence of the weak or cowardly and therefore has no potency. If we bear malice and hatred in our bosoms and pretend not to retaliate, it must recoil upon us and lead to our destruction." In practice this philosophy led not only to civil disobedience and boycotts, but to the self-discipline evident in one of Gandhi's most effective tactics: his fasts unto death.

The truth of Gandhi's philosophy can be seen in the contrast between the power of his own fasts—which could, and did, stop incipient civil wars—and the ineffectiveness of the Irish Republican Army's fasts unto death in Britain's Maze Prison. The IRA fasts, while tactically nonviolent, were far less effective than Gandhi's fasts in changing public opinion. This occurred at least in part because the IRA's previous commitment to violence undercut the nonviolence of the fasts.

It would be a mistake to assume that Gandhi's philosophy and methods can be adopted in toto by social change movements in non-Indian cultures. Each country is different and in each one the philosophy, strategy, and tactics of nonviolence will differ. Thus in the Southern United States, Martin Luther King, Jr., drew upon Gandhi's experience *and* the black Christian tradition of which he was a part to develop methods and philosophy suited to conditions where he was.

Some of Gandhi's critics argue that in some ways he cooperated with the British in maintaining peace in India. While it is perfectly true that Gandhi's methods avoided outright civil war, it does not follow that he was in any way cooperating with the British. On the contrary: British resistance to Gandhi's campaign was clear from the outset and included use of military force, imprisonment of Gandhi and his followers, and other violent tactics.

It is unfair to judge the results of Gandhi's campaign by looking at India's current problems or its present commitment to the use of military force. Gandhi's life ended almost simultaneously with the achievement of India's liberation. He himself could not directly influence events when dead. India's later difficulties should not obscure Gandhi's positive achievements. In a world which had known only violent revolutions, he organized and brought to completion a nonviolent revolution. His campaign remains the most successful and largest national liberation movement in history. His contributions to nonviolent philosophy were invaluable not only for the power of their thought, but also for the practical experience that pervades them.

(See also: BRAZIL, NONVIOLENCE IN, KING, MARTIN LUTHER, JR.; NONVIOLENCE)

Golden Rule and Phoenix: The voyages of the *Golden Rule* and the *Phoenix,* two small, wind-driven ketches which tried to sail into the United States nuclear test zone near Eniwetok in 1958, were among the most courageous and imaginative actions in the history of the peace movement. Both craft sailed as a protest against atmospheric testing of nuclear weapons. The *Golden Rule* carried a crew of four pacifists, all men. The *Phoenix* carried Earle and Barbara Reynolds and their family.

The first of the ships to set out was the *Golden Rule* on February 10, 1958. Heavy seas and bad weather forced the ketch to turn back. On a second sailing, the crew of the ship was arrested as it entered the test zone in April 1958. The four men were charged with violating off-limits restrictions and returned to Honolulu, where a federal judge ordered them not to sail out of Honolulu Harbor. When they tried to do so on April 24, they were jailed for contempt of court.

The *Phoenix* crew encountered similar difficulties with federal authorities. *Phoenix* had left Honolulu June 11, bound for Hiroshima. It deliberately sailed into the Eniwetok test zone, where it was intercepted. Earle Reynolds was arrested and charged with violating Atomic Energy Commission regulations. He was convicted and sentenced to six months in prison. On appeal, his case was sent back to the district court for a new trial. Following his second trial, Reynolds was again sentenced to six months in prison. His case was reversed on appeal because the AEC regulations he violated had not been authorized by the Atomic Energy Act.

Although these two actions did not stop nuclear testing in the Pacific, they received widespread publicity—in part because the crews of the vessels were clearly prepared to die in a nuclear explosion. They focused public attention on testing in the Pacific and, along with other actions such as witnesses at test sites in the Nevada desert, helped to pressure the U.S. government to seek an end to atmospheric testing. Although atmospheric testing of nuclear weapons ended in 1961 with the Test Ban Treaty,[1] underground testing continues. Pacifist witness against such testing also continues.[2]

(See also: CIVIL DISOBEDIENCE, DAY, DOROTHY, NON-VIOLENCE, NUCLEAR WEAPONS AND WAR, WAR RESISTANCE)

1: The Test Ban Treaty affected only atmospheric testing. An overall treaty to ban nuclear testing remains an urgent need. See *Defense Monitor*.
2: This account taken from Central Committee for Conscientious Objectors *News Notes*, Vol. 10, No. 2 (Feb.-March 1958); Vol. 10, No. 3 (April-May 1958); vol. 10, No. 4 (June-Sept. 1958); Vol. 10, No. 5 (Oct.-Nov. 1958); Vol. 10, No. 6 (Dec. 1958); Vol. 11, No. 4 (June-Sept. 1959); Vol. 11, No. 5 (Oct.-Nov. 1959); Vol. 13, No. 1 (Jan.-Feb. 1961).

Guerrilla Warfare: Guerrilla warfare takes its name from the Spanish popular resistance to Napoleon's armies.[1] Guerrillas are soldiers who live among the population, usually supported by them (whether willingly or not), and fight using ambushes, hit-and-run attacks on conventional forces, and sabotage. Guerrilla forces are particularly difficult to defeat by traditional military tactics. They do not fight battles, preferring if possible to avoid battle in favor of sudden, surprise attack and quick withdrawal. They are hard to find because they live among the population and often do not wear military uniforms.

Over the years traditional armies fighting guerrillas have developed tactics suited to the methods of their opponents. Called counterinsurgency warfare, these tactics include direct attacks on the civilian population, destruction of the environment and the food supply, destruction of civilian houses and villages, and extensive use of "population relocation" and concentration camps. Prisoners are tortured to force them to divulge what they know about the guerrillas' operations. In Vietnam forests were sprayed with powerful and dangerous weed killers (defoliation) to make the guerrillas easier to see and expose their supply lines. In that same war, wells were poisoned, a practice which has been outlawed by international agreement since the Middle Ages.

These appalling tactics are no accident. Counterinsurgency warfare aims to destroy the guerrillas' means of support. Since those means are almost always the means of support for the people at large, a counterinsurgency army must destroy the country. It was common in Vietnam for policymakers and field commanders alike to speak of "destroying the country in order to save it." (A further discussion will be found under INDOCHINA WAR.)

Guerrilla warfare is commonly associated with revolutionaries of the Left, as in El Salvador or Vietnam. Nothing, however, prevents groups of the Right from using guerrilla tactics, and in fact this has happened. The Boers used guerrilla tactics against the British in the war which bears their name (1899–1901). The British responded with counterinsurgency tactics that included concentration camps and farm burnings. The Boers fought, not for a Socialist cause, but for their freedom to run South Africa along the racist lines now formalized as *apartheid*. They were notorious for the deliberate and pointless slaughter of the African population.

It is fashionable on the Left to support or express solidarity with guerrilla movements, or "armed liberation struggles." These movements pose a difficult issue for many pacifists, as they should for all who support their aspirations. On the one hand, the goals of the insurgents may be desirable. On the other hand, their means, which are violent and occasionally involve ruthless tactics, are likely in the long run to undercut the goals they seek.

Facile condemnation of revolutionary guerrillas, however, would be as mistaken as is facile support for everything they do. It is important to distinguish between supporting a movement's chosen means and understanding the pressures that drove them to use those means. One can understand why an insurgent movement has turned to violence without supporting that violence. And in the light of this understanding, one can seek nonviolent alternatives to guerrilla warfare.

In South Africa, for example, the South West African People's Organization (SWAPO) originally sought a nonviolent end to *apartheid*. The pressures for violence, however, were enormous. The South African government's arms industry is one of the largest in the world. Its army is one of the most ruthless in counterinsurgency fighting, with little compunction about using similar tactics against civilians and soldiers, violent and nonviolent alike.

Whether better nonviolent discipline or strategy would have led to nonviolent change is unknowable. What happened instead was that SWAPO felt compelled to adopt guerrilla tactics. Thus the South African government's military response to a nonviolent movement brought on the very war which the military buildup was supposed to prevent. A blanket endorsement or facile condemnation of armed struggle does little justice to such a complex and tragic situation. Either position may be a substitute for the far more difficult work of seeking creative ways for outsiders to help end the injustice.

It has never been true that the alternative to guerrilla warfare is acquiesence in oppression. Gandhi's liberation of India, which remains the largest and most successful anticolonial movement in history, was nonviolent. It was based not on passivity but on tough-minded, creative political strategy. It succeeded not because the British were civilized—in their treatment of Gandhi's movement, they were not—but because nonviolence properly used is a powerful force for change. Thus in the struggle for justice, violence is not and has never been inevitable.

182

To say that there are alternatives to guerrilla warfare, however, is not to suggest that the same tactics will work under all conditions. Each situation, whether in South Africa, El Salvador, Chile, or elsewhere, will require a different strategy. Outsiders cannot determine such strategies. They can, however, encourage nonviolent change by seeking to end the sources of oppression and violence where they live.

A study by the American Friends Service Committee (1983) showed that U.S. sales of high-technology equipment to the South African government have tripled under the Reagan administration. Such equipment, though it is not weapons, could have military uses or could (as, for example, with computer technology) be used to enforce *apartheid*. It will almost certainly raise the level of violence and opppression in South Africa. The appropriate nonviolent response is to expose and try to change such a policy.

So with the bloodshed in Central America, where the United States has consistently raised the level of violence by arms shipments and other aid to several governments, without regard for those governments' brutalization of their own people. Those who hope for nonviolent change in that region will not succeed unless they can change U.S. policy, which is the source of much of the violence in that unhappy area.

(See also: CENTRAL AMERICA, COLD WAR, CONVENTIONAL WAR, GANDHI, MOHANDAS K., HELICOPTER, INDOCHINA WAR)

1. B. H. Liddell Hart, *Strategy: The Indirect Approach* (New York and Washington: Praeger, 1972), p. 373.

Helicopter: The helicopter is a peculiar instrument of war. It is on the one hand highly mobile and undeterred by many obstacles (forests, for example) that might stop a ground vehicle. It is on the other hand slow, noisy, and easily crippled or destroyed by antiaircraft fire from the ground. Thus in pitched battles fought with modern weapons it would probably be of little use.

Nonetheless all major armies have large numbers of helicopters. These range from small vehicles much like those in civilian use, to large helicopter gunships which have no civilian parallel. If not brought down by opposing fire, helicopter gunships can be very deadly indeed. They can carry heat-seeking missiles, cannon, and machine guns. They are particularly well adapted for firing at targets (people and villages) on the ground, and can reach many such places where standard aircraft would have extreme difficulty.

The primary use of helicopter gunships and combat helicopters generally has been in counterinsurgency warfare and in putting down civil disturbances. In the Indochina War helicopters transported troops to battle zones where ground vehicles could not go. In El Salvador helicopter gunships regularly patrol the jungles, firing indiscriminately at buildings and movements on the ground. Eyewitness reports make clear that most of these targets are civilians, not the guerrilla troops who are the ostensible targets. The Soviet Union has used helicopter gunships in its counterinsurgency war in Afghanistan. The British army uses helicopters in Northern Ireland to put down civil disturbances there.

Helicopter supporters have argued that their primary use is not for counterinsurgency warfare at all, but for more traditional combat such as a major land war in Europe. This is the rationale—along with the army's desire to have its own aircraft—for the U.S. Army's extensive use of helicopters.

A major land war in Europe is unlikely to remain a conventional war for more than a few days; both sides rely too much on nuclear weapons. But even if NATO and the Warsaw Pact somehow confined themselves to use of non-nuclear weapons, the helicopter's vulnerability to ground fire would mean quick death for nearly all helicopter crews in the war. (The army's Redeye missile, for example, which is designed to attack much faster fixed-wing aircraft, is fired from a hand-held launcher. It would make short work of a helicopter.)

There are two possible explanations for this apparently foolish expenditure of money. Either the army is following the usual military practice of spending millions of dollars for weapons that will not work to counter threats that do not threaten, or the military planners know perfectly well what

184

they are doing, and what they are doing is *not* a preparation for European land war. Possibly both are true.

Whatever the rationale, and whatever the real reasons underlying it, the fact is that in actual use the helicopter kills far more civilian peasants than enemy soldiers. Thus while saying that it is arming itself for a major European war, the army is in fact arming for war against guerrillas and the unlucky civilians who happen to be in the path of the fighting.

(See also: CENTRAL AMERICA, CONVENTIONAL WAR, GUERRILLA WAR, INDOCHINA WAR, NATO AND WARSAW PACT, NUCLEAR WEAPONS AND WAR)

Hiroshima and Nagasaki: On the morning of August 6, 1945, the American bomber *Enola Gay*, accompanied by two other aircraft, appeared over the city of Hiroshima, Japan. The Hiroshima authorities, who had at first sounded the air raid warning sirens, concluded from the small number of aircraft that *Enola Gay* was on a reconnaissance flight. They sounded the all-clear. Thus the citizens of Hiroshima had come out of their shelters and returned to their normal business when the first nuclear weapon ever used in combat detonated over their city. The intense blast and heat leveled and burned much of the city at once. It was followed by a firestorm similar to the ones in Tokyo, Hamburg, and Dresden. Tens of thousands of people, most of them civilians, were killed outright. More died from radiation sickness. The total dead, which is still not known precisely to this day, was at least seventy-eight thousand and possibly as high as one hundred thousand or more.

Three days later U.S. planes dropped a nuclear bomb on the city of Nagasaki. The effects, except for the firestorm, were similar to those at Hiroshima. Two days after the destruction of Nagasaki the Japanese government offered unconditional surrender.

The Hiroshima and Nagasaki bombing raids were not in and of themselves the most destructive of World War II. That dubious distinction must go to the raid on Tokyo (250,000 dead), which used the conventional firebombing techniques developed by the Allied air forces in the European theater of the war. But Hiroshima and Nagasaki marked the end of war as the world had known it and the beginning of the nuclear age in warfare. So powerful was the new weaponry that *one* bomb at Hiroshima wreaked as much havoc as an all-night firebombing by many squadrons of aircraft would have done. So horrifying were the effects of the bomb on human flesh that even hardened observers could not bear the sight of the dead and wounded at Hiroshima and Nagasaki.

It was widely believed at the time that the use of the atomic bomb had shortened the war in the Pacific by as much as a year and saved up to half a million American lives (Gen. Douglas MacArthur's estimate of casualties in a proposed invasion of the Japanese homeland). This theory, like most historical speculations, is untestable. It is worth remarking, however, that by 1945 the Japanese were all but defeated. Their navy was destroyed. Their air force was in shambles, reduced to kamikaze (suicide) raids on American ships—a tactic which was rapidly killing their skilled pilots and destroying their few remaining aircraft. The Japanese army had five million soldiers and was prepared to fight on, but the end of the war in Europe and Russia's entry into the war against Japan might well have made conventional military victory far less costly than MacArthur believed. On military grounds, therefore, the use of the atomic bomb was probably not as urgent as its proponents argued.

The decision to use the atomic bomb was opposed by many of the scientists who created it, including Leo Szilard. Szilard argued that the U.S. should make a "demonstration explosion" in an uninhabited place to show the Japanese government the power of the bomb. Szilard's counsel and that of other scientists who opposed using the bomb on a city reached few ears in Washington and was kept from those who made the final decision. The general public, which was not informed until afterward that the U.S. was developing the atomic bomb, had no role whatever in the decision. Nor did the Congress.

On military grounds the decision to bomb Hiroshima and

Nagasaki was questionable. There is no such question about its morality. Even President Truman, who publicly defended the use of the bomb and gave the order to use it, stopped a proposal to bomb further cities because he could not bear the thought of killing thousands more children. The raids on Hiroshima and Nagasaki remain the only combat use of nuclear weapons. They are one of the great atrocities of military history.

Recent research has demonstrated conclusively that the motivation for using the atomic bomb was not solely a quick end to the war. The bombing raids were valued as much for their effect on Stalin and the Soviet Union as for their effect on Japan. This thinking was far too callous and cynical for public consumption, but recently released government archives make clear that Truman and his advisors viewed the bomb as a way of "containing" Stalin. The raids did not, of course, do so. They became the first stage in a nuclear arms race that continues to this day.[1]

The Hiroshima bomb, terrible as its effects were, was small by modern standards: 12.5 kilotons. Modern tactical nuclear weapons are frequently many times this size, and strategic weapons dwarf it altogether. Those who speak lightly of using "small" nuclear weapons in combat, or of "small" nuclear wars, would do well to study the destruction of Hiroshima and Nagasaki. What happened to these cities proves that there are no small nuclear weapons.

(See also: AREA BOMBING CAMPAIGN, DETERRENCE, NUCLEAR STRATEGY, NUCLEAR WEAPONS AND WAR)

1. The full story of the bomb's role in the early Cold War will be found in Gregg Herken, *The Winning Weapon: The Atomic Bomb in the Cold War, 1945–1950* (New York: Alfred A. Knopf, 1980).

Hitler, Adolf: The tragic history of Germany in the 1930s and 1940s centers on Adolf Hitler, who ruled that nation from 1933 to 1945, and his National Socialist (Nazi) ideology. Hitler and his ideas were at the center of World War II in

Europe, which resulted in tens of millions of military and civilian dead. He was responsible for the Holocaust and the deliberate massacre of some ten million "undesirables." In death he has become a symbol—as his career was the reality—of evil run rampant in the world.

One's first reaction on reading even the most bald account of Hitler's career is simple disbelief. Concentration camps, deliberate slaughter of innocents, violently anti-Semitic speeches, Jews and homosexuals (among others) forced to wear identifying marks—such is the stuff of nightmares. Yet the ideas underlying these appalling practices were widely shared at the time and continue today in other guises.

Nazi ideology was nationalistic, racist, and militaristic. Hitler believed quite literally that the Germanic peoples (Aryans) were superior to others and destined to rule. Though he reserved his most intense hatred for the Jews, other "inferiors" such as Gypsies, homosexuals, and Slavs were considered fit only for death or slavery. Nazi planners constructed elaborate schemes for breeding a "pure" Aryan race. Nazi politics relied on the trappings of military pomp—uniforms, universal conscription, and mass orchestrated demonstrations—to maintain control over the German population.

Hitler's career is commonly cited as proof that military preparedness is necessary or that pacifists are wrong. In fact it proves no such thing. Hitler's ascendancy was the result of a complex series of events and shocks to the German public. Military action, far from preventing Hitler's rise to power, contributed to it. The German defeat in World War I led to the Treaty of Versailles, which was regarded as unfair by the German public (and as time went on by much of the rest of the world). At Versailles the Allies proceeded on the assumption that Germany was solely responsible for the war and that the remedy for future wars was containing Germany. Thus they disarmed Germany but not themselves, demanded financial reparations from Germany, and decreed that parts of prewar German territory should become part of France.

The provisions of Versailles combined with the fact of German defeat gave impetus to the extreme right wing in Germany. Hitler's Nazi party was only one among many at

188

the beginning. All of these parties sought a strong German military and revenge against the Allies. (General Erich von Ludendorff, the primary German strategist in World War I and later leader of an abortive fascist coup against the Weimar Republic, advocated a program even more militaristic than Hitler's.)[1]

To the shock of defeat was quickly added the shock of the German inflation of the 1920s, followed by depression and unemployment on a scale never before seen in Germany. Though neither of these was a direct result of World War I, many Germans blamed Germany's economic chaos on war reparations. Thus it is fair to say that World War I and its aftermath were major factors in Hitler's rise to power and the willingness of Germans to follow his lead. Military preparedness not only could not have stopped this process, it was irrelevant to it. (An Allied "preemptive invasion" of Germany, for example, might have left the German people more, not less, willing to follow a Hitler.)

The military historian Alistair Horne suggests another way in which World War I may have contributed to the rise of Hitler. German battle casualties in the trenches, which approximated 1.7 million dead, included artists, philosophers, journalists, writers—all of whom might have lived to oppose Hitler—and, above all, potential leadership. "One might in truth [say] that the bloodletting . . . contributed to a vacuum of leadership in Germany into which rushed the riff-raff of the Himmlers and Goebbels."[2]

In the political infighting which led to Hitler's ascent to power, the German Communist Party (KPD) played a strange and ultimately disastrous part. Calling the Socialist Party (SPD) "social fascists," the KPD refused to cooperate with them. They did this in the belief that Germany needed a period of Nazi rule to better appreciate the Communist revolution when it came. This incredible strategy proved to be a blunder. Whether unity on the Left could have prevented the rise of Hitler is unknowable, but there is little doubt that the KPD's commitment to disunity was one factor in Hitler's success.[3]

World War II, like World War I, was not the product of a single man's mind or a single set of events. But in a Germany economically strong, not subject to war reparations, and not forced to sign a humiliating treaty, Hitler might have remained a failed postcard painter dreaming of a glory that would never be his.

A far more difficult question is how the world can deal with unbalanced and expansionist national leaders. Traditional diplomacy could not control Hitler once he was in power. Nor, without great bloodshed, did a traditional military response. Whether nonviolent resistance could have succeeded at less ultimate cost than these methods is moot. It is clear, however, that once Hitler was in power with a mass army at his disposal, any response to his actions would have led to great suffering. The choice was between evils—not between a "good" war and a bad alternative response. No response was, or could be, wholly good, wholly without pain, or wholly without undesirable aftermath.

That this is so is evident from the aftermath of World War II. The war against Hitler and the Japanese resulted not only in fifty million dead, but in incalculable destruction of property. The strategic bombing tactics used by the Allies and the Germans are the direct ancestors of the plans for mass slaughter that have become accepted in military strategic practice today. Nuclear weapons, though used against Japan, were originally intended also as a response to Hitler's armies. The shape of contemporary Europe and the tensions there can be traced to World War II. In the short run, the war defeated Hitler. In the long run, it helped create the conditions for a conflict in which Hitler, were he alive, would see himself revenged indeed upon the Allies.

A less concrete but equally dangerous legacy of Hitler is the demonology which now pervades international relations. Nations which before Hitler might have compromised on issues between them find compromise more difficult because of fears that they will be seen as weak. It is far too easy to call compromise "appeasement" and paint one's adversary as "another Hitler." President Reagan's reference to the Soviet Union as the "evil empire" is one example of such thinking. Demonology adds nothing to our understanding of the world. It poisons the international climate and makes war more, not less, likely.

The historical Hitler died in 1945. Racism, nationalism, and militarism did not begin with him, and they did not die with him. Yet the peculiar combination of circumstances that led to Hitler's rise is unlikely to recur. More important than speculation on whether another Hitler will rise to power is learning what we can from the history of Germany in the 1930s and 1940s. It is ironic that so many draw from that history the lessons that Hitler might have drawn: that military preparedness must be paramount; that other nations are evil and only understand force; that negotiation and compromise are more dangerous than a tough stand; and that our side is always right.

(See also: AREA BOMBING CAMPAIGN, DRESDEN, THE HOLOCAUST, LE CHAMBON, NATO AND WARSAW PACT, NONVIOLENCE, TOTALITARIANISM, NAZIS AND NUCLEAR WEAPONS AND WAR)

1. B. H. Liddell Hart, *Strategy* (New York: Praeger, 1972), pp. 225–226.
2. Alistair Horne, *The Price of Glory: Verdun, 1916* (Middlesex, England: Penguin Books, 1964), p. 342.
3. I am grateful to Murray Polner for this suggestion.

The Holocaust: Adolf Hitler's attempt to exterminate "inferior races" during the 1930s and 1940s remains one of the great crimes of human history. Most of Hitler's victims were Jews, and for them the Holocaust was unique. All Jews were marked for death simply because they were Jews. But other groups—particularly Gypsies, Slavs, and homosexuals—suffered as well. "Inferiors" were made to wear identifying marks, such as the Star of David for Jews and a pink triangle for homosexuals.

In the early days of the Holocaust, victims were lined up beside mass graves and shot. This method of execution proved too inefficient for the Nazis: they designed and built special death camps where victims, most of them Jews, were systematically starved, worked to the point of death, gassed, and cremated. Many were subjected to brutal "medical experiments" before death. Hitler's "Final Solution" resulted in the death of approximately 72 percent of the Jewish population in Nazi-controlled territory. In all, about six million Jews and four million other "inferiors" and political prisoners died at the hands of the Nazis.

No words can adequately portray such horrors. Nor is it possible even today to assess fully the significance of the Holocaust. The repercussions of these terrible events are still with us and likely to remain so far into the future. Some conclusions, however, seem clear.

The fact of the Holocaust does not justify further violence. At the end of World War II some commentators excused the Allied bombing campaign, whose military and moral justification was questionable at best, because of the Nazi death camps. The Holocaust has also been cited to justify other violence.

This is a grave error. No violence can bring back the victims of the Holocaust or undo the damage the Nazis did. Nor will violence eradicate the racial hatred which lies at the root of attempts to exterminate whole groups of peoples. If the only lesson drawn from the Holocaust is a justification for violence, the suffering of those in the death camps could become the basis for new suffering. This would be an insult both to the victims and the survivors.

The war was not "about" the Holocaust. Before the war the Allies had little interest in saving the Jews. The U.S. Congress, for example, defeated a bill to permit twenty thousand Jewish children to enter the United States.[1] During the war, although much of what the Nazis were doing was known, the Allies made little or no effort to hinder the operations of the death camps or to organize a rescue effort.[2]

The war was primarily "about" German expansionism and the growth of German power, and only secondarily about internal Nazi policies. Whether it would have been fought solely to stop Hitler's extermination policies is unknowable.

The war did not prevent the Holocaust. Nor, until almost the last hours of the Nazi regime, did the war stop the slaughter. It is likely that the extermination camps worked more and more frantically as German defeat became inevitable.

The Holocaust was not the first mass slaughter of Jews.
European history contains many instances of such slaughter
and of deliberate efforts to drive Jewish people out of certain
countries. The Nazis were more systematic than previous
anti-Semites, and they killed far more people. But they were
by no means the first.

Nor were they the last. Stalin's atrocities, for example,
included the murder of Jewish cultural leaders in 1948, and in
1953 an effort to deport all European Jews in the Soviet Union
to Siberia and Central Asia.

Mass slaughters have occurred frequently in human history.
The massacre of Armenians by the Turks during World War I,
though its scale is still unknown, may have been an attempt to
exterminate an entire race.[3] Since World War II, there have
been large-scale executions in Burundi, Uganda, Brazil, and
Cambodia, among other places. The Holocaust differed from
these campaigns in its scale and uniquely anti-Jewish nature.
But the record of humanity, which is full of horrors, shows
that racial and class hatred and persecution have not been
confined to Nazi Germany. To suggest that they were, or that
the potential for genocide ended with the end of the Third
Reich, is a mistake.

The lesson of the Holocaust is that racial hatred, in whatever form, is always dangerous. The best way to prevent
another Holocaust is not, as some have suggested, through
armaments and determination to fight back. It is through a
determined effort to end racial and class hatred and establish
justice in society.[4]

(See also: HITLER, ADOLF, LE CHAMBON, NAZIS, NON-
VIOLENCE AND, STALIN)

1. Peter Calvacoressi and Guy Wint, *Total War: The Story of World War II* (New
York: Pantheon Books, 1972), p. 238.
2. See generally, Arthur D. Morse, *While Six Million Died* (New York: Random
House, 1968).
3. On the Armenian massacres, see the startling eyewitness account, Kerop Bedoukian, *Some of Us Survived: The Story of an Armenian Boy* (New York: Farrar,
Straus, Giroux, 1978).
4. On the Holocaust, see generally, Nora Levin, The Holocaust: The Destruction
of European Jewry (New York: Schocken, 1973); Lucy Dawidowicz, *The War
Against the Jews, 1933-1945* (New York: Holt, Rinehart & Winston, 1975); Raul

Hilberg, *The Destruction of the European Jews* (Chicago: Quadrangle Books, 1971); Gerard Reitlinger, *The Final Solution*, 2d Ed. (South Brunswick, N.J.: Thomas Yoseloff, 1968) and David Wyman, *The Abandonment of the Jews* (New York: Pantheon, 1984). On genocide, see Leo Kuper, *Genocide* (New Haven and London: Yale University Press, 1981).

Indochina War: The large peninsula of the southeastern tip of Asia known as Indochina is divided into six countries: Burma, Thailand, Malaysia, Laos, Kampuchea (formerly Cambodia), and Vietnam. From 1950 through 1975 the United States tried to defeat insurgent guerrilla forces in Vietnam: first with military aid, then with covert intelligence operations, then with military advisers, and finally with direct military intervention. The air war in Indochina, in which American aircraft dropped a higher tonnage of bombs than during World War II, extended also to Laos and Cambodia, as did American ground combat with insurgent forces.

The United States war, like the French war before it, failed. In failing, American forces lost more than fifty thousand dead and hundreds of thousands of wounded. American military power destroyed the Vietnamese countryside, economy, and social fabric. Over four million Vietnamese died, along with hundreds of thousands in Laos and Cambodia. After the war the revolutionary Kampuchean regime of Pol Pot engaged in mass slaughter with deaths estimated at between one and two million.

American policy, based as it was on the assumption that the Indochina War was part of a worldwide "struggle to contain communism," was doomed from its outset. It was perfectly true that the insurgents in Vietnam were Communists, and their government now has strong ties to the Soviet Union. But the insurgency in Vietnam was first and foremost a nationalist war, giving it the special tenacity that soldiers always display when fighting on their own soil. The Vietnamese, who had been fighting foreign invaders since at least 208 B.C., did not fit the stereotypes of the Cold War, any more than do insurgents today in Latin America. The U.S. forces, which supported corrupt and unpopular governments, could

194

not hope to defeat an opponent which was willing to accept even the most appalling losses rather than submit. American policymakers never fully understood this.

The Beginning of the War

Western influence in Indochina began with French missionaries in the seventeenth century. In 1861 French forces conquered Saigon, the major city in the South. By 1863 French control had extended to Cambodia, and by 1887 the French had consolidated their hold over the territories now known as Vietnam, Kampuchea, and Laos. During World War II, Vietnam, along with much of the rest of Indochina, was occupied by the Japanese. Vietnamese guerrillas, led by Ho Chi Minh, helped to defeat the Japanese forces. French authority in the area was restored in 1945. Despite an agreement between Ho Chi Minh and the French, French forces attacked Haiphong, a key harbor in the north of the country, on November 23, 1946. This, and Ho Chi Minh's withdrawal to the countryside, signaled the beginning of the Vietnam War proper.

French combat involvement in Vietnam continued until the siege of Dienbienphu in 1954. Following the French defeat there, nine nations meeting in Geneva in July 1954 sought a political settlement to the war. The Geneva agreement called for division of Vietnam into North and South, to be followed shortly by national elections which would form a unified government. The United States did not agree to this solution.

As the date for the proposed elections approached, the American-supported ruler of the South, Ngo Dinh Diem, refused to take part in any nationwide election. The United States supported this decision. American involvement, which earlier had been confined to military aid to the French, now began to encompass direct aid to Diem's government. American military advisers, only a few hundred at first, trained South Vietnamese troops in counterinsurgency warfare. In 1964, following a reported confrontation between U.S. intelligence ships and North Vietnamese patrol boats in the Gulf of Tonkin, the U.S. Congress passed the Tonkin Gulf Resolution—in effect a declaration of war against North Vietnam.

(The Tonkin Gulf Resolution was repealed in 1973. Testimony at that time showed that reports of a direct attack on U.S. ships were exaggerated or false.)

By 1967 American ground troops in Vietnam numbered half a million. At its peak in 1968 the U.S. troop strength was 540,000. These ground troops were supplemented by naval bombardment, aerial bombardment, and South Vietnamese troops trained and to a great extent financed by the United States. Even as U.S. ground troops were being withdrawn in 1969 through 1973, the U.S. bombardment of Indochina not only continued but increased in size and destructiveness.

Nature of the War

The war in Vietnam was in nearly every way a supreme example of counterinsurgency warfare, United States policies included destruction of villages and farmland, internment of civilians in concentration camps, defoliation of jungle with powerful and toxic weed-killers, extensive bombing of both military and civilian targets, indiscriminate use of antipersonnel weapons, and even poisoning of wells. All of these policies were aimed at destroying the infrastructure, or sources of support, of the antigovernment insurgents (Viet Cong). That the Viet Cong infrastructure was also the source of support for the civilian population at large mattered little to U.S. military planners. In any case, on the ground, U.S. troops could not distinguish between guerrilla soldiers and civilians—with the result that many civilians were killed out of fear that they might be guerrillas.

Unlike conventional wars, the Vietnam War had no definable front. Combat could and did occur at any time and in any place. During the 1968 Tet Offensive, Viet Cong troops even invaded the capital city of Saigon, and nineteen specially trained commandos attacked the United States Embassy.

Because the fighting was spread over the entire country with no stable combat zones, the destructive effects of American military power were also widespread. Half of Vietnam's inland forest was destroyed, along with 41 percent of its coastal forest. Four percent of Vietnam's bird species and 3 percent of its plant species became extinct during the fighting.

In South Vietnam, 40 percent of all rubber plantations—a major factor in the country's economy—were destroyed.

Conventional standards for judging military victory and defeat did not apply in Vietnam. Instead, U.S. policymakers deliberately fought a war of attrition in which U.S. firepower was supposed to "grind down," that is, kill, Viet Cong and North Vietnamese forces. Success was measured in so-called body counts, which often included civilians, animals, and even—to inflate the totals—trees. This grisly method of measuring military effectiveness was reminiscent of the attrition methods practiced by generals in World War I, but in Vietnam death occurred everywhere, striking military and civilians alike. The vast majority of casualties, by some estimates as high as 95 percent, were civilians.

The weapons used in Vietnam, though not advanced by today's standards, included fragmentation bombs, versions of the cluster bombs later used in Lebanon; napalm, a sticky, inflammable substance which can cling to human flesh while burning at high heat; conventional aerial bombs; and an elaborate electronic minefield known as the automated battlefield. Jungles were destroyed using the dioxin-based weed killer Agent Orange, whose effects on the environment and the human body are still not fully understood. Bulldozers cleared thousands of square miles of forest. The Stockholm International Peace Research Institute estimates that most of South Vietnam will take forty years or more to recover from the environmental effects of the war, and that some areas will never recover.

The Antiwar Movement

Although the Tonkin Gulf Resolution passed Congress with only two senatorial dissenters, Ernest Gruening of Alaska and Wayne Morse of Oregon, public opposition to the war grew as American ground troops entered the fighting. By 1968 the anti-Vietnam War movement had become a significant factor in U.S. politics. The antiwar candidate Eugene McCarthy almost defeated the incumbent president, Lyndon Johnson, in the New Hampshire presidential primary.

The obvious public support for McCarthy, combined with

American losses in the Tet Offensive, caused Johnson to withdraw from the presidential election. His successor, Richard Nixon, would probably have increased the air war over Indochina even more than he did, had it not been for mass opposition such as the Vietnam Moratorium, which brought half a million people to Washington, D.C. for a demonstration in October 1969, and which sponsored similar demonstrations around the United States.

The size and persistence of the opposition to the Vietnam War were unprecedented in American history. Public figures opposed to the war included members of Congress such as Senator Morse and Senator William Fulbright, leaders of the nonviolent peace and civil rights movement such as Dr. Martin Luther King, Jr., and A. J. Muste; and entertainment personalities such as Robert Vaughn and Richard Dreyfus. Ordinary citizens by the millions participated in demonstrations. Many who faced the draft refused induction or returned their registration cards to the Selective Service System. Thousands of draft resisters fled the country—most of them to Canada—as did thousands of military personnel who were absent without leave. Military units occasionally refused en masse to go into combat.

Figures from the Vietnam era resistance are startling. The Selective Service System reported 570,000 incidents of draft resistance between 1964 and 1973, a figure that is probably low because it leaves out "silent" resisters who did not register for the draft and were never caught. (The actual figure is probably closer to 1.5 million.) Half a million incidents of AWOL were recorded by the military during the war, and at some points over three hundred military personnel went absent without leave every day. The total number arrested for civil disobedience connected with demonstrations is unknown, but was probably in the millions. And over 250,000 soldiers were discharged with other than honorable discharges during the war, an index both of poor conditions within the military and of in-service dissent.

By the end of the war the majority of Americans opposed the U.S. intervention in Indochina. Despite the high levels of dissent and resistance, however, the peace movement had not become a majority. Public opinion polls consistently showed

198

that Americans believed the war had been a mistake, but were not yet prepared to raise more basic questions. This is hardly surprising. Prior to the Vietnam era Americans had been led to believe that their country's forces always allied themselves with the good and democratic forces in the world. The period of greatest and most public dissent from the Vietnam War lasted approximately seven years (1966–73), with the most publicized antiwar activity occurring between 1968 and 1972. This was not long enough to overcome twenty years of Cold War indoctrination.

Nonetheless the accomplishments of the Vietnam era peace movement were many and significant. For the first time opponents of a U.S. interventionist war were able to open up broader questions about United States intervention policies generally. Many of the ad hoc peace groups began during the Vietnam era, such as Clergy and Laity Concerned About Vietnam, continued after the war and dealt effectively with a variety of issues. (To symbolize its broader concerns, CAL-CAV shortened its name to Clergy and Laity Concerned, or CALC.) Older established peace groups such as the War Resisters League, the Fellowship of Reconciliation, and SANE, gained significant new membership during the war which did not entirely melt away once the immediate crisis was past.

Most important, the Vietnam era peace movement helped to make it more difficult for a president to commit U.S. troops to a war of foreign intervention. The Vietnam precedent remains a strong factor in American politics.

The Media and Vietnam

Vietnam has been called the first television war. This characterization is accurate as far as it goes; there is little doubt that repeated scenes from the war on evening television news helped to build American disquiet about the fighting. It is significant that in the Falklands (Malvinas) War and the U.S. invasion of Grenada, television coverage was forbidden by military censors. Military officers, who have historically been suspicious of war correspondents, had learned from the Vietnam experience that in order to go about their business they had to restrict public scrutiny of what they were doing.

199

Media coverage of Vietnam was extensive and in its way highly sophisticated. The reporters themselves, however, admitted that it had serious flaws. One major deficiency, probably the most important, was the reporters' lack of knowledge about Vietnamese history. This led many of them, at least until late in the war, to adopt an essentially supportive attitude toward the war. The result was that an atrocity like the My Lai massacre, in which American troops deliberately slaughtered an entire Vietnamese village, went unreported by representatives of the regular American press. The story was first broken by Seymour Hersh, then a freelance reporter based in the United States. Had regular correspondents known more of the history of Vietnam, it is likely that their coverage of the war would have been less superficial and more critical than it was.

At home coverage of the peace movement had serious flaws with effects that outlasted the war itself. The media's tendency to focus on personalities rather than on issues, and on spectacular events rather than more quiet but potentially more significant developments, distorted the public's picture of the peace movement. Opposition to the war was far more decentralized than the public media ever showed, and much peace movement activity involved day-to-day organizing (such as counseling and legal aid for potential draftees) which went virtually unreported. At the same time, because the media concentrated on the spectacular and—in the case of television—the visual, the public came to believe that the opposition to the war was more violent than it actually was. Violence is far more visual than nonviolent resistance or quiet organizing.

Reporters and columnists routinely exaggerated the size and influence of the peace movement, asserting that the country had become "antimilitary." This had enough basis in fact to ring true but it implied a thoroughgoing opposition to the military which most Americans did not feel. The effects of this distortion were two-fold. On the one hand, it reinforced right-wing fears about dissent and helped begin a process that in the late 1970s culminated in a fear campaign based on alleged U.S. "unilateral disarmament" and Soviet military "superiority."

On the other hand, the media's exaggeration of the peace movement's size, combined with the well-founded feeling that America was in crisis, led many in the antiwar movement to expect "the revolution" far more quickly than was realistic. The inevitable disillusion when the revolution did not occur caused some activists to turn to violence, which in its turn received exaggerated media coverage and made quiet, long-term nonviolent organizing more difficult. For example, public memory of the Students for a Democratic Society, which began as a nonviolent group in the early 1960s, is confined almost entirely to the final days of SDS and the activities of the very violent Weathermen faction. The Weathermen and the coverage they received helped in the final destruction of SDS as an effective group, though they were only two among many factors.

Vietnam Veterans

The most lasting effect of the war on the U.S. has been the presence of approximately two million military veterans who served in Vietnam. Although frequently portrayed as unstable, potentially violent drug abusers, most Vietnam veterans have gone on to live productive lives. Nonetheless the physical and emotional scars of their duty in Vietnam—especially for those who were in combat—will never leave them and remain a serious problem for American society as a whole.

An unknown but probably very large number of Vietnam veterans were exposed to the defoliant Agent Orange. Some studies have found that the main ingredient in Agent Orange, dioxin, is linked to illnesses ranging from cancer to birth defects among children of Agent Orange veterans. The full effects of Agent Orange exposure are unknown.

It is common, also, for Vietnam veterans to suffer from post traumatic stress disorder, or PTSD. This emotional reaction, similar to World War I shell shock and World War II battle fatigue, has its own effects unique to Vietnam veterans. Combat conditions in Vietnam were quite different from those in the two world wars. There was no front, as discussed above. Moreover soldiers were not sent to Vietnam, or sent home, as part of a unit, but as individual replacements. This meant that a returning soldier might arrive home alone, going in a few days from the horrors of Vietnam combat to a normal American environment where many people did not wish to hear about Vietnam, and where many others considered American soldiers to be war criminals.

In order to survive at home, many Vietnam veterans have tried to repress their response to their combat experience, only to have it come out later in the form of nightmares, aimlessness, and occasionally physical violence. PTSD has thus become a major problem not merely for individual veterans and their families, but for American society. The agonies of Vietnam veterans have deepened the tragedy of the war itself.

The Reevaluation of Vietnam

At present the American intervention in Vietnam is being reevaluated, not only by historians but by writers generally and to a lesser extent the public. This reevaluation has included publication of significant histories, such as that of Stanley Karnow, novels and memoirs such as those of Philip Caputo and W. D. Ehrhardt, and Guenter Lewey's revisionist study, *America in Vietnam*. The U.S. Army has contributed to the reevaluation with studies purporting to show that U.S. troops committed almost no atrocities during the war—a thesis firmly rejected by hundreds if not thousands of Vietnam veterans who testified during the Winter Soldier investigations while the war was going on and by the Peer Inquiry report on the murders at My Lai.

Historical reevaluation of wars, as of other events, is normal and desirable. It would be tragic, however, if the current effort to arrive at new understandings of the Vietnam War resulted primarily in apologies for the war. The objections to the war are unlikely to change as a result of historical research. On the contrary. In the past, as in World War I, historical research has frequently reinforced or added to objections raised at the time of the war. Nor can any arguments justify the attrition and counterinsurgency tactics used during the war. They were brutal and inhumane in 1967, and similar tactics in Central America are equally brutal and inhumane.

202

The lessons of Vietnam are clear. One is the folly of America's attempt to control world events. Another is the urgent need for the U.S. to base policy on a real understanding of events, not on Cold War stereotypes. A third is the horrific nature of counterinsurgency warfare. In Vietnam, U.S. troops, following American policies, committed acts which the public had thought possible only by soldiers of other countries. Whether the public has learned or forgotten all this only the future will tell.

The Reagan government in particular, which would like to believe we have gone "beyond Vietnam"—i.e., that military intervention has become acceptable again—has unquestionably learned from the Vietnam experience. Little of its learning has been worthwhile, though. Military officers have learned to restrict media coverage of military operations. Administrations since Vietnam, while for the most part eschewing use of U.S. ground troops, have learned other methods of intervention such as the revival of the CIA's covert war-making function, as in the illegal war against Nicaragua.

The basic thrust of U.S. policy, which was at issue in the Vietnam era debate, has changed little. American dollars and weapons still support corrupt and dictatorial regimes and, under the Reagan administration, in 1983 U.S. troops even invaded Grenada, a small island whose government the Administration found unacceptable. Whether, in the long run, the U.S. will learn to be a better citizen of the world because of the Vietnam debacle is impossible to predict. Historical research can help it to move in more positive directions. We shall learn nothing, however, if the current reevaluation becomes simply an occasion for rationalization of the most unjust war in U.S. history.

(See also: CONSCIENTIOUS OBJECTION, CONSCRIPTION, GUERRILLA WARFARE, LAWS OF WAR, WAR RESISTANCE)

Jagerstatter, Franz: Franz Jagerstatter, an Austrian peasant and a devout Catholic, refused induction into the Nazi army in 1943. He was tried and convicted in that year. Despite the pleas of many around him, including his wife, his friends, his lawyer, and even a German military court, he refused to make any compromise with the Nazi regime. Jagerstatter was beheaded. In his home village of St. Radegund, there is a monument to his memory.

Jagerstatter's war resistance grew out of his Catholic faith. It is not clear from the available records whether he objected to all wars or solely to Hitler's aggression, but the issue is of little importance. The evil Jagerstatter faced was so great that there was no need to think about other wars and other times.

After his death, Franz Jagerstatter became known to the American peace movement through Gordon Zahn's biography, *In Solitary Witness: The Life and Death of Franz Jagerstatter.*[1] His resistance set an example for many war resisters during the Indochina War. His courage in the face of certain death will continue to serve as an inspiration for war resisters in all times and places.

(See also: HITLER, ADOLF, NAZIS, NONVIOLENCE AND, TOTALITARIANISM, NONVIOLENCE AND)

---

1 Gordon Zahn, *In Solitary Witness: The Life and Death of Franz Jagerstatter* (Collegeville, Minn.: The Liturgical Press, 1981).

Just War Theory: Originally formulated by St. Augustine (A.D. 354–430), the Just War theory is an attempt by Christian theologians, while rejecting pacifism, to limit the brutality of war and set standards for deciding between acceptable and unacceptable wars. It was a departure from the teachings of the early church, which were pacifist.

Theologians disagree on the Just War standards, their number, substance, utility, and validity. As usually codified by its supporters, however, the Just War theory requires that any acceptable war must meet seven standards:

- War must be the last resort and used only after all other means have failed.
- War must be declared to redress rights actually violated or for defense against unjust demands backed by the threat of force.
- War must be openly and legally declared by a legal government.
- There must be a reasonable chance of winning.
- The means used must be in proportion to the ends sought.
- Soldiers must distinguish between armies and civilians and not deliberately attack civilians.
- The winner must not require the utter humiliation of the loser.

Objections to this theory are many. No government has ever followed it in determining policy, though many governments claim they are Christians fighting for a just cause. Even Hitler's government claimed that its cause was just. The theory finds little or no support in the New Testament. Most telling, the Just War theory has allowed the church to sanction virtually every war in Western history, giving its blessing in many of them to *both* sides—an impossibility under any reasonable reading of the theory.

These objections are of less importance today because no modern war meets or can meet the Just War criteria. At the simplest level modern wars are no longer openly declared. The military's need for surprise has rendered such formalities dangerous to the army which tries to follow them.

At a more complex level, attacks on civilians are now a commonplace of warfare. Counterinsurgency warfare consists of little else. Strategic bombing is a military euphemism for dropping tons of high explosive on civilians. Nuclear missiles are regularly targeted on cities of no military importance. And on and on.

The Indochina War met none of the Just War standards. It violated the first six outright, and it is likely that the U.S. intended something like the utter humiliation of North Vietnam. Even World War II, in which the Allies arguably did have a just cause, violated the prohibition against attacks on civilians, the injunction to proportionality, and the injunction against requiring utter humiliation. It is unlikely that any war fought under modern conditions could meet all seven standards, as a war must do to be acceptable under the theory.

Just-War objectors who maintain that a just war is now impossible have qualified for conscientious objector status under U.S. law.[1] The American Bishops' Pastoral Letter of 1983, which came close to rejecting nuclear weapons outright, was also a step away from traditional applications of Just War theory.[2] It is likely that the Just War theory will gradually die, as it should, a natural death.[3]

(See also: AREA BOMBING CAMPAIGN, CONSCIENTIOUS OBJECTION, CONVENTIONAL WAR, GUERRILLA WARFARE, NUCLEAR PACIFISM, NUCLEAR WEAPONS AND WAR, WAR RESISTANCE)

1 U.S. v. Berg, 310 F.Supp. 1157 (D.Me. 1970).
2 Cf. Gerard A. Vanderhaar, "Bishops Praise War Resistance," CCCO News Notes, Vol. 35, No. 3 (Autumn, 1983), p. 10.
3 For a brief account of the just war theory, see Richard J. Niebanck, Conscience, War, and the Selective Objector (Board of Social Ministry, Lutheran Church of America, 1972). Fuller accounts and critiques will be found in Roland H. Bainton, Christian Attitudes Toward War and Peace (New York: Abingdon Press, 1960) and Richard McSorley, S.J., The New Testament Basis of Peacemaking (Washington, D.C.: Georgetown University Center for Peace Studies, 1979).

King, Martin Luther, Jr.: In 1954 the Supreme Court of the United States held that racial segregation in public schools is unconstitutional. This decision, which by inference outlawed all other racial segregation, had little practical effect until the people most directly affected, using nonviolent direct action, forced the nation to confront the evils of racial discrimination. The most important figure in the nonviolent civil rights movement was the Rev. Martin Luther King, Jr.

Martin Luther King, Jr., was educated at Emory University, Atlanta, Crozer Theological Seminary, Chester, Pennsylvania, and Boston University. At Crozer, he studied nonviolence in theory. In 1956, in the Montgomery bus boycott, he learned to apply it in practice. During the boycott, black citizens of Montgomery, Alabama, stopped riding the segregated Montgomery buses, sometimes walking miles to work, until they were no longer required or expected to sit in the backs of the buses.

King's achievements in the nonviolent campaign for civil rights are too many to list in a brief article. He founded the Southern Christian Leadership Conference, whose nonviolent action and grassroots work throughout the southern U.S. helped to transform the life of that region. He led many successful nonviolent actions, such as the Selma-Montgomery March (1965), and in 1963 organized the March on Washington for Jobs and Freedom, which brought approximately half a million people to the capital. His major legislative success was the campaign for passage of the Voting Rights Act of 1965. In 1964 he received the Nobel Peace Prize. He was assassinated in 1968. King's legacy includes the Martin Luther King, Jr., Center for Nonviolent Social Change in Atlanta.

Martin Luther King, Jr., is now so widely respected that his birthday became an American holiday in 1985. This was not always the case. Like his followers, King spent much time in jail during the early years of his career. His "Letter From Birmingham Jail" has become one of the classic statements on the need for racial equality and the philosophy of civil disobedience. During his lifetime King was harassed by the Federal Bureau of Investigation and regularly vilified by the press, particularly in the South.

Toward the end of his life, King began to speak out not only against racial segregation, but against the Indochina War and the nuclear arms race. His critics rather condescendingly suggested that civil rights, not peace, was King's purview, and that he should confine his public statements to civil rights matters. In fact, however, King's antiwar stand was neither accident nor aberration. He was a committed pacifist who had studied Gandhi's nonviolent campaign, traveled to India, and been influenced by A. J. Muste. He was a member of the Fellowship of Reconciliation, one of the major pacifist groups in the world. His death cut short much of his theological work, but there is no doubt that during his lifetime he was one of the major nonviolent theorists and practitioners of the twentieth century. Those who argue that King's antiwar position diverged from his other thinking or was a foolish stand underestimate him both as a human being and theologian.

King's contributions to the nonviolent movement have been second only to those of Gandhi. Except for Gandhi's liberation of India, the nonviolent civil rights campaign was the most successful nonviolent campaign to date. King was its spiritual leader, spokesperson, and architect. As writer and speaker, he was unsurpassed in eloquence. His own statement of his pacifist position is a sample:

If we assume that humankind has a right to survive, then we must find an alternative to war and destruction. In a day when sputniks dash through outer space and guided ballistic missiles are carving highways of death through the stratosphere, nobody can win a war. The choice today is no longer between violence or nonviolence. It is between nonviolence or nonexistence.[1]

(See also: GANDHI, MOHANDAS K., MUSTE, A. J., NONVIOLENCE)

1 Martin Luther King, Jr., "My Pilgrimage to Nonviolence" (1960), reprinted in *The Catholic Worker*, Jan.–Feb. 1983.

Laws of War: Attempts by the nations to limit the brutality of war by agreeing on what may or may not be done in combat have on the whole failed in their main purpose. The laws of war are a mixture of international conventions, precedents such as those established at the Nuremberg Trials following World War II, and generally accepted custom. No neutral agency enforces them, and enforcement remains the weakest part of international law generally.

In some cases, such as the treatment of prisoners, the laws of war have been relatively well observed. Most countries are signatories to the Geneva Convention on prisoners of war, and even in particularly savage conflicts such as the Iraq-Iran War (1980–present), prisoners of war have not been slaughtered. Killing prisoners war was common practice in ancient warfare.

More often, particularly in combat, laws of war are (sometimes routinely) violated. In the Indochina War, American and South Vietnamese troops regularly attacked and killed civilians—a direct violation of international law. Many of these atrocities received little or no public notice. The only one which did, the massacre at My Lai, resulted in court-martial for the officer immediately in charge, but no penalty for those above him in the chain of command. Like the slaughter itself, this represented a violation of the laws of war. Under the Nuremberg Principles, a commander—even up to the commander-in-chief—bears responsibility for violations of the law by soldiers under his command. Thus in principle even the president of the United States could have been criminally liable for the My Lai slaughter.[1]

The most famous of the Nuremberg Principles holds that not only commanders but individual soldiers can be held to account for war crimes. This has led the U.S. military to provide a sort of "Nuremberg defense" for soldiers accused of refusing to follow orders. If the soldier can prove that the order violated the laws of war, he or she will be acquitted. But since the burden of proof is on the soldier this particular provision has never been invoked. It would be unrealistic to expect anything else. Combat is such a confused and frightening situation that outright refusal of direct orders under fire is very rare. The U.S. military's provisions assume that soldiers will know the laws of war and be willing to invoke them, and gamble that a court-martial will agree.[2]

The laws of war are so complex in any case that soldiers rarely know them or have any hope of applying them in combat. Moreover soldiers quite naturally develop some cynicism about a body of law which protects them only from the weapons which the nations find it expedient to outlaw. In World War I, for example, notched bayonets were outlawed by international convention; machine guns and artillery were not. The bayonet was a poor weapon in hand-to-hand combat in a trench, and soldiers quickly learned to use entrenching tools (sharp-pointed shovels) instead. This made hand-to-hand combat more brutal. Worse, the acceptable weapons were responsible for the most battle deaths of any used in the war.

After the war an international convention outlawed poison gas which though much feared had not proved as lethal as its reputation. No convention outlawed the machine gun or the cannon and none does to this day. Both are far more destructive than were the gasses used in World War I.[3]

Despite an impressive body of international law, warfare has become more, not less, destructive in the twentieth century. Scholars argue that many weapons and tactics of modern warfare—strategic bombing, nuclear weapons,[4] nerve gas, and so on—are violations of the laws of war (or would be in use). No such prohibitions attach to "smart" weapons, which have in theory increased the deadliness of the battlefield by a factor of ten or more. New laws concerning such weapons could be developed, but the history of laws respecting the most useful weapon is not encouraging. Militarily useful weapons tend to remain in use and untouched by the laws of war.

The difficulty with the laws of war lies with the nature of combat itself. Combat has a life of its own and a logic which is directly in conflict with the rule of law. For a military force, the mission—defeating the opposing army—is paramount. Legal considerations are secondary. Flagrant violations of international law, such as the My Lai incident, may be punished, but the military will probably not punish them in a way that will put serious curbs on its freedom to pursue the mission.

This amoral "morality"—whatever accomplishes the mission is good, whatever hinders it, bad—is one of the prime objections to war. Within the context of combat, no level of brutality is completely forbidden if it contributes to military victory. Laws of war directly challenge this logic but there is no one to enforce them in combat.

Nonetheless international law and the laws of war have the potential for much good. They are likely to be effective on the level of policymaking if they are backed by popular pressure. Much American opposition to the Indochina War was based on the belief that U.S. troops were being forced to commit war crimes in Vietnam, Cambodia, and Laos. The soldiers in combat did not make the policies that led to these crimes; one could hardly expect them to enforce the laws against what they were ordered to do. A courageous unit or, on occasion, a courageous individual might refuse orders. But stopping the crimes meant stopping the war.

This is hardly surprising. In combat the rule of law has succumbed to the rule of force. If laws of war are to have any meaning at all, they must be enforced, not against individual soldiers but against those who decide that there will be combat, the kind of combat involved, and the kind of tactics that will be used. This means the high command, and it means civilian policymakers. These leaders will not accuse themselves of crimes. The public, as in the Indochina War, must do so.

(See also: AREA BOMBING CAMPAIGN, ANTIPERSONNEL WEAPONS, CONVENTIONAL WAR, GUERRILLA WARFARE, INDOCHINA WAR, NUCLEAR WEAPONS AND WAR, "SMART" WEAPONS)

1. A general discussion of Vietnam and the Nuremberg Principles will be found in Telford Taylor, *Nuremberg and Vietnam: an American Tragedy* (New York: Times Books, 1970).

2. See Barton Stichman and Robert Rivkin, *The Rights of Military Personnel* (New York: Avon, 1977), pp. 103–104.

3. Casualty figures for World War I, broken down insofar as possible, will be found in E. L. Bogart, *Direct and Indirect Costs of the Great War* (1920), quoted in C. R. M. F. Crutwell, *A History of the Great War* (Oxford: The Clarendon Press, 1934), p. 630 ff.

4. On the legality of nuclear weapons, see Elliott L. Meyrowitz, "Are Nuclear Weapons Legal?", *Bulletin of the Atomic Scientists*, Vol. 39, No. 8 (October, 1983), pp. 49–52; and Burns H. Weston, "Nuclear Weapons Versus International Law: A Contextual Reassessment," *McGill Law Journal*, Vol. 28, No. 3 (July, 1983), pp. 542–590.

Le Chambon: The commune of Le Chambon sur Lignon is a small village in the southern French Alps.[1] During the Nazi Occupation of France and the rule of the puppet Vichy government (1940–44), Le Chambon became a refuge for thousands of Jews fleeing the Gestapo and the Vichy authorities. Without violence, and at great risk to themselves, the villagers of Le Chambon took in Jewish refugees and arranged for them to reach Switzerland and safety.

Prior to the Occupation, Le Chambon had been a center of pacifist activity. The Cevanol school, founded in 1938, drew pacifists from all over France (it continued its work after the war). During the Occupation the school harbored many refugees, both as teachers and students. Eduard Theis, the head of the school, procured false identity papers for the refugees—a serious offense under Vichy French law.

The Vichy French government did not cooperate reluctantly in the persecution of French Jews. On the contrary, President Petain and his colleagues were eager to arrest and deport Jews in order to curry favor with their Nazi overlords.

The cooperation of the Vichy government extended to arresting those who tried to save the Jews, including the leaders of Le Chambon. Andre Trocme, who founded the Cevanol school, Edward Theis, and Roger Darcissac, who had made Le Chambon a place of refuge, themselves spent time in an internment camp. They were released unharmed. Andre Trocme's cousin, Daniel, was not so lucky; he died at the hands of the Gestapo in the death camp at Maidanek, Poland.

Though they operated in secret, even to the point of dividing themselves into thirteen separate cells who did not know each other's plans, the villagers of Le Chambon were not without support from outside. The American Friends Service Committee, a Quaker relief agency, provided substantial help in the effort. By agreement the joint work of AFSC and Le Chambon was concentrated on saving Jewish children.

Despite this outside support, credit for the remarkable achievements of Le Chambon belongs to the villagers themselves and their leaders, particularly Andre Trocme, who organized the rescue. Their work stands as an example of how good can occur even in the midst of great evil. It stands also in contrast to the failures of the Allies, both before the war and during it, to take serious action to save Europe's Jews.

Those involved in the rescue effort at Le Chambon probably would not see it this way. Philip Hallie, who interviewed the villagers extensively while preparing his book on the rescue, says:

In almost every interview I had with a Chambonnais or a Chambonnaise there came a moment when he or she pulled back from me but looked firmly into my eyes and said, 'How can you call us "good"? We were doing what had to be done. Who else could help them? And what has all this to do with goodness? Things had to be done, that's all, and we happened to be there to do them. You must understand that it was the most natural thing in the world to help these people.[2]

(See also: THE HOLOCAUST)

1. The full story of Le Chambon will be found in Philip Hallie, *Lest Innocent Blood Be Shed: The Story of the Village of Le Chambon and How Goodness Happened There* (New York: Harper & Row, 1979). This article is based on Hallie's book.
2. *Ibid.*, pp. 20–21.

Marxism: (See Communism, Soviet Union, Stalin)

Middle East: The countries of western Asia and North Africa include Iran, Iraq, Syria, Lebanon, Egypt, Israel, Jordan, Kuwait, Saudi Arabia, Qatar, Bahrain, the United Arab Emirates, Oman, North and South Yemen, Libya, Tunisia, and Algeria. Since 1945 they have been the site of at least fifty-five wars.[1] These conflicts have ranged from the guerrilla war in Algeria (1954–62) to the 1967 and 1973 wars between Egypt and Israel which were fought with modern conventional weapons and tactics. Active wars in the region include the bloody World War I-style conflict between Iran and Iraq, and the complex civil war in Lebanon. In addition, the Middle East has been the site of extensive terrorism.

Ethnic and Religious Rivalries

The variety of ethnic and religious groupings in the Middle East is staggering and should give pause to outsiders who believe—as the Great Powers apparently do—that they can control events in the region. In Lebanon alone the military forces involved in the civil war include Maronite Christians,

213

Druse Muslims, Shiite Muslims, regular Syrian troops, regular Lebanese troops whose multi-ethnic composition has led to unit breakdowns under fire, and various factions of Palestinian fighters. In addition Israeli troops, while not originally directly involved in the civil war, contributed to the violence in Lebanon by invading the country in 1982. The Iran-Iraq War, which began in 1980, is a conflict between an Arab and a Persian state and all the more bitter because of an ethnic rivalry that goes back to ancient times.

Complicating the situation further is the fact that ethnic and religious divisions in the Middle East do not follow national borders. This has led to approximately twenty-three civil wars and six regional uprisings in the Arab and Persian countries since 1945. These wars have been far more costly than is generally realized in the United States. Syria, for example, has experienced fifteen years of war since 1945. Approximately two-thirds of this fighting has been internal, including the bloody suppression of two regional uprisings in the early 1980s (1980 and 1982).

It is evident that conflict in the Middle East is not solely between Arabs and Israelis or between Israelis and Palestinians. These two conflicts, while severe and difficult to resolve, have probably accounted for less bloodshed than the many civil wars and the fighting among the Arab states. Resolving the Arab-Israeli and Israeli-Palestinian conflicts will not, by themselves, bring peace to the region.

Nor will the various ethnic conflicts in the Middle East be solved by military means. On the contrary, they can only be made worse by continued fighting. Many of them, like the rivalry between Arabs and Persians, have their roots in ancient times. Military force has failed in the Middle East, as it has failed elsewhere, because it cannot bring resolution to a conflict. It can bring defeat to one of the combatants, but the history of the Middle East demonstrates that military defeat frequently makes the defeated side wish for revenge—leading, in the long run, to continued violence, insecurity, and destruction for both sides.

The Iran-Iraq War is a case in point. Rivalry between Arabs and Persians began centuries ago and today is so intense that the war between Iraq (an Arab state) and Iran (a Persian state) became the bloodiest in the region's recent history. Although both sides apparently observed the Geneva Convention on treatment of prisoners of war, the fighting on the border between the two countries combined the savagery of trench warfare with the destructiveness of modern weapons. Iranian troops attacked Iraqi positions in human waves reminiscent of the offensives on the Western Front in 1914–18. Many of these "soldiers" were children aged twelve years or even younger, some of them roped together in groups of twenty and used as human minesweepers. In retaliation, Iraqi forces resorted to the use of poison gas, napalm, and various other antipersonnel weapons. Joint casualties, though impossible to determine with any certainty, probably were well over one hundred thousand by mid-1985. Yet, as on the Western Front in World War I, the military situation was locked in a brutal stalemate. No military solution was possible, and the defeat of one side would in any case have been no solution at all. It would have led to the desire for revenge and thus to further combat in the long run.

The difficulties of the Palestinians also cannot be resolved by military or terrorist means. Palestinian use of terror tactics has been self-defeating. By increasing Israeli fears it has undercut the possibility of negotiations for a Palestinian homeland. At the same time it has decreased support for Palestinian aspirations in the Arab world, leading in some cases (as in Jordan) to the expulsion of Palestinian fighters from Arab territories. On the other hand it is clear that the various Palestinian terrorist groups cannot, in the long run, be defeated militarily—just as they cannot prevail. The Israeli attempt to do so by invading Lebanon in 1982 was opposed by many Israeli citizens and created much controversy and popular opposition in Israel.

So with the many other ethnic conflicts in the Middle East. Peace in the Middle East is no closer than it was forty or even a thousand years ago.

Great Power Interference

In a complex situation like the Middle East, outsiders do well to use caution lest they make the conflicts worse. The United

States and the Soviet Union, however, have done the opposite, thus increasing the danger not only of regional war but of nuclear war. Between 1961 and 1978 the major military powers of the Middle East and their lesser rivals purchased $4,312,000,000 in weapons, primarily from the U.S. and the Soviet Union. The United States arms countries on both sides in the Arab-Israeli conflict. U.S.-supplied arms supported the Shah of Iran until his regime was overthrown, and they were used extensively in the Iran-Iraq War. The Soviet Union supplies weapons and technical personnel to many of the Arab countries. Syria's air force uses Soviet-built fighter planes, for instance, and its troops in Lebanon were accompanied by large numbers of Soviet military advisers.

The primary reason for Western interference in Middle Eastern affairs is oil. Many countries in the region, including Saudi Arabia, Algeria, Bahrain, Iran, Iraq, Kuwait, Libya, Oman, the United Arab Emirates, and North and South Yemen, are oil producers. Fears of Soviet interference with oil shipments to the West prompted the so-called Carter Doctrine, announced in early 1980 by President Jimmy Carter. Under this doctrine, the United States officially considers any threat to Middle Eastern oil shipments to be a direct attack on U.S. interests. The Rapid Deployment Force, an expensive and dangerous intervention force, was developed to counter perceived Soviet threats to Middle Eastern oil shipments.

Whether or not the Soviet Union seeks control of Middle Eastern oil fields, it is clear that no military action can assure or protect oil shipments. U.S. plans in the event of a Middle Eastern oil war include use of tactical nuclear weapons which would render the areas defended a radioactive wasteland. The U.S. would be ten thousand miles from the war zone with consequent difficulties for supplies and logistics. In addition the oil fields would be open to sabotage, oil facilities would be destroyed either during the fighting or by defenders following a scorched-earth strategy, and an occupation of the Middle Eastern oil fields on a large scale would be nearly impossible because of local resistance. An oil war would also risk general nuclear war. Any Soviet attempt to conquer the oil fields, while not subject to the same problems of distance and logis-

216

tics, would also encounter local resistance and would result in destruction of the oil fields.

The futility of war for oil has been extensively documented by researchers at the Center for Defense Information in Washington, D.C.[2] The danger of the Great Powers' attempt to gain military ascendancy in the Middle East by proxy is also evident. By seeing Middle Eastern events primarily as a playing-out of the U.S.A.-U.S.S.R. struggle, both sides distort an already complicated situation. By arming the combatants in the various Middle Eastern wars, they have contributed to increased bloodshed and suffering for the people of the region.

The Israeli Peace Movement

Israel, which is probably the major military power in the Middle East, is also the home of the only independent peace movement in the region. Since the Israeli invasion of Lebanon this movement has become a significant political force. Many Israeli soldiers even resisted deployment on the West Bank of the Jordan River, where a largely Palestinian population is subject to Israeli military control, and to Lebanon.

Following the invasion of Lebanon, the broadly-based Peace Now movement organized a demonstration of one hundred thousand Israelis to call for an end to the war. The demonstration, held in Tel Aviv on July 5, 1982, was the largest of its kind in Israel up to that point. An even larger demonstration (approximately four hundred thousand) followed the massacre of Palestinians by Christian militia in the Sabra and Shatilla refugee camps.

In proportion to the population of Israel these two demonstrations and the peace movement they represent are among the largest in the world, if not the largest. Though not pacifist, they unite in opposing Israeli territorial expansion and use of military force to solve Israel's foreign policy difficulties. The growing peace movement in Israel is one of the more hopeful signs amid the Middle Eastern conflicts of the last ten years.

It is tragic that there were no similar movements in the

Arab world. The success of the peace movement in Israel demonstrates the importance of an independent peace movement. Without such movements on both sides, resolving the Middle East conflicts will be far more difficult. An independent peace movement can provide a corrective to government policy which in the absence of opposition may become too enamored of military force or, worse, become a proxy for the Great-Power conflict.

Most of the Arab countries are authoritarian in structure. Yet even in authoritarian countries a strong popular movement may accomplish much. Although it ultimately led to a repressive and warlike government, popular opposition in Iran, for example, led to the abdication of the Shah, whose secret police were notorious for their use of torture.

The Potential of Peace

Although resolution of the conflicts in the Middle East will be difficult, it is clear that the many wars and the militarization of the region have done nothing but harm to the peoples there. A region whose culture and civilization go back thousands of years, and whose contributions to world civilization are almost immeasurable, has instead become the focus of world conflict. The resulting costs have been great. Hundreds of thousands of soldiers and civilians have been killed in the various Middle Eastern wars. No major country in the region has avoided war and some, such as Egypt and South Yemen, have experienced nearly twenty years of war since 1945.

Yet peace in the Middle East is not impossible. It has never been true, for example, that security for Israel must be bought at the expense of the Arabs, or that the Arab countries will gain security by their attempts to overcome Israel. On the contrary: the rivalry between the two exacerbates fears on both sides, leads to a potentially disastrous military competition, and makes each side less, not more, secure. So with the rivalry between Arabs and Persians whose cost in blood and money has been incalculable. And so with the many rivalries among Arabs. In the Middle East, as everywhere, there is no security in military might.

Despite their many rivalries, the peoples of the region have common interests—in economic development, in security, and in peace itself—which can eventually overcome the divisions among them. Outsiders can aid the movement toward peace by encouraging the growth of independent peace movements throughout the region, but especially in the Arab countries. And the Great Powers can do much good by recognizing that conflicts in the Middle East are not simply reflections of the East-West rivalry. Even simple steps such as conservation of oil can help.

All the same, none of this may be enough. A Middle East in which ethnic, religious, and national rivalries are resolved with military force and bloodshed, in which the Great Powers arm the combatants, in which terrorism is common and innocent bystanders are regularly killed and maimed, is not only a region of great danger for its own people but for the people of the world.

But there is the potential for another Middle East, one in which Arabs, Israelis, Persians, and Palestinians alike contribute. Such a Middle East would be a region whose economic strength and prosperity would be unrivaled in the world. This is the potential of peace.

(See also: ANTIPERSONNEL WEAPONS, COLD WAR, CONVENTIONAL WAR, NUCLEAR WEAPONS AND WAR)

1. Data from "War 1945–82: Europe, Middle East, Africa," in Michael Kidron and Dan Smith, *The War Atlas* (New York: Simon & Schuster, 1983). Statistics elsewhere in this article are also taken from this invaluable source.
2. "The Oil Crisis: Is There a Military Option?", *Defense Monitor*, Vol. VIII, No. 11 (December, 1979).

Military-Industrial Complex:[1] The interdependence of the U.S. Department of Defense and the weapons industry is well known. Defense contractors such as Lockheed, Boeing, and General Dynamics are now in many respects wards of the state. They would collapse or suffer serious reverses without weapons orders. At the same time these corporations influence weapons procurement and military policy. Retired military officers frequently become high-ranking officers in the weapons industry, creating interpenetration between buyer and seller. All this is well-documented in the public media.

Less well-known is the fact that the Soviet Union has its own military-industrial complex. Soviet design bureaus, such as Sukhoi and Mikoyan-Gurevich, are a rough equivalent of American weapons makers. They work closely with Soviet military authorities, much as do Lockheed and Boeing. As in the United States, major weapons makers are not permitted to fail. And, as in the U.S., the weapons makers have an economic and business interest in a continued military buildup.[2]

In both countries the influence of the military-industrial complex has distorted policy, increased government spending, and made ending the arms race more difficult.

The most publicized effect of the military-industrial complex is its cost. There is no doubt that much military spending in the U.S. and the U.S.S.R. is militarily superfluous. Excessive military costs result from simple overcharging, as when the U.S. Air Force spends hundreds of dollars for a simple bolt for an aircraft body; from cost overruns, or expenditures well over those originally budgeted (such overruns are an everyday occurrence); and from purchase of weapons systems whose military value is dubious. These systems are sometimes conceived by the weapons makers as a way of recouping the cost of designing and building systems which have failed in the civilian market. The AWACs radar aircraft, for example, was originally designed as an airliner. After it failed in the civilian market it was redesigned as a radar plane.[3]

Most often, however, the Pentagon (and Soviet authorities) order dubious systems because of the influence of the weapons makers in the procurement offices. This, while it leads to great expense for small military impact, is by no means the most dangerous effect of the military-industrial complex.

Far more disturbing is the practice of "threat inflation." Both the weapons makers and the military participate in this. They are aided by politicians who have an interest in exaggerating their adversary's power and by pressure groups such as the Committee on the Present Danger in the U.S. Threat inflation occurs in the United States and the Soviet Union.

A typical example of threat inflation was the U.S. arms establishment's treatment of the MiG-25. This fighter plane was hailed by officials as "the finest interceptor in the world today." The secretary of defense said that it might cause the U.S. "to reappraise our entire approach to the strategic technological balance." As a result of this exaggeration Congress willingly appropriated money for a new U.S. fighter plane, the F-15, in 1976. When, however, a Soviet pilot defected with his MiG-25, the plane was found to be not at all a superweapon; its top speed was 2.5 times the speed of sound, for instance, not the 3.3 times that U.S. officials had claimed. Thus the F-15 fighter, which had serious operational problems, became a weapon that did not work designed to meet a threat that did not exist.[4]

But threat inflation is not merely a danger to American and Soviet government budgets. It exacerbates tensions between the two nations, thrusting policy into an oversimplified fantasy world in which "we" are five feet tall, thin, and weak, and "they" are ten feet tall, muscular, and strong. The results of such exaggeration are a renewed Cold War, a speeded-up arms race, and military expenditures which may cripple the economies of both superpowers.

Closely related to threat inflation is the dependence of the superpower economies on weapons production. Major weapons contractors are not allowed to go out of business. The government rescues them with large military contracts. Entire areas of the United States, such as Seattle, are so dependent on weapons production that the collapse of their local weapons plants would lead to economic disaster for the community. The peace movement has tried to meet this particular obstacle by developing ways to convert military production to civilian uses. Peace conversion programs point the way toward ending the weapons industry's grip on the U.S. economy.

Both the U.S. and the U.S.S.R. pay dearly for their weapons expenditures—and not only in money. Weapons, which are nonproductive, drain resources from the economy. Expenditures on them are inflationary and contribute nothing to economic development beyond the immediate employment they offer. By using immense stocks of capital for weapons, the superpowers have wasted money desperately needed for economic development. They have turned thousands of their best engineers and scientists to developing unproductive military hardware. And they have retarded genuine community development by substituting military contracts for the creation of more lasting sources of wealth; a contract to refurbish an aircraft carrier substitutes for rebuilding the industrial base in Philadelphia, for example.

Thus even when there is no war the military-industrial complex has been disastrous for the U.S. The same is true of the Soviet Union whose economy is at best far less productive. Controlling the two nations' respective military-industrial complexes would be a major step toward peace.

(See also: COLD WAR, SOVIET UNION, UNITED STATES)

1. An excellent source of information on the military-industrial complex is National Action and Research on the Military-Industrial Complex (NARMIC), 1500 Race St., Philadelphia, PA 19102.

2. See Andrew Cockburn, *The Threat: Inside the Soviet Military Machine* (New York: Random House, 1983), ch. 5.

3. A full description of the "interpenetration" process will be found in Gordon Adams, *The Iron Triangle: The Politics of Defense Contracting* (New Brunswick, N.J.: Transaction Books, 1981).

4. Cockburn, pp. 14–15.

Military Training: Military training has three purposes: to break down the identities of trainees so that they can become part of a military unit; to teach them military skills and by constant repetition make performance automatic; and to try to make soldiers obey orders absolutely, even when the orders are absurd. Insofar as it achieves these purposes, military training makes possible not only the killing, but the dying, that are central to war.

The three-fold purpose of military training explains its brutality. Soldiers are forced to obey arbitrary orders not by chance but by design. They are deprived of sleep, forced to eat quickly, forced to perform humiliating rituals, subjected to random inspections of their quarters, punished as a group for infractions by individuals—all the while undergoing a rigorous physical routine. Drill instructors routinely abuse soldiers mentally. Physical abuse also occurs in some instances.

222

All of this seemingly pointless behavior is actually well-planned and controlled. In the documentary film *Soldier Girls*, which traces three female recruits through basic training, the contrast between drill sergeants when they are off duty and on is startling. The forms and content of abuse heaped upon recalcitrant recruits vary little from one sergeant to another. It is as if all the sergeants had learned their lines at drill instructor school—as, in all likelihood, they did. The officers in command of the training know quite well what they are doing and why.

By repetition recruits learn to respond automatically. By constantly having to obey unpredictable changes in orders—if they do not they and their units face severe punishment—they learn obedience. And by being under constant stress they store up anger and hostility which, at least in theory, are meant to erupt when required for combat purposes.

Curiously while anthropologists and psychologists debate whether humans are naturally warlike, experienced military planners constantly assume that they are not. If war came naturally to humans, military training would be far different. Soldiers would learn skills, they would learn to obey orders, and they would drill as part of a group; but they would not need "breaking down" and remolding. Training would be a matter of channeling their already violent impulses. Instead it deliberately builds anger—whether toward other countries, or other races, or merely the drill sergeant.[1]

Advertising for the U.S. All-Volunteer Army has led recruits to expect that military training will prepare them for civilian jobs upon discharge. Nothing could be further from the truth. Military jobs have few civilian counterparts in the first place. And, worse, military jobs are broken down into small easily-learned tasks so that soldiers qualified for a particular skill can be replaced without difficulty if killed in combat. Thus a military mechanic does not learn to repair an entire engine; he or she only learns to repair one specific part.[2]

(See also: CHAIN OF COMMAND, COMBAT)

1. This article draws on extensive discussions with military personnel seeking counseling on discharges. I am grateful also to Jim Crichton, "Brainwashing and Basic Training," unpublished article.

2. Phyllis Larimore, "Going Somewhere?" (Philadelphia: Central Committee for Conscientious Objectors, 1984).

Muste, A. J.: A. J. Muste, who died in 1967, was little-known to the general public, yet he was one of the most influential figures in the peace movement. The list of his achievements is staggering. From 1940 to 1953 he was Executive Secretary of the Fellowship of Reconciliation. He helped to found, among other groups, the Central Committee for Conscientious Objectors (1948) and the National Mobilization Committee to End the War in Vietnam (1966). He was on the editorial board of *Liberation,* the major journal of nonviolent thought in the late 1950s and early 1960s. And his influence, in one way or another, extended to virtually every action and group in the nonviolent peace movement, as well as to groups such as the National Committee for a Sane Nuclear Policy (SANE) which were not comitted to nonviolence.

Muste's chief virtues were three: a consistent and courageous pacifist stand; an ability to work with a mediator among a wide variety of political groups; and a tough-minded and penetrating political understanding. He was a war tax resister who, in "Of Holy Disobedience," made one of the classic statements on the case for draft resistance. In the political infighting of the 1950s and 1960s Muste repeatedly helped groups of divergent views to work together on common projects without abandoning his own principles.

Muste's political insights were far more penetrating than those of most mainstream political analysts. After an early commitment to pacifism, he became, during the 1930s, a Trotskyite Socialist. When he once again committed himself to pacifism, he incorporated his radical economic views and much of the analysis underlying them into his pacifist thought. His essays in *Liberation,* for which he regularly wrote editorials, not only present the case for nonviolence but also show persuasively the fallacy of so-called alternatives to nonviolence. His statement of the peace movement's role, written in the mid-1960s, might still serve as a guide for action:

There is now no Socialist and Labor movement committed to basic social change, and therefore the peace movement either has to take part in the development of new political forces and new political organizations, or it has itself to be somehow or other a force for political change in the sense in which the peace movement was not in the old days—when pacifism was an individual matter.[1]

Yet Muste was well aware of the difficulties of making revolution—either violent or nonviolent:

It is quite true that we can only dimly discern what the new society will be like. This has always been true in revolutionary periods. The future did not correspond to the blueprints if men ventured to make blueprints. . . . [But it] is better to go out, not knowing whither we go, precisely because the city of peace and fraternity which we seek has yet to be built and must not be like what we now know and can readily describe.[2]

Muste, the most revolutionary pacifist of all, showed by his life and thought that pacifism is neither passive nor fuzzy-minded. This is perhaps his most important legacy.

(See also: KING, MARTIN LUTHER, JR.)

1. Nat Hentoff, *Peace Agitator: The Story of A. J. Muste* (New York: A. J. Muste Memorial Institute, 1982), p. 231.
2 Ibid., p. 232.

NATO and Warsaw Pact: Following World War II, the United States and several other Western countries formed the North Atlantic Treaty Organization (NATO) as one means of containing Soviet territorial ambitions. In response, the Soviet Union, with several Eastern European countries, formed the Warsaw Pact alliance. Today NATO includes the United States, Canada, Belgium, Denmark, West Germany, Greece, Italy, Luxembourg, The Netherlands, Norway, Portugal, Spain, Turkey, and Great Britain. The U.S. remains dominant in the alliance, though its hegemony is being questioned. Countries in the Warsaw Pact include the U.S.S.R., East Germany, Czechoslovakia, Poland, Hungary, Romania, and Bulgaria. The Soviet Union maintains its dominance of this alliance, though some other Warsaw Pact nations have begun to question Soviet policies.

The two alliances face each other in a Europe more heavily armed than at any time in history. Equipped with the most modern armaments—tactical nuclear weapons, "smart" weapons, tanks, aircraft—the mass armies of NATO and the Warsaw Pact prepare for war with each other, run military exercises, and maintain an atmosphere of tension which could result in nuclear holocaust if one side miscalculates.

The decision by the NATO governments to deploy U.S. cruise missiles in Great Britain and Italy, and Pershing II missiles in Germany, has raised the level of tension and made nuclear war far more likely than it was even two or three years ago. The Pershing II missile can reach Moscow in eight minutes, striking with the force of so-called strategic missiles. The cruise missile, which can carry a sizeable nuclear device, has become a threat unlike any in the past. It is launched from a mobile launching pad and because of its low flight path is invisible to ordinary radar.

Both of these missiles are first-strike weapons, useful primarily for attack rather than retaliation. This increase in first-strike power should surprise no one who is familiar with NATO military doctrine. On the assumption that Warsaw Pact armies are larger and better-armed and could therefore defeat NATO armies in conventional combat, NATO doctrine has long held that the main deterrent to a Warsaw Pact invasion of West Germany is NATO's willingness to attack an advancing Warsaw Pact force with nuclear weapons. Thus, when the Soviet Union formally renounced first use of nuclear weapons—a move which helped the Soviet public image but would probably make little difference in a full-scale conflict—NATO did not respond in kind because its doctrine depends on first use. The NATO governments did not explain this for public consumption; in the face of the largest European peace movement in history, such an explanation would have been too embarrassing.

As it happens the very dangerous deployment of the cruise and Pershing II made little sense even from a military standpoint. The so-called nuclear balance in Europe is roughly equal. NATO governments publicly stated that Europe was out of balance because of the Soviet SS-20 missile. NATO, they said, was behind the Warsaw Pact by "1,000 to nearly zero." This argument left out of account the many NATO-controlled sea- and air-based missiles and French missiles which are not under NATO command. All could be unleashed against the Soviet Union.

One effect of the NATO missile decision was the growth of the European peace movement. In each of the European NATO countries the movement rapidly became a major factor in the debate over the cruise and Pershing II and over NATO policy in general. (The peace movement is discussed in the article on EUROPEAN PEACE MOVEMENT.)

Deliberate attack by either side in the European stalemate is in reality highly unlikely. While NATO planners may or may not be interested only in defense, as they claim, they are unlikely to attack the Warsaw Pact simply because they are not fools. The history of attacks over land on the Soviet heartland, for that is what an invasion of the Warsaw Pact would probably mean, is deterrent enough for all but madmen. Hitler and Napoleon met disaster in Russia. The Allied intervention following World War I was a failure. A NATO army would be likely to meet a similar fate. It might also experience resistance from within its ranks.

On the Warsaw Pact side, a deliberate invasion is unlikely because the risks of such an operation would likewise be great and its results equally questionable. Western European countries, which would be populated with potential guerrillas and nonviolent resistance, would be an administrative nightmare for Warsaw Pact armies. Those armies are in any case unreliable. An invasion of Western Europe could lead to the end of the Warsaw Pact.[1]

Thus the two alliances are reduced to posturing, deploying ever more destructive weapons systems, and trying to gain "security" while becoming ever more insecure. Their military exercises are expensive and not only in financial terms. The NATO "Reforger" war games accidentally kill or injure several civilians and do millions of dollars worth of property damage annually. The military usefulness of preparations for such a highly improbable war is dubious. The sanity of such policies, however, is not in question. They are clearly insane. A tank commander who misreads a map and crosses the border could precipitate a serious incident. A routine patrol lost in the fog could start World War III. This is not security but a kind of mutual suicide pact.

The NATO-Warsaw Pact confrontation is convenient for the U.S. military and U.S. policymakers, though—as it is for their Soviet counterparts. It is far easier to persuade Congress to support a replay of World War II (the "good war") than to support counterinsurgency training. Thus when appropriations are discussed the "Soviet threat in Europe" is regularly trotted out. When the Pentagon talks about the draft, the "need" to mobilize for a European land war provides the rationale for draft registration, as it may do someday for renewed inductions. The weapons developed for this hypothetical conflict, and the troops recruited for it, are then adapted and trained for the only wars in which Western armies are now used: wars of intervention in the Third World.

Scenarios which depict a mass European land war, though they may appeal to Congressional nostalgia for the 1940s, have little to do with reality. Such a war would quickly lead to nuclear war. Even if—as European peace activists rightly fear—the holocaust was confined to Europe by unspoken agreement between the superpowers, it would kill hundreds of millions. More terrible still it would almost certainly release more than the 100 megatons of explosives which could be enough to trigger the "nuclear winter" discussed under NUCLEAR WEAPONS AND WAR. Thus a European war could in the long run result in human extinction.

To suggest that risking such a result is grossly irresponsible understates the case. Yet this is what passes for responsible policy every day among the NATO and Warsaw Pact policymakers.

(See also CONVENTIONAL WAR, HELICOPTER, NUCLEAR WEAPONS AND WAR, "SMART" WEAPONS)

1. *The War Atlas* rates three of seven Warsaw Pact armies as "barely reliable." Of the other four, only that of East Germany is rated "reliable." The remaining three are rated "probably reliable." "The International Military Order," in Michael Kidron and Dan Smith, *The War Atlas* (New York: Simon & Schuster, 1983).

228

Neutron Bomb: The neutron bomb, or enhanced radiation weapon, is a nuclear device designed to kill people with minimal damage to buildings, roads, and vehicles. Detonated in the air above its target, it emits lethal radiation over considerable distances but creates little or no blast, heat, and electromagnetic pulse effects as compared to ordinary nuclear weapons. It was first tested by the United States in 1963 and has also reportedly been tested by the Soviet Union.

In the United States, development of the neutron bomb was abandoned until the late 1970s, when antitank missiles with enhanced radiation warheads were proposed for use by NATO troops in Europe. Public outcry forced NATO to delay deployment of the weapon. The Reagan administration went ahead with production of neutron warheads during the early 1980s, but as of 1985 no neutron bombs had been deployed in Europe. The neutron bomb was, however, still under consideration as a possible NATO weapon.

The moral arguments against the neutron bomb are evident from its nature. It is a weapon whose sole function is to kill people. While all weapons kill, the neutron bomb couples with its killing power a brutal selectivity of targets which is practically impossible with ordinary explosives. Its radiation will not damage a building, but it will cause the people in that building to sicken and die very painfully over a period of hours. Thus it preserves property at the expense of human life.

Equally telling against deployment of the neutron bomb is the argument that it makes the use of nuclear weapons, up to and including large-scale "strategic" weapons, more likely. In its most recent form, the enhanced radiation device would be used on the battlefield. Its rays are capable of penetrating tank armor and disabling or killing the crew. For a commander facing a tank attack, the temptation to use antitank missiles with neutron warheads would be great indeed.

The U.S. military's procedures for using battlefield nuclear weapons are elaborate and, in theory, would prevent an unauthorized attack with neutron weapons. In theory they would also control the use of strategic weapons. Under combat conditions, all such safeguards would quickly disintegrate. *Any* use of nuclear weapons would breach the psychological barrier between nuclear and conventional war.

The theoretical distinction between tactical and strategic weapons, so important in academic nuclear strategy, would become meaningless. Use of the neutron bomb would be one step toward general nuclear war and the end of civilization.

(SEE ALSO: NATO AND WARSAW PACT, NUCLEAR PACIFISM, NUCLEAR STRATEGY, NUCLEAR WEAPONS AND WAR)

Nazis, Nonviolence and: Following World War II the military historian and strategist B. H. Liddell Hart interviewed a number of German generals for his book *The German Generals Talk*. He found that almost without exception the generals had had little difficulty containing violent resistance to the Nazi regimes, but reported significant problems or even failure in countering nonviolent resistance. Liddell Hart attributed this astonishing finding to "the *relatively* humane tradition in which [the German generals] had been brought up."[1] It is, however, equally a tribute to the power of nonviolent resistance.

The most significant nonviolent resistance to the Nazis occurred in Denmark, Norway, and Holland. In France, the rescue of Jews in Le Chambon (see separate article LE CHAMBON) was probably the most important nonviolent effort. Nonviolent resistance also occurred in Belgium and, most impressively, in Nazi Germany itself. Resistance there included individual war resistance such as that of Franz Jagerstatter (see separate article) and resistance to Nazi policies such as that of German Quakers and the White Rose. Actions by German Quakers included attempts to supply warm clothing to Jews being transported to death camps; foster care for Jewish orphans; hiding Jews from the Gestapo; and public opposition to Nazi atrocities.[2] The White Rose, a student-based group in Bavaria, distributed anti-Nazi literature. Most of its members were executed. One who survived, Franz Mueller, is still active in the German peace movement. In Berlin in 1943, a group of Jewish prisoners' non-Jewish wives stopped the Gestapo from transporting their husbands to the death camps. In 1954 Annedore Leber collected and documented the histories of sixty-four men and women who resisted the Nazis, most at the cost of their lives.[3]

The German generals interviewed by Liddell Hart were baffled by nonviolent resistance; it had no parallel in their experience and they had neither the training nor the knowledge to cope with it. In common with the various guerrilla movements in Europe, nonviolent resistance did not threaten the direct overthrow of the occupation regimes. But it limited their power in ways not possible for more violent movements.

In Norway in 1942 the government of Vidkun Quisling tried to establish a fascist corporative state modeled on Mussolini's Italy. Quisling selected teachers as the first corporation and created a compulsory teacher's organization. At the urging of the underground, between eight thousand and ten thousand teachers out of twelve thousand signed a petition refusing to participate in the corporation. The resistance persisted despite government threats to dismiss all teachers, the arrest of one thousand male teachers, and other repressive actions. Quisling was eventually forced to abandon his plans.[4]

Danish resistance continued throughout the occupation. Because the resistance mixed nonviolent methods with more violent ones such as sabotage, it is difficult to arrive at a clear evaluation of the effects of nonviolence in Denmark. One historian concludes that "The most reliable authorities on the resistance in Denmark hold the view that it was the work of the sabotage groups which set off reactions amongst the civilian population generally, giving rise to nonviolent forms of resistance such as strikes and boycotts, and not *vice versa*.[5] It is clear, however, that one of the most spectacular achievements of the Danish resistance—the rescue of approximately sixty-five hundred of Denmark's seven thousand Jews—was a purely nonviolent action. Following the collapse of the Danish government in August 1943, the German military assumed power in Denmark. In October of that year Hitler's government ordered the arrest of all Danish Jews. Warned by a German official, Georg Duckwitz, the Danish resistance managed to transport all but five hundred Danish Jews to Sweden, mostly in fishing boats.

Duckwitz' role in the escape of the Danish Jews "showed

that such an inhumane policy could cause opposition amongst the Germans themselves so that they were prepared to risk the consequences of giving a warning."[6] It is unlikely, however, that Duckwitz or any other German official would have acted to save the Jews in the absence of a resistance movement.

None of these resistance movements was planned. Failure to plan in advance—by establishing criteria for civil servants to follow in resisting an occupation government, for instance—led to unwitting collaboration in some cases, notably in the Netherlands.[7] Nonetheless the resistance movements were successful in limiting the power of occupation governments. Considering the totalitarian conditions under which they operated this was a significant achievement indeed.

(See also: HITLER, ADOLF, THE HOLOCAUST, LE CHAMBON, NONVIOLENCE)

1. B. H. Liddell Hart, "Lessons from Resistance Movements—Guerrilla and Non-Violent," in Adam Roberts, ed., *Civilian Resistance as a National Defense* (Middlesex, Eng.: Pelican Books, 1969), p. 240.

2. Michael Seadle, *Quakers in Nazi Germany* (Chicago: Progresive Publisher, 401 E. 32nd St., Chicago, IL 60616).

3. Annedore Leber, ed., *Conscience in Revolt: Sixty-Four Stories of Resistance in Germany 1933–45* (London: Vallentine, Mitchell, 1957).

4. Gene Sharp, *The Politics of Nonviolent Action* (Boston: Porter Sargent, 1973), quoted in Murray Polner, ed., *The Disarmament Catalogue* (New York: The Pilgrim Press, 1982), p. 171. See also Magne Skodvin, "Norwegian Non-Violent Resistance During the German Occupation," in Roberts, *op. cit.*, pp. 162–181.

5. Jeremy Bennett, "The Resistance Against the German Occupation of Denmark 1940–45," in Roberts, *op. cit.*, p. 195–196.

6. *Ibid.*, p. 199.

7. Theodor Ebert, "Organization in Civilian Defense," in Roberts, *op. cit.*, pp. 299–301.

Nonviolence: The search for alternatives to war has led to many proposals, ranging from William James' "moral equivalent to war" to world law. Most far-reaching of these is that which would substitute nonviolent, civilian-based resistance for conventional military defense.

Among pacifists the proposal has an obvious attraction. It would provide a morally acceptable answer to the question of national security. It also provides a way out of the dilemmas posed by totalitarian regimes. Among nonpacifists, such as Commander Stephen King-Hall, nonviolence is seen as the only feasible response to military threat in a nuclear age.

Nearly all programs for nonviolent action include proposals for nonviolent peacemaking—mediation, steps toward disarmament, and so on—and conflict resolution. This article discusses nonviolent action only as a possible substitute for military defense. (Discussion of some other peacemaking programs can be found in separate articles on NUCLEAR FREEZE MOVEMENT and NUCLEAR FREE ZONES.)

Nonviolence, Social Change, and Defense

The virtues of nonviolent action as a method of achieving social change are clear. Although the most famous nonviolent campaigns are those of Gandhi and Martin Luther King, Jr., nonviolent tactics—ranging from persuasion to voter registration to strikes and boycotts—have in fact been used extensively and effectively. This has been true even in countries where governments have been highly repressive, such as Chile and Brazil.

Supporters of military defense dismiss nonviolent defense, however, usually on the ground that it "would not work." While this argument is in part based on a gross overestimate of the benefits of military defense, it is also based on ignorance. Historical examples such as the Czech resistance of 1968 and Norwegian resistance during World War II show that nonviolent resistance, undertaken even without prior planning or organization, can cause serious difficulty for an invading or occupying army. The British military historian B. H. Liddell Hart reported that German generals he interviewed after World War II had more difficulty containing nonviolent than violent resistance. Again this occurred in countries which before occupation had no plan for nonviolent resistance, no strategy, and a population largely untrained in nonviolent tactics.[1]

Thus though never tried on a large scale as a substitute for military defense or other uses of military force, nonviolence clearly has potential. It is, at minimum, an alternative strategy to military defense. Whether it is more than this is a separate question discussed below.

The Uses of War

War is commonly held to serve four "legitimate" functions: settlement of international disputes; struggle against injustice (e.g., guerrilla wars of liberation); deterrence; and defense of national territory. Other, less legitimate functions of war include territorial expansion and intervention in the affairs of other countries.

Whether or not war can actually accomplish its functions, the public believes that it can. Thus if nonviolence is to be accepted as a substitute for war, it must be seen as capable of settling disputes, overcoming injustice, deterring attack, and defending territory. That nonviolence is unsuited to territorial expansion and interventionist adventures says more about these functions of war than it does about nonviolence. It is the purported function, not the tactic used, that is wrong.

It is clear that nonviolent methods can settle international disputes. In a world less committed to the use of military force this would be obvious beyond the need for argument, for war has long ceased to be—if it ever was—a means of settling disputes. The costs of modern warfare, in human and material terms, far outweigh any conceivable benefits. Its aftermath is almost invariably the destruction of one adversary or both, though in some cases there is no aftermath because the war becomes a long and bloody stalemate and the problems allegedly solved, as in Europe after World War I, usually resurface in another, often far more terrible form. Thus nonviolent means are the *only* ones which offer real hope for settlement of international disputes.

At the same time the use of nonviolence by King and Gandhi, among others, demonstrates that nonviolence is a potent force against injustice. It is improbable that Gandhi could have achieved the liberation of India by violence, and it would have been flatly impossible for King to have achieved what he did by using violence. In the one case the British would have been even more ruthless than they were in re-

234

pressing the independence movement, and in the other, the civil rights movement would have forfeited nearly all popular support, and not only among whites.

Violent tactics undercut the justice which those who use them are seeking. This is so partly because the disciplines of violence are unsuitable for any but totalitarian governments. Violence, which is difficult to control in the best of circumstances, cannot achieve any end but destruction without centralized discipline. The leaders of violent movements, who acquire totalitarian and repressive habits, usually cannot change these habits the instant they seize power. There are exceptions, but in general violence and violent tactics tend toward totalitarianism and elitism, not toward democracy and shared power.

As to the third function of war, deterrence, it is possible—though by no means certain—that by providing a defense which is difficult to counter by standard military methods nonviolence could function as a deterrent to an invader. The difficulty with any such prediction is the difficulty with all deterrence theory: it is untestable because so many factors would be involved in a decision on whether to invade. Nonetheless there is no doubt that, as in Czechoslovakia in 1968, nonviolent resistance could make an invasion very troublesome indeed. It could also undermine the aggressor army's morale. Thus the existence of an organized and well-publicized nonviolent defense program would surely be one factor—and a weighty one—in a decision on whether or not to attack another country.

There remains the question of defense of territory. Nonviolent strategists argue with some force that nonviolent defense, particularly in a nuclear age, is the only means which *can* defend territory. Their critics suggest that nonviolence could not defend a country's borders.

This dispute, though fundamental, is at least partly a matter of definition. If "defend the country's borders" means literally "stop an invading army at the border," nonviolent tactics have little chance of providing defense. Nonviolent strategists generally concede that resistance to an invasion can begin with delaying tactics at the border, but because nonviolent tactics take time to become established and to work a country using civilian-based defense would have to accept at least some period of occupation.

To suggest, however, that this proves the virtues of military defense is to ignore history. There are almost no instances where a military force has stopped an invasion at the borders of the country it was defending. World War I on the Western Front was fought entirely on French and Belgian territory, some considerable distance beyond the borders of those countries, yet, at bottom, it was a defense against an invasion. World War II in Europe was largely a matter of invasion and counterinvasion; first by the Germans into France, Eastern Europe, and Russia, and then by the Allies into Germany. Military resistance did not stop these invasions at the border, and the French attempt to do so—the Maginot Line—is today cited as quintessential military folly.

The examples could easily be multiplied. Yet even assuming that military resistance might in the past have stopped an invasion at a country's border, "defending the border" is not a meaningful term in today's warfare. Aircraft, missiles, and the increased mobility of armies have rendered such defense not only meaningless but highly dangerous for the peoples being defended.

A clear example of the folly of military defense is the border between East and West Germany. This inner German border is heavily guarded by military forces on both sides. Its defense would consist of extensive use of modern conventional weapons, possible use of nuclear weapons, and in general the destruction of the territory being defended. It is hard to see how this could benefit anyone or be in any way worse than a nonviolent defense which impeded the invasion only nonviolently and resisted occupying troops from within. In the strictest of cost-benefit analyses, military defense today must inevitably be found wanting.

Nonviolence as Strategy and Commitment

The difficulty with considering nonviolence as one strategy among others, as "pragmatic" nonviolent strategists are prone to do, is twofold. On the one hand widespread use of nonviolence would transform the system and human relations in

236

ways which, though not totally foreseeable, would differ sharply from the effects of any chosen military strategy. On the other hand effective nonviolent action is difficult or impossible without a firm commitment to nonviolent discipline—a commitment generally going beyond that required to choose one strategy as against another. Thus Gandhi says that nonviolence begins in the mind, and, if it does not, it is likely to fail.

From the pragmatic point of view, however, maintenance of nonviolent discipline is also essential. A break in the discipline would allow an occupying army an opportunity for violent repression. As Liddell Hart says:

[The German generals] were experts in violence, and had been trained to deal with opponents who used that method. But other forms of resistance baffled them—and all the more in proportion as the methods were subtle and concealed. It was a relief to them when resistance became violent, and when nonviolent forms were mixed with guerrilla action, thus making it easier to combine drastic suppressive action against both at the same time.[2]

Thus for nonviolent resistance to be most effective, deep commitment to nonviolent discipline is needed and, preferably, training in maintaining it.

The Dynamics of Nonviolence

Gene Sharp, one of the major theorists of nonviolence, has said that nonviolence involves a kind of "moral jiu-jitsu." This characterization, though terse, encapsulates the particular nature of nonviolent action. Nonviolence is not passive. Though it can involve persuasion, it is not merely this. Nor is it a form of coercion like that used by the military. Nonviolence seeks to establish a human bond between the resister and those being resisted. In the long run this changes the oppressor and can transform the system which has created the oppression in the first place.

The most basic assumption of nonviolent theory, and especially of nonviolent civilian defense, is that government—and, by extension, occupation—functions only with the consent of the governed. This means literal physical cooperation. If such cooperation is withdrawn in a nonviolent way the government faces two choices. It can modify its policies, or it can repress the resistance. The latter choice is not in general attractive because the resisters have provided no excuse for violence. To enforce repression against unarmed people who resist without fighting back risks undermining the morale of the occupying army. This is too great a risk for many regimes to take. Nonviolence which uses "go-slow" tactics and other more subtle forms of resistance can baffle an occupying force, since it can make ordinary administration difficult or impossible while providing no focus for repression.

This does not suggest that nonviolent resisters will not suffer terribly. Gandhi's movement and King's movement accepted great suffering as the price of their freedom. But in the end both prevailed because it became impossible to enforce repression against people who would not respond to it with violence.

Techniques of Nonviolence

Gene Sharp lists 198 distinct nonviolent techniques which have been used in history.[3] Sharp summarizes these techniques as follows:

- Protest and persuasion: Including leafletting, picketing, marches, and teach-ins.
- Social Noncooperation: Including student strikes and social boycotts.
- Economic Noncooperation: Including war tax resistance, consumer boycotts, and labor strikes.
- Political noncooperation: Including draft resistance and refusal to obey unjust laws.
- Nonviolent Intervention: Civil disobedience generally, nonviolent blockages, sit-ins, nonviolent obstructions.

Some pragmatic strategists include sabotage of property as a nonviolent technique. While arguable, this position poses serious difficulties. In a property-conscious society, sabotage of property is often considered a form of violence which justifies violent repression. Thus the use of property sabotage carries risks which outweigh its potential benefits.

Far less dangerous and more clearly acceptable is sabotage of bureaucratic systems. This technique is frequently not only low in risk but completely legal. An example is the breakdown of the Selective Service System in the early 1970s, which was brought on by a combination of civil disobedience and mass use of rights which were provided by law. In the event the hundreds of thousands of legal appeals filed by men subject to the draft were probably the determining factor in making the draft unworkable.

In an occupation or totalitarian situation, sabotage of bureaucratic systems may take the form of a perfectly legal slowdown undertaken in a cordial and smiling way. It may include losing papers, "accidentally" erasing computer tapes, and so on. The possibilities are limited primarily by the imagination of the nonviolent resister. Such actions would be difficult to repress, and they would make administration of the government a matter of extreme difficulty. In order to be most effective, however, they should be part of a coordinated campaign so that if one resister is fired from a bureaucratic job the next person in the post will continue the resistance, perhaps in different ways.

Obstacles to Nonviolent Defense

The obstacles to the use of nonviolence as defense are not those usually cited by militarists. They relate instead to the more general problems of defense in modern warfare and to acceptability of nonviolence to governments as now constituted.

Military defense is, as shown above and in other articles, extremely costly in material and human terms. More than that, however, it is impossible in the case of missile attack and to a lesser extent in aerial bombardment generally. This is also true of nonviolent defense for there is no complete effective defense against such attack.

None of this invalidates nonviolence. It suggests, however,

that nonviolent defense of one country is not sufficient to end war or increase national security. What is required is a strategy which will prevent missiles from being deployed and launched in the first place. Military defense and preparations for it cannot provide such a strategy. They are *built around* deployment of missiles and the threat to use them. Thus while it provides no defense against aerial attack, in the long run nonviolence offers the real hope of stopping such attacks before they begin—which is the only way they will be stopped.

A far more serious obstacle to widespread use of nonviolent resistance is the fact that it is a technique based not in an elite or a government but in the population at large. It cannot work without popular participation. Thus it is the only inherently democratic form of national defense. Moreover because it seeks to change those who enforce the system being resisted, to break through to them as human beings, nonviolence in principle undercuts *all* oppressive systems.

This is an obvious threat to governments, which even among the democracies engage in some degree of repression. Although a democratic government operates to a greater or lesser extent by popular consent, it does not empower the public in the way that nonviolent training would. Thus it is an open question whether any current government would accept nonviolent defense as national policy—not because such defense would fail, but because a people trained in nonviolent resistance would be a constant check on government abuses. From the government's point of view, an obedient and disciplined army which follows its leaders without question would be far more desirable than a nonviolently-trained citizenry which can if it chooses block government actions it finds unacceptable.

This suggests strongly that nonviolent strategists must look beyond the question of national defense to the larger question of transformation of the war system itself. If governments will not adopt nonviolent defense, then the public must learn to defend itself against the government's military follies.

This is in fact being done. In Europe the nonviolent peace movement seeks to interpose itself as a neutral force between the Eastern and Western alliances. It does this in the name of

Europe, but even more so in the interest of humanity. Based on this model nonviolence would be not simply a "better" form of national defense, but a defense for humanity against the destructive forces the nations are now empowered to unleash.

Transformation of the system thus becomes the overriding goal of nonviolent action. National defense is of far less importance for if the war system does not change there will sooner or later be no nations to defend.

Nonviolence and the United States

Despite the difficulties of considering nonviolence solely as a form of national defense, it is worthwhile to imagine how civilian resistance could be used in one country. This can show the feasibility of nonviolent defense, and it can also show how one country's adoption of nonviolent defense could begin to transform the war system.

Paradoxically one obvious candidate for successful nonviolent defense is also the greatest military power: the United States. Strategically the U.S. is well situated for any form of defense. It is bordered on the north and south by friendly neighbors and on the east and west by oceans thousands of miles wide. The nearest hostile bases are in Cuba, ninety miles from American shores. The U.S. is large geographically, complex politically, and administered by bureaucracies which an invader could not replace without extreme difficulty.

All this means that the defense of the United States could be accomplished with far smaller military forces than are currently at the president's disposal. It also means that the country is ideally situated for nonviolent defense.

There is, as noted above, no adequate defense against aerial attack, particularly missile attack. An invader would, however, gain little by such an attack. If the bombardment were conventional, the attacker could not expect to annihilate all defenders; the history of aerial bombardment shows that this has never occurred. An occupation army following after the bombardment would find defenders (either nonviolent or military) still alive, while means of transportation, roads, and so on, would be severely damaged. This would make occupation against any form of resistance difficult. If the bombardment were a large-scale nuclear attack, it would render most of the U.S. uninhabitable and, as shown in the article NUCLEAR WEAPONS AND WAR, might precipitate a "nuclear winter" and amount to suicide for the attacker.

Despite the objections to a preliminary bombardment, such tactics are common military practice and would be likely in any conventional attack on the U.S. The logistics of the occupation that followed, however, would frighten any sane general. An army is only as good as its line of supply and cannot easily cross three thousand miles of ocean, let alone sustain itself, once at its destination. Its troops would be far from home and thus liable to drastic declines in morale. Confronted with a nonviolently trained citizenry, they would face the choice of regularly using violence against unarmed people or seeing the occupation's administration break down. Their own bombardment would have made getting around and obtaining local supplies far more difficult. The occupying army would be dependent on a three thousand-mile line of supply. They would be forced to unload their own ships, arrange their own transportation, and perhaps set up their own administration. This would lead to the phenomenon that Liddell Hart calls "overstretch." For a military force overstretch leads to collapse.

It is impossible to predict whether any of this would in fact occur should the United States adopt nonviolent defense. The difficulties of an invasion and the possibility of widespread citizen resistance would in all likelihood be strong deterrents in themselves.

The positive effects of a nonviolent policy would, however, be incalculable. United States military forces would no longer be available to intervene in civil wars. The U.S. would no longer threaten the world with mass destruction. And abandonment of violence would lead to an immediate decrease in the general level of violence in the world—by, for example, stopping U.S. arms sales. America's role as world policeman, with all its terrible results, would end.

Whether the change in United States policy would lead to a larger transformation in the world system is unknowable. One can only speculate. However, the U.S. is not about to adopt a nonviolent policy. Quite the contrary. Thus like the peace movement elsewhere, the American peace movement cannot look to its government to change the system. It must instead seek, as it has done, to change the system directly.

Two Spurious Objections

It is commonly suggested that Gandhi and, to a lesser extent, Martin Luther King, Jr., succeeded with their nonviolent campaigns only because they were dealing with civilized oppressors or, in the case of King, a country in which the basic law and social consensus favored them. Critics of nonviolence also suggest that because nonviolent strategies often depend on influencing public opinion, nonviolence is somehow a failure. Nothing could be further from the truth.

Gandhi's nonviolent campaign succeeded *despite* British civilization. The British record, particularly in the nineteenth century, had been as bloody and racist as that of most other nations, save Hitler's Germany and Stalin's Russia. In repressing a Moslem revolt, British troops slaughtered ten thousand Dervishes at Omdurman (1896): the architect of the slaughter, Lord Kitchener, earned a peerage for his troubles.[4] British troops had repressed violent rebellions in India with heavy casualties for the rebels. They showed little compunction about firing into crowds of unarmed Indian civilians during Gandhi's campaign. Thus the suggestion that the British were especially civilized, while flattering to the British, is unsupported by the facts.

So, too, with King's campaign, which while its aims were far more limited, encountered entrenched and violent opposition that led to beatings, jailings, and even death for nonviolent resisters. Nor did the social consensus favor King's campaign. Though his name is remembered now with a holiday, Martin Luther King, Jr., was considered by many to be a dangerous radical while he was alive and was harassed by the FBI. His support among the general population was by no means widespread, and racism in various forms persists in the United States today. King's campaign succeeded because of the power of nonviolence and the steadfastness of its resistance, not because he reflected an existing consensus.

243

The argument that nonviolence somehow does not work if it seeks to change public opinion is unworthy of extensive comment. It is perfectly true that Gandhi tried to influence British public opinion and that King sought to change American public opinion. This was an effective and nonviolent way of achieving their goals. When a military force uses similar tactics it is called "psychological warfare," and is considered a respectable tactic even though it seldom works.

The ability of nonviolent movements to change public hearts and minds is in fact one of their strengths. Violence, whether in India or in the southern United States, would have failed utterly in this regard and led to bloody repression of the two movements. It is hardly surprising that a military force generally fails to influence enemy public opinion, while a nonviolent movement succeeds more frequently than not.

By changing the hearts and minds of people in Britain, Gandhi gained independence. King made major gains for civil rights in the same way. These results hardly show that nonviolence fails; they are instead one of the enduring strengths of nonviolent action.

Nonviolence and Revolution

Critics of nonviolence argue that it cannot overthrow an entrenched, ruthless and unjust power structure. According to this argument, nonviolence, though in principle revolutionary, cannot reasonably promise success if those in power have no scruples.

Questions about the best methods for achieving social change are difficult and painful not only for pacifists but for all who seek justice and peace. They are also, however, impossible to answer with certainty. No route to social change can guarantee success. On the contrary: Movements, whether violent or nonviolent, frequently fail or lose their initial impetus. Ideals are betrayed; liberation becomes oppression. History provides ample evidence that justice is never easily or perfectly achieved.

The difficulty of social change, however, is not a defect of nonviolence. It is part of the human condition. We cannot predict all of the consequences of our acts. When a movement seeks major social change, it cannot determine the outcome; it can control only the means used to seek that outcome. If those means are violent, the movement—whether it succeeds or fails—will do extensive damage to people or property or both. Violence, far from building a movement for social change, frequently increases factionalism and destroys the movement from within. The aftermath of violence is bitterness and division. The aftermath of failed violence is almost always increased government repression. This destruction is not an accidental by-product. It is a consequence of the means chosen.

A simple example will illustrate. A nonviolent sit-in may not achieve its objectives, but it will not destroy the building where it takes place. Nor, unless it is met with police violence, will it result in death or injury. But a time bomb placed in the same building will inevitably do damage to the building and to anyone who happens to be within range of the explosion. Government repression, decrease in popular support for social change, media fascination with the violent and spectacular—all make peace and justice more difficult to achieve. The consequences of violence are all too evident from history.

It is clear that violence is, at best, an untrustworthy and risky means of achieving social change. More significantly, the use of violence does nothing to change the balance of power between the established order and those who seek change. The established order is based on violence. It is far better armed than those who would overthrow it. In modern industrial society, armed revolutionaries who confront the system openly would be quickly annihilated by government forces. Those who have sought revolution through terrorism or other violent means have developed little or none of the popular support needed to mount and sustain a genuine revolution. Persuading the public not to cooperate with the established order is the aim of all revolutionary movements. But violent means have generally done no more than frighten the public, in some cases turning them against all social change. The historical examples of this process are many. The popular reaction against terrorism and the utter failure of violent revolutionaries in the United States during the Vietnam era are among the best-known.

Nonviolence, on the other hand, can build popular support and give the people—even the weakest among them—a means of seeking justice. It can change the balance of power between the established order and the public because it takes advantage of government's fundamental weakness: its dependence on the cooperation of the governed.

In the Third World, where violent revolution and guerrilla warfare are far more common than they are in the West, the record of nonviolence is encouraging. Gandhi's nonviolent campaign in India remains the largest successful movement of national liberation. Following the ill-fated Falkland War, Argentina, by early 1985, had achieved without violence a democratic government pledged to prosecute government officials responsible for the outrages of the older dictatorship. Brazil, home of the largest nonviolent movement in the world, had held democratic elections for the first time in twenty-one years. And the most effective pressures against the South African *apartheid* system, both from inside and from outside the country, were nonviolent.

In the early 1980s, attacks on the Sandinista regime in Nicaragua by right-wing rebel forces (the *contras*) raised difficult questions for pacifists and others committed to peace in Central America. The Sandinista regime had wide popular support and had begun a major program of social reform. The *contras*, who were supported by the United States, fought with little scruple and posed a serious threat to the Sandinistas.

Many who supported the Sandinistas argued that the *contras* must be fought by military means. The Nicaraguan government did in fact arm its citizens and take strong military measures against the *contras*. But the key to stopping the *contra* attacks was not to be found in the jungles of Central America, but in the White House, the Congress of the United States and peace proposals made by other Central American countries (the *contadora* process). The *contra* operations were dependent on support from the U.S. As long as there was U.S. support, the *contras* could not be defeated on the ground. But they could be stopped by halting the aid and pressuring the United States to join the *contadora* process in good faith. These were purely nonviolent means—and the only ones which promised long-term success.

Nonviolence and Aggression

The basis of nonviolent resistance and its possible application to the United States are discussed above. There remains the question of whether such a defense would be effective against ruthless aggression.

No good answer is possible to this question, primarily because nonviolence has never been tried on a large scale. On a small scale, it has produced results which belie the assumption that it will inevitably fail. The Czech resistance of 1968 held out for weeks in a militarily untenable situation. Hundreds of thousands of Jews were rescued from the Holocaust by nonviolent means. Nonviolent resistance made Norway virtually impossible for its Nazi-sponsored government to rule.

There are other examples. But these were hastily improvised responses to aggression. Nonviolent resistance in these cases was not ultimately successful. Critics of nonviolence suggest that these historical defeats prove the futility of civilian resistance.

This conclusion is unwarranted. Makeshift military resistance against overwhelmingly superior forces has failed repeatedly. Does this "prove" that military defense will not work? No advocate of military defense would accept such an argument. Yet it is commonly assumed that any defeat for nonviolence disproves the case for all nonviolence. This is an error. There has been no real test of civilian-based resistance.

The difficulty with all such argument is that it addresses the wrong question. It assumes that nonviolence is merely an alternative form of national defense. It inserts this narrow form of nonviolence into a desperately flawed system without other substantial changes. It then demands that nonviolent, civilian-based resistance produce miracles.

Substituting one form of defense for another, however, will not end the system that produced the problem. Aggression has roots in history, in social conditions and in policies made

247

by governments. Thus the debate should not be about whether nonviolent resistance could have stopped Hitler, but about why there was a Hitler at all. Once an aggressor like Hitler comes to power with a large military force at his disposal, the situation is *already* lost. Neither violent nor nonviolent resistance is guaranteed to succeed, and both will lead to heavy casualties.

World War II did not represent the inevitable triumph of good over evil; nor did it vindicate the war system. But for Hitler's own military blunders, it might have led to defeat for the Allies and the entrenchment of Nazism in Europe for many years. Neither military means nor nonviolence could have guaranteed the defeat of Hitler once he was in power. The time to defeat him was *before* he came to power.

History cannot be changed, but it provides object lessons for the future. Hitler's rise to power was made possible in part by World War I and its aftermath. The rise of Pol Pot and the monstrous direction his revolution took was made possible in part by the U.S. intervention in Kampuchea (Cambodia). Violence in both cases helped to create the evils which, it is argued, only violence could destroy.

Nonviolent resistance alone does not promise a way out of the trap into which the war system has led us. Other nonviolent paths to peace—reasoned debate, negotiation, conflict resolution—must supplement it. The end to which these means would lead us is, like all human goals, likely to be changed by the very process of achieving it. But nonviolent means, in their many forms, give hope that the war system can be ended. This cannot be said of violence. It was violence that made the trap we are in. We cannot expect to free ourselves by using the very means that imprisoned us.

(See also: CONVENTIONAL WAR, CZECH RESISTANCE, GANDHI, MOHANDAS K., KING, MARTIN LUTHER, JR., NAZIS AND NONVIOLENCE, TOTALITARIANISM, NONVIOLENCE AND, NUCLEAR WEAPONS AND WAR)

1. B. H. Liddell Hart, "Lessons from Resistance Movements—Guerrilla and Non-Violent," in Adam Roberts, ed., *Civilian Resistance as a National Defense* (Middlesex, Eng.: Pelican, 1969), p. 239.
2. *Ibid.*, p. 240.

3. See generally, Gene Sharp, *The Politics of Nonviolent Action* (Boston: Porter Sargent, 1973).

4. Alan Morehead, *The White Nile* (New York: Harper & Bros., 1960), p. 337.

Nonviolent Intervention Forces: Nonviolent intervention in conflict situations takes a variety of forms. Among the methods that have been used are mediation, legal action, silent witness, legislative lobbying, and civil disobedience.

A relatively recent development has been the attempt to develop trained groups of volunteers to intervene in war zones or areas of international tensions. The first such experiment, called the World Peace Brigade (WPB), was begun in late 1961 at a conference at Rumanna Friends School near Beirut, Lebanon. Among its sponsors were A. J. Muste, Bertrand Russell, Martin Buber, Danilo Dolci, and Vinoba Bhave, who had become spiritual leader of the nonviolent movement in India following the death of Gandhi.

The Beirut conference called for establishment of a group of one thousand volunteers who would be ready "to give substantial blocs of time and to be on call for emergency service in international projects related to the abolition of war and the use of nonviolent attitudes and methods in the achievements of national independence and basic social change eliminating poverty and exploitation."[1]

The WPB had its greatest success in Africa, where it helped establish a nonviolent training center in Dar es Salaam, Tanganyika (now Tanzania), and aided the movement for the liberation of Zambia. A later project, the voyage of the *Everyman III* to protest Soviet nuclear testing, failed. Financial difficulties finally brought about the end of the Brigade.

A more recent effort, sponsored by a coalition of churches in cooperation with Peace Brigades International, was the Witness for Peace. This tried to develop a nonviolent presence on the Nicaragua-Honduras border, where United States-funded right-wing guerrillas regularly attacked Nicaraguan territory. Organizers of the effort hoped the presence of a nonviolent witness on the border would deter the guerrillas, or *contras,* from their operations. At the same time those who participated were able to report to the American public on conditions in Nicaragua. Doctors and nurses, and others with technical skills, also provided direct and immediate help to the people of Nicaragua.

Because this kind of nonviolent intervention is a new development, it is too early to evaluate its effects. The World Peace Brigade was probably unrealistic in hoping to recruit a standing nonviolent force. The Witness for Peace, on the other hand, was an ad hoc effort to which volunteers committed what time they could, without being on call for emergency intervention around the world. As such it may provide a realistic and workable model for future nonviolent intervention.

It is clear, however, that direct nonviolent intervention alone could not stop the U.S. covert war on Nicaragua. The source of the violence on the border was the U.S. Central Intelligence Agency and, more broadly, U.S. policy in Central America. The weapons of the *contras* were supplied by the U.S. Thus the border presence was most effective when supplemented by pressure on the U.S. government to end its attempt to overthrow the government of Nicaragua.

(See also: CENTRAL AMERICA, GUERRILLA WARFARE, MUSTE, A. J., NONVIOLENCE, UNITED STATES)

1. Nat Hentoff, *Peace Agitator: The Story of A. J. Muste* (New York: A. J. Muste Memorial Institute, 1982), p. 221. A brief history of the World Peace Brigade will be found on pp. 220–228.

Nuclear Free Zones: A nuclear free zone is an area from which nuclear weapons have been excluded, either by treaty or by legislative action. The prohibition on nuclear weapons can extend to deployment, manufacture, transportation of weapons through the zone, or various combinations of these prohibitions. Declaring an area nuclear free serves several purposes. It protects the zone from the immediate effects of an accidental nuclear explosion or other nuclear accident. In theory it makes the area a less likely target in the event of nuclear war. And most important, it makes a public statement against nuclear war and preparations for nuclear war.

Treaties creating nuclear free zones have had mixed success. The Antarctic, which has at present little military value or interest, is nuclear free by treaty. This situation is likely to continue despite international frictions over mineral rights in the area, since deploying nuclear weapons there, much less using them in combat, could serve no conceivable purpose.

The first continent to become a nuclear free zone was South America under the 1967 Treaty of Tlatelolco. Whether this treaty will continue to have any effect remains to be seen. Latin American countries such as Brazil and Argentina are capable of producing nuclear weapons in the near future and have not signed the Nuclear Non-Proliferation Treaty. It is also possible that nuclear weapons have already been brought into the zone, in violation of the treaty, on nuclear-capable British ships used in the Falklands (Malvinas) War. These ships, which are normally used for NATO purposes and which normally carry nuclear weapons, were not refitted before setting out for the South Atlantic.

Japan, which has been a nuclear free zone since World War II, has been far more scrupulous about nuclear weapons than about conventional rearmament. Although Japan's constitution prohibits any Japanese army, the Japanese Defense Force—an army in all but name—numbers 245,000 and is armed with modern conventional weapons, many of them supplied by the United States. Because of popular pressure stemming from the Hiroshima and Nagasaki bombings, however, the Japanese government has not sought nuclear weapons. When a nuclear-armed U.S. Navy ship entered Japanese waters in 1982, popular pressure forced the ship's withdrawal.

An encouraging development has been the growth of many local nuclear free zones. The most spectacular of these is the Greater London area, whose council declared nuclear-free status in response to the Thatcher government's call for cities to initiate civil defense programs. The council also provided assistance for a study of the effects of nuclear attack on London, now published as *London After the Bomb* (1982).[1]

In the United States no major city has declared itself nuclear free. Many have refused to cooperate with the government's civil defense programs, however, and some have adopted ordinances which amount to declaration of nuclear-free status. Cambridge, Massachusetts, commissioned a detailed study of a nuclear attack on Cambridge and distributed the results to its citizens. Many smaller towns, particularly in New England, have adopted nuclear-free ordinances.

A single local nuclear free zone is small and unlikely by itself to have much effect. But many together could make nuclear strategy a near impossibility because they would make deployment and transportation of nuclear weapons extremely difficult. Administration spokespersons have actually expressed fears about the growth of the nuclear-free zone movement. Administration fears, in this case, are grounds for hope that the nuclear-free zone movement can be an effective tool against nuclear war.

(See also EUROPEAN PEACE MOVEMENT, NATO AND WARSAW PACT, NUCLEAR STRATEGY, NUCLEAR WEAPONS AND WAR)

1. *London After the Bomb* (Oxford and New York: Oxford University Press, 1982).

Nuclear Freeze Movement: The most successful action by the peace movement during the 1980s was the campaign for a bilateral (U.S. and U.S.S.R.) freeze on production, testing, and deployment of nuclear weapons. City councils and voters across the United States approved resolutions supporting such a freeze; the proposal had widespread though ambivalent support in Congress; and on June 12, 1982, the freeze movement organized the largest peace demonstration in U.S. history, bringing approximately one million people to New York to support the proposal.

Popular support for the nuclear freeze was so great that even the Reagan administration, which had budgeted $305 billion for military expenditures in fiscal year 1985 alone, tried to cut the ground from beneath the movement. The administration's proposals included Strategic Arms Reduction Talks, a change of name from the previous Strategic Arms Limitation

Talks; an alternative freeze proposal; and the so-called build-down proposal.

The START talks predictably, failed, becoming merely a new name for the political maneuvering associated with arms talks in recent years. The administration's freeze proposal was no such thing: it would have allowed the president's proposed military buildup to proceed apace and *then* have sought a negotiated freeze. Build-down, which would destroy two (or three) older weapons for each newer one deployed, is a cruel hoax. It would allow "force modernization"—i.e., the creation of ever more terrible instruments of death—while disposing of older weapons that might have been destroyed in any case.

These responses to the nuclear freeze movement are hardly responsive. It is, however, significant that they were made at all. By following a strategy which combined public demonstration with grass roots organizing, the freeze movement had forced a response from an administration which had committed itself to the futile search for advantage in the arms race, or peace through strength. This was no small achievement.

The freeze proposal, though complex to implement, was simple, straightforward, and what is far more important not biased toward either side in the Cold War. Under it both sides would simply stop where they are in the arms race. They would not build new weapons. They would not test or develop them. They would not deploy them. Each side would have the right to verify the other's good faith adherence to the agreement.

Verifying the nuclear freeze would present few technical problems. United States and Soviet military planners already know each other's major weapons, deployments, and capabilities. Satellite technology, which has revolutionized military intelligence gathering, has developed to the point that a satellite camera today can produce a relatively clear and readable photograph of an automobile license plate. Verification and other "technical problems" with the freeze have thus become primarily political problems. They can be solved if the parties to the negotiations wish to solve them.

The U.S. cruise missile, which is small and hard to detect by ordinary means, will make verifying the freeze more difficult when it is deployed. It is likely, however, that each side will develop methods of detecting cruise missiles and their positions in due course. In this case, as in others, technical problems can be overcome.

The more serious problems are political. Critics of the nuclear freeze fall in general into three categories. Those on the political right argue either that the movement is orchestrated by the Soviet Union, or that it would freeze the arms race with the U.S. at a disadvantage. The first of these arguments, which has no foundation in fact, would be unworthy of reply had it not been taken up by the president himself in mid-1982. The documentation for such charges is nonexistent; the major source for the president's allegations was an article in *Reader's Digest* that gave no documentation at all.

The suggestion that the freeze would leave the U.S. at a disadvantage also has no foundation in fact. To the uninitiated, comparisons of the two nations' nuclear arsenals are roughly as comprehensible as the oracles of Nostradamus. But there is general agreement among experts on these matters that the U.S. and the Soviet Union have parity, or approximately equal ability to destroy each other. Thus the freeze would not lock in some arcane advantage. In any case, advantage is a term without content in discussions of nuclear war. Each side can destroy the other many times over. Ten or twenty or a hundred more weapons on one side confers no advantage in any meaningful sense of the term.

Political liberals who favor deterrence have argued that the freeze would somehow render deterrence ineffective. Leaving aside the highly debatable assumption that deterrence works, and without regard for the morality of deterrence, it is simply false to state that the freeze would end deterrence. The arsenals of the superpowers would be frozen at levels so high that they could easily make an attack by either side into a form of deliberate suicide.

A small number of pacifists criticize the freeze proposal on precisely the opposite ground. They argue that the freeze, if viewed as an end in itself, would leave the U.S. and the U.S.S.R. with unacceptable destructive power. This is certainly correct. It does not, however, follow that the freeze is a bad proposal. Proponents of the freeze have never viewed it as anything but a first step toward disarmament. The proposal's originator, Randall Forsberg, has been at pains to show how the freeze could lead to both nuclear and conventional disarmament. She has also emphasized the connections between the arms race and superpower intervention in the Third World.

That the freeze proposal could be distorted as some pacifists fear is undeniable. Something like this happened in Congress in 1983. The administration-supported freeze would have led to an increase in U.S. destructive power, and the build-down proposal became fashionable as an alternative to the freeze. The uncertainties of dealing with Congress, however, do not invalidate the freeze proposal. They point instead toward the kind of grass roots strategy which the freeze movement has followed.

Thus in the matter of nuclear war, as with many issues, the best hope lies with the people most directly affected. That means everyone. The great achievement of the nuclear freeze movement was that it had, more than any other recent peace effort, reached the people who must act if humankind is to survive.

(See also: ARMS CONTROL AND DISARMAMENT, COLD WAR, CONVENTIONAL WAR, NUCLEAR FREE ZONES, NUCLEAR PACIFISM, NUCLEAR STRATEGY, NUCLEAR WEAPONS AND WAR, SOVIET UNION, UNITED STATES)

Nuclear Pacifism: The advent of nuclear weapons is widely, and rightly, considered a sea change in the nature of war. Before Hiroshima and Nagasaki, it was plausible to speak of winners and losers in war. Now it is not: there would be no winners in an all-out nuclear war. Nuclear weapons have thus led many nonpacifists to question whether wars can ever again be fought on the old terms.

Nuclear pacifism, or objection to the use of nuclear weapons, is one response to this new situation. Nuclear pacifists

255

are willing to accept conventional war as a dreadful necessity at times; they do not accept that nuclear weapons can ever be rightly used.

Nuclear pacifists differ when it comes to the practical implications of their thinking. Some are seeking disarmament but accept the use of nuclear weapons for deterrence. Others, the majority, oppose the entire theory of deterrence.

Few nuclear pacifists are faced personally with orders to use or maintain nuclear weapons. Most of those who are, are in the military and often run afoul of military law. Some go absent without leave or refuse orders. Others find the threat of nuclear weapons so all-pervasive that they object to all wars and can qualify for discharge as conscientious objectors.

The nuclear pacifist position is not without difficulties. Primary among these is the problem of determining when the nuclear threshold has been or will be crossed. Modern nuclear weapons come in all sizes, from tactical weapons no larger than a big artillery shell to strategic weapons which can incinerate cities. It is unlikely that a combat soldier could avoid nuclear weapons entirely.

More difficult still for the nuclear pacifist is the growing interdependence of nuclear and conventional warfare. Nearly all doctrines of conventional warfare espoused by the nuclear powers hold that tactical nuclear weapons can be used in a similar manner to non-nuclear explosives. Worse, conventional weapons are, in some cases, actually more destructive than nuclear weapons. Thus the line between nuclear and conventional warfare has become so blurred that a pure nuclear pacifism is becoming less and less possible.[1]

These are, however, theoretical difficulties. The areas of agreement between pacifists and nuclear pacifists are far larger than the areas of disagreement. While some nuclear pacifists advocate substantial increases in conventional armaments, most do not. In nearly all respects most nuclear pacifists oppose not merely nuclear war but war generally. As the powers of conventional weapons increase it is likely that more and more nuclear pacifists will move toward a complete pacifist position.

(See also: ARMS CONTROL AND DISARMAMENT, CONSCIENTIOUS OBJECTION, CONVENTIONAL WAR, DETERRENCE,

1. A good discussion of the blurring of the nuclear "firebreak" will be found in Michael T. Klare, "Leaping the Firebreak," *The Progressive*, Vol. 47, No. 9 (September, 1983), pp. 31–33.

Nuclear Strategy: From the military point of view, the difficulty with nuclear weapons is that they serve no military purpose. War fought with them would be absolute war—war with no political end in view, whose only purpose is destruction.[1] It is impossible to use such weapons to defend territory or take positions, two traditional aims of military operations. The territory being defended would quickly become a radioactive wasteland of no use to anyone; and the position taken would be so radioactive that soldiers would not dare enter it and hold it against further attack.

This fundamental problem has led to contradictory responses among military thinkers. Some have argued, as Lord Louis Mountbatten did, that "wars cannot be fought with nuclear weapons,"[2] and sought to limit or abolish such weapons. These have been in the minority. The majority of strategists have opted to ignore the military uselessness of nuclear weapons. Confronted with it, they have devised theories which justify nuclear weapons and provide a rationale for their use.

Primary among these theories is the doctrine of deterrence, (see separate article on DETERRENCE). This has been the conventional wisdom since 1945.

Less conventional but more and more in the ascendant are theories of nuclear strategy that seek to win a nuclear war. Under such theories nuclear weapons are military weapons much like others. They are larger and more destructive and they have more lasting effects, but in planning they are treated as if they could, properly used, gain military victory. This school argues that nuclear weapons can be used to fight wars.

President Reagan's Secretary of Defense, Caspar Weinberger, has said that the goal of U.S. policy is to "prevail" in a "protracted" nuclear war. This position, called the nuclear warfighting school of strategy, suggests that nuclear war could proceed by stages and that attacks at each stage could be met and deterred or defeated by a controlled response. Thus a conventional Soviet attack in Europe would be met by a conventional defense. If that failed, tactical nuclear weapons would be used. If these failed, a Soviet city might be bombarded with nuclear weapons after suitable warnings to Soviet authorities. And so on up to all-out nuclear holocaust.

A related doctrine, known as counterforce, holds that the purpose of military attacks is to disable an opponent's military forces. Proponents of this theory, including (since presidential directive 59) the U.S. government, advocate targeting weapons on Soviet weapons installations, command centers, manufacturing centers, and so on. Counterforce requires a high degree of accuracy in missile guidance systems—accuracy which in practice may be impossible to achieve. It also requires willingness to strike first since destroying an opponent's missile bases serves no purpose whatever if one's own missiles strike empty launching pads. This "need" for first-strike capability is the most dangerous aspect of counterforce.

The destructiveness of nuclear weapons is such that the kind of rational war-by-stages envisioned by the nuclear warfighters would almost certainly be impossible. This is doubly so because one of nuclear war's first effects, desired and sought after by both sides, would be to disrupt communications. Thus a commander-in-chief wishing to proceed to the next stage might find that his or her computer had gone dead, making it impossible to give the necessary order or to control the growth of the conflict. Such a war could easily acquire its own momentum toward the end of the human race.

At the same time, counterforce doctrines and nuclear warfighting doctrines require a new generation of nuclear weapons which are more accurate and more threatening to an opponent than older weapons. Such an increase in one's power cannot fail to bring a response in kind, leading to yet another effort to gain an advantage, and so on to oblivion. Counterforce, even more than deterrence, is a doctrine which can lead only to a more desperate arms race and greater likelihood of war.

Were it not that they have now been accepted as official United States policy, it would be easy to dismiss nuclear warfighting and counterforce as the ravings of a few maniacs. For all its flaws and inherent dangers, even the doctrine of deterrence is not as dangerous as the newer schools of nuclear strategy. If such thinking prevails, the final holocaust will be closer than it has ever been.[3]

(See also: CONVENTIONAL WAR, DETERRENCE, NATO AND WARSAW PACT, NUCLEAR WEAPONS AND WAR)

1. Definition of absolute war: Roger Parkinson, *Encyclopedia of Modern Warfare* (New York: Stein and Day, 1977), p. 1.
2. *Defense Monitor*, Vol. IX, No. 4 (May 1980).
3. Full accounts of nuclear strategy and its history will be found in: Peter Pringle and William Arkin, *S.I.O.P.: The Secret U.S. Plan for Nuclear War* (New York: W.W. Norton, 1983); and Fred M. Kaplan, *The Wizards of Armageddon: Strategists of the Nuclear Age* (New York: Simon & Schuster, 1983).

Nuclear Weapons and War: On July 16, 1945, at Alamagordo, New Mexico, the United States exploded the first nuclear bomb. Three weeks later, on August 6, 1945, an American bomb destroyed the city of Hiroshima, Japan. Three days after that another atomic bomb destroyed Nagasaki.

Since the bombings of Hiroshima and Nagasaki nuclear weapons have not been used in combat. Scientists in the United States, the Soviet Union, and the other nations which possess these weapons have developed them to levels of destructiveness unimaginable in the prenuclear age, until today nuclear weapons could kill every man, woman, and child on earth more than ten times over. (The rationale for this appalling development is discussed in the articles on NUCLEAR STRATEGY and DETERRENCE.)

Nuclear weapons pose a threat unique in the history of warfare. Useless as a military weapon, they could nonetheless be used in a war which might mean the extinction of the human race. Thus they have become a major focus of public debate. This article discusses and evaluates the types of nuclear weapons, their purported uses, their effects, the effects of nuclear war, and how such a war might start.

The Language of Nuclear War

Nuclear strategists and planners use a peculiar vocabulary all their own which often conceals the reality of what nuclear weapons do. In order to understand nuclear war and its effects, however, one need not have full command of this language; terms used in this article are defined as they are used.

The explosive power of nuclear weapons is measured in equivalents of TNT; a one-ton yield, for example, would mean that the weapon in question explodes with the force of a ton of TNT. No nuclear weapon is this small. The most usual measures of nuclear destructive force are the *kiloton* and the *megaton*. A kiloton yield weapon explodes with the force of a thousand tons of TNT. A megaton yield weapon explodes with the force of a thousand kilotons of TNT, or a million tons. A megaton of TNT would fill three hundred boxcars.

Strategic and Tactical Weapons

Nuclear strategists divide nuclear weapons into two types: strategic and tactical. The terms do not refer to size, although in general strategic weapons are larger than tactical weapons. They refer to purported use. The basis of this division is not always clear. Nor is it likely that the division would make much difference in the event of nuclear war. The overlap between the categories is also likely to increase with the deployment of missiles such as the U.S. Pershing II and cruise.

Strategic nuclear weapons are those intended for use at long range to strike at the enemy's homeland. Thus a nuclear-armed missile (long-range guided rocket) whose target is the Soviet Union, and whose base is in North Dakota, would be considered a strategic weapon.

260

Tactical nuclear weapons are those intended for use on the battlefield—e.g., in a European conflict. Thus a nuclear-armed artillery shell or land mine whose ostensible target is enemy troops would be considered a tactical nuclear weapon.

A third term frequently used by nuclear planners is *theater* weapons. This term refers partly to purported use and partly to where the weapon is located, or deployed, and would in theory be used. Thus weapons designed for use in Europe are considered theater weapons. The distinction between strategic and theater weapons—which was artificial to begin with—has recently broken down almost completely as the United States has deployed theater weapons which though ostensibly for use in a European conflict can reach cities in the Soviet Union with about seven minutes warning. These weapons should properly be considered strategic weapons since they can strike at the Soviet heartland.

Nuclear strategists, politicians, and arms negotiators make much of the distinctions among the three kinds of weapons. But in practice these distinctions are meaningless. Tactical nuclear weapons can sometimes be several times the size of the Hiroshima bomb and their use would cause devastation well beyond that of the Hiroshima bomb. To suggest that this is somehow different from the devastation caused by a strategic bomb is ludicrous: a city destroyed by a tactical bomb—as many would surely be in a European land war—would be destroyed. It would not matter what kind of bomb did the damage.

Sizes of Nuclear Weapons

Nuclear weapons range in size from small tactical weapons whose yield may be one-half to one kiloton, to strategic weapons yielding twenty megatons or more of explosive force. American weapons for the most part are designed for accuracy rather than sheer size, whereas Soviet designers seek large explosive yield. (The largest single bomb ever made, 54 megatons, was a Soviet weapon.) Thus comparisons between U.S. and Soviet weaponry, of which politicians and generals are inordinately fond, are not only misleading but nearly impossible. Such comparisons mean little because each of the two superpowers can destroy all of humankind several times over.

Delivery Systems

Originally nuclear weapons were dropped from aircraft, as ordinary bombs had been throughout World War II. Since 1945, however, military planners and researchers have developed the guided missile, or long-range rocket, to such a degree that in the Soviet arsenal it is the primary means of delivering strategic nuclear explosives. The U.S. still relies on long-range bombers, but these have become part of the so-called triad, which consists of land-based missiles, missiles based on submarines, and bombs delivered by aircraft. The supposed vulnerability of land-based missiles led to the U.S. decision to deploy the MX missile, a supposedly less vulnerable weapon. Submarine-based missiles are nearly invulnerable, but are considered less accurate than the other two legs of the triad.

A modern nuclear missile is a fearsome weapon. Its range allows it to fly from the U.S. to any city in the Soviet Union, or vice-versa. It carries not one nuclear weapon but several. These weapons, contained in self-propelled *warheads*, separate from the missile at a predetermined point in its flight. Each of them can be aimed (targeted in nuclearese) at a separate target. Thus a missile carrying four warheads can actually destroy four cities since each warhead may yield several megatons of explosive power.

The U.S. triad is designed to assure that if the Soviet Union should strike first and demolish one leg of the triad, the other two would be ready to retaliate. It is likely that the Soviets have similar plans to hold a substantial number of weapons in reserve, though official secrecy makes it hard to determine whether this is so. In addition U.S. warfighting plans call for placing a major reserve of nuclear weapons in a submarine under the Northern ice cap, so that after a major nuclear exchange the U.S. could threaten what remains of the Soviet Union with nuclear destruction in a kind of World War IV.

A recent and disturbing development has been U.S. deployment of the cruise missile in Europe. This missile—which flies close to the ground, correcting its course as needed using a built-in computerized map of the route to its target—is essentially an offensive, or first-strike weapon. Ordinary radar cannot detect it in flight; it is highly mobile because it can be launched from a base small enough to be transported by ordinary ground vehicles. Thus it can strike almost entirely without warning. A 1983 study by the Center for Defense Information concluded: "The small size and mobility of the cruise missiles will make it almost impossible to verify nuclear arms reduction agreements. . . . Cruise missiles threaten an end to effective arms control."[1]

Death of a City

The destructive power of nuclear weapons is best understood by describing what a nuclear explosion would do to a specific city or area. Jonathan Schell's description of the destruction of Manhattan is probably unmatched in the literature of nuclear war:[2]

. . . Burst some eighty-five hundred feet above the Empire State Building, a one-megaton bomb would gut or flatten almost every building between Battery Park and 125th Street, or within a radius of four and four-tenths miles, or in an area of sixty-one square miles, and would heavily damage buildings between the northern tip of Staten Island and the George Washington Bridge, or within a radius of eight miles, or in an area of about two hundred square miles. . . . "[T]he blast wave of a sizeable nuclear weapon endures for several seconds and can surround and destroy whole buildings.

Within the area of destruction, buildings which had not been immediately flattened would collapse. "[T]he people and furniture outside would be swept down onto the street." People already on the street would be picked up and hurled away from the blast just as would inanimate debris. Even ten miles from ground zero—the center of the blast—debris such as glass would be thrown away from the blast at lethal speeds. In midtown, "the walls [of the buildings] would fall and the ravines [streets] would fill up." The avalanche would include not merely stone, brick, and glass, but people. Those in the streets would be crushed.

Two miles or so from ground zero, "winds would reach four hundred miles an hour, and another two miles away they would reach a hundred and eighty miles an hour. Meanwhile, the fireball would be growing, until it was more than a mile wide and . . . six miles [tall]." Within a radius of nine miles, the fireball would cause third-degree burns and probably kill all those who were out in the open. People near ground zero would simply be charred and killed instantly. "From Greenwich Village up to Central Park, the heat would be enough to melt metal and glass." Inflammable material such as paper and dry leaves would catch fire in all five boroughs, and as far west as Passaic, New Jersey. These fires would create an area of two hundred eighty square miles in which mass fires might break out.

Fires there would be—such fires as the world has not seen since the death of Hiroshima. Broken gas mains, oil tanks, wood and flammable materials near ground zero—all would be ignited, and "a strong, steady wind would begin to blow in the direction of the blast." This could produce a whirlwind, as happened at Hiroshima. The individual fires could form a mass fire, or firestorm, much as individual fires did in Tokyo, Dresden, Hamburg and Hiroshima. People in shelters would be asphyxiated because the firestorm would suck all available oxygen out of the air. If not asphyxiated, they would be cremated alive.

After the fire, chaos. Medical services would be nonexistent. Most of the police force would be dead or dying. Firefighters would also be dead, or dying, and in any case could not cope with a firestorm. Water, electricity, fuel, food supplies—all the paraphernalia which mean life to a modern city—would cease to exist in the blast. Those who did survive would be shocked and disoriented, probably unable to cope with the simplest matters, let alone life after a nuclear blast. Many would be slowly dying of radiation sickness.

Such carnage, difficult as it may be to contemplate, is the very stuff of U.S. and Soviet nuclear policy. Nuclear weapons aimed at cities obviously are designed to kill civilians. Less obviously, those targeted on military installations will, by the

264

government's own admission, do immense "collateral damage"—that is, they will bring a frightful death to millions of civilians.

The Effects of Nuclear Weapons

The immediate effects of nuclear weapons are four: blast, heat, radiation, and electromagnetic pulse. Long-term effects of a large nuclear exchange are discussed under the next two sub-headings.

Blast: As described above, the most immediate effect of a nuclear explosion is a blast wave. This powerful and highly lethal wall of compressed air takes shape within a fraction of a second of the explosion. It moves away from ground zero at about 750 miles per hour. The blast creates overpressure—air pressure above and beyond the normal—in varying amounts. Five pounds of overpressure is enough to collapse buildings within range of the blast wave. People can withstand up to two hundred pounds of overpressure, but are unlikely to withstand the collapse of the buldings around them.

Heat: At the center of a nuclear explosion the temperature reaches millions of degrees. This creates two thermal pulses. The first, which is very short, does little damage. The second, which follows almost immediately on the first, travels at the speed of light and thus precedes the blast wave. Within the killing zone, which varies with the size of the explosion, people are charred beyond recognition. Those outside the killing zone may suffer third- or second-degree burns, depending on how far they are from ground zero. The second thermal pulse may also ignite the firestorm described above. Whether there will be a firestorm, what kind it will be, and its effects, are unpredictable.

Radiation: Following the initial explosion, vast quantities of dirt would be made radioactive and lifted into the air in what is known as fallout. The effects of such fallout are unpredictable, since they depend on the size of the explosion, whether the weapon was detonated on the ground or in the air, and wind conditions. It is likely, however, that in any major nuclear exchange fallout would keep the environment lethally (or at least dangerously) radioactive for a considerable time.

Electromagnetic Pulse: When a nuclear explosion takes place in mid-air, the collision of intense gamma radiation with the air creates an electromagnetic pulse which can overload and destroy electrical equipment for miles around the center of the blast by causing a powerful surge of voltage through conductors such as power lines, antennas, pipes, and railroad tracks. "The Defense Department's Civil Preparedness Agency reported in 1977 that a single multi-kiloton nuclear weapon detonated one hundred and twenty-five miles over Omaha, Nebraska, could . . . damage solid-state electrical circuits throughout the entire continental United States and in parts of Canada and Mexico."[3]

The electromagnetic pulse could destroy nearly all command and control systems. Since these systems have until recently been designed without taking the pulse effect into account, they are likely to be vulnerable—as will be the computers without which a modern military force cannot function. At the same time both sides have deliberately targeted each other's command and control systems, so that in addition to the danger from pulse there is the danger of direct destruction by blast or other effects. It is likely that in a nuclear exchange the two military giants will thrash blindly at each other until both are dead—and the people of the world with them.

Effects of Nuclear War

In any probable nuclear war not merely one but many cities would be destroyed. Tens, hundreds, or even thousands of nuclear explosions would occur. Taken together these explosions would affect the atmosphere, the earth and water, and human society in ways which are only partly predictable. Their effects would probably be far greater and more destructive than the sum of the explosive power expended in the war.

An all-out nuclear exchange between the superpowers

could involve a total of 11,200 megatons or more of explosive power. It is far more likely, however, that the total explosive expended would include only a fraction of each power's arsenal—though still enough to destroy the fabric of both societies. A one thousand megaton bombardment of the U.S. would result in about 140.5 million dead and another twenty-nine million injured. The Soviet Union would suffer similar damage.[4]

Deaths and injuries would be only the immediate effects, though. A nuclear war on the scale assumed here would cover much of the world with radioactive fallout which in itself would be lethal for a considerable time. Recent studies, discussed under "The Nuclear Winter," below, suggest that fallout would be far more lethal for a far longer time than has been assumed. Thus fallout shelters and bombshelters generally—even those whose inhabitants had not been roasted alive—would probably be of little value for surviving such a massive exchange.

Those who did survive would face a society whose fabric had been destroyed. Although nuclear strategists argue that the American economy could recover from all-out nuclear war, their conclusion is, like most of their reasoning, questionable. In the face of all the evidence they assume that civil defense programs could keep deaths below ten million. Unlikely as this is (and no independent scientific authority supports it), it would still be a catastrophe virtually without precedent. The two world wars caused death on this scale, but these deaths took place over several years and were not accompanied by the extensive environmental and social damage that would occur during a nuclear war. The shock of casualties on this scale, all occurring within a few hours or days, is most closely comparable to the shock caused by the Black Death in the fourteenth century. In that catastrophe, death occurred over a few months and resulted from forces utterly beyond the control or understanding of anyone in society. Panic, incipient psychosis, obsession with death, and mass depression, combined with the loss of about a third of the European population, so strained the fabric of European civilization that the social order did not fully recover for nearly a century.[5]

The analogy is, of course, far from exact. The shock of nuclear war would be far greater, with consequent greater disorientation.

The more likely casualty figures—approximately five hundred million deaths worldwide—could not conceivably be absorbed by any society.

It is likely that the immediate deaths would be only the beginning of the catastrophe, however. While environmental damage in a nuclear war is difficult to predict, studies have suggested two possible outcomes which, while apparently contradictory, could easily occur in succession. The first would be a period of artificial winter. The second would be significant destruction of the atmosphere's ozone layer resulting in greater penetration to the earth's surface by ultra-violet rays from the sun. This would not merely increase the incidence of skin cancer; it might cause living creatures to be fried alive. Severe damage to the ozone layer could result in extinction not merely of animals and plants, but of humanity itself.

Even assuming that extinction did not occur, deaths would continue for years following a nuclear exchange. Some would be direct results of radiation, burns, and radiation sickness, and would occur shortly after the war. Others would result from cancers brought on by the radiation which remained after the war. It is likely that the living would envy the dead.

A so-called limited nuclear war—for example, a war fought entirely in Europe—would have similar effects within the area where it was fought. The long-term effects of fallout from such a war are difficult to predict, but it is likely that the whole world would suffer from some radiation deaths and radiation-induced cancer. In addition even a "small" nuclear war might produce the "nuclear winter."[6]

The Nuclear Winter

In 1983 a group of American scientists led by the astronomer Carl Sagan, in cooperation with a group of Soviet scientists, used computer models to predict the effects of the dust which any major nuclear exchange would throw into the atmosphere. Using models derived from studies of dust on Mars, they found that a protracted nuclear exchange could result in long periods of subfreezing temperatures, darkness, and greater exposure to radioactivity than had previously been projected.

In a 5,000-megaton exchange, with 20 percent of the explosive power targeted on cities, smoke and dust resulting from the many explosions could absorb enough light to cause darkness for several weeks. Beyond that time the light filtering through the dust clouds would be too weak to sustain photosynthesis; this would kill plants or limit their growth, thus disrupting the food chain. The same lack of sunlight would cause subfreezing temperatures. Occurring quite suddenly, these temperatures would very likely kill or damage crops. Animals would die of thirst because surface water would be frozen over. Fallout would be greater than had previously been assumed. In addition disruptions in wind patterns could lead to similar winter conditions in the Southern Hemisphere, which had previously been thought relatively safe. Said the scientists' report:

> The extinction of a large fraction of the earth's animals, plants, and microorganisms seems inevitable. The population size of *Homo Sapiens* conceivably could be reduced to prehistoric levels or below, and the extinction of the human species itself cannot be excluded.

This nuclear winter might result not only from a massive nuclear exchange, but from a much smaller exchange of the sort heretofore called limited nuclear war. The report considered projections based on exchanges as small as 100 megatons. Although such an exchange would not have effects on the scale of a larger nuclear war, it would still result in damage far beyond previous projections. In effect, the paper says, a "small" nuclear war is a practical impossibility. Any such war would have environmental effects far beyond the mere discharge of explosive power.

Ethics and Prediction

Supporters of U.S. and Soviet nuclear policy have argued that projections of human extinction, extensive environmental damage, and so on are not conclusively established. This is true, but it does not follow, as nuclear supporters suggest, that we are thereby made morally free to choose our current suicidal policies. In moral reasoning prediction of consequences is nearly always impossible. One balances the risks of an action against its benefits; one also considers what known damage the action would do. Thus a surgeon in deciding whether to perform an operation weighs the known effects (the loss of some nerve function, for example) and risks (death) against the benefits, and weighs also the risks and benefits of not performing surgery.

Morally, however, human extinction is unlike any other risk. No conceivable human good could be worth the extinction of the race, for in order to *be* a human good it must be experienced by human beings. Thus extinction is one result we dare not—may not—risk. Though not conclusively established, the risk of extinction is real enough to make nuclear war utterly impermissible under any sane moral code.[7]

The Nuclear "Club"

In the early years of the nuclear age the United States was the only country with nuclear weapons. The secrets of nuclear fission and fusion, and thus of nuclear weapons, are no secret at all, however. They are well-known to physicists in all countries. Thus the Soviet Union soon joined the United States as a nuclear power (1949). In 1952 Great Britain acquired nuclear weapons; in 1960 France; in 1964 China; and in 1974 India.

It is likely that this trend will continue unless steps are taken to reverse it. Nuclear weapons are so easy to make that given access to the necessary materials, a bright college physics student could construct one in a home laboratory. Delivery systems, while far more expensive and difficult to acquire, could be adapted from missiles already available in the world weapons market. Worse, many Third World countries seek, almost as if by reflex, the most modern and devastating weaponry: witness the rush to buy Exocet missiles after the Falklands (Malvinas) War.

Ground Zero, an American nuclear information group, believes that Israel and South Africa are already secret members of the nuclear club. In addition they suggest that in the next ten years Argentina, Brazil, South Korea, Taiwan, Iraq, Libya, and Pakistan may acquire nuclear weapons.[8]

With each country that possesses nuclear bombs and missiles, the chances of nuclear war increase. One obvious example is Latin America, which though technically a nuclear-free zone could well see the development of nuclear weapons by one or more countries before the year 2000.

Because nuclear fission and fusion are no longer secret, it is also possible that independent terrorist groups might acquire nuclear weapons—probably fission weapons, which are cheaper and easier to build without high technology.

Thus to the danger of war between the superpowers must be added the danger of war between Third World nuclear powers. Efforts to control this proliferation of nuclear weapons have on the whole been less than successful. The countries that are among the most likely to develop nuclear weapons, or which may already secretly have them, have been among those which have refused to sign the Nuclear Nonproliferation Treaty of 1968. Although one hundred twenty-five countries have signed, the lack of these crucial signatures vitiates much of the treaty's force.

How It Could Start

Nuclear war could begin in a number of ways, some more likely than others.

Deliberate Attack: Nuclear strategists and advocates of deterrence frequently project a nuclear war which begins with one side attacking the other. Known as a first-strike scenario, this sort of projection never suggests that "our" side might attack first. A typical first-strike projection assumes that Soviet leaders would strike first, using extremely accurate missiles, in order to destroy most of the U.S. retaliatory capability, and thus prevail quickly and "painlessly." New weapons, and more of them, are the suggested remedy for this threat. In fact, however, such a first strike is highly unlikely except as the result of accident or miscalculation—both of which have been made more probable because of the nuclear arms race and the system of mutual deterrence. (See the separate article on DETERRENCE.)

European War: Following World War II, Europe quickly became the most heavily armed territory on earth. Today the armies of NATO and the Warsaw Pact, each armed with the most modern of weapons, face each other daily, and posture and threaten. American military planning is based to a great extent on a projected European land war, with the Warsaw Pact as the assumed aggressor.

NATO strategy (see NATO AND WARSAW PACT) depends heavily on nuclear weapons. In addition to the Pershing II and cruise missiles, the NATO arsenal includes tactical weapons ranging from nuclear land mines to missiles delivering explosive power greater than the Hiroshima and Nagasaki bombs combined. These weapons would soon come into use in any major European conflict. It is also likely that either the U.S. or the Soviet Union would attack the homeland of its primary adversary, leading in short order to all-out nuclear war.

Independent military experts consider a European conflict highly unlikely except by accident or miscalculation.

Proxy War: Both the U.S. and the Soviet Union regularly arm and train the armies of countries where they have influence. They are the largest suppliers of arms in the world. It is possible that in an area where each nation's vital interests are at stake, a war between two proxies could spread to the superpowers and thus lead to nuclear war. The best current example is the Middle East, where American arms and aid support Israel, and Soviet arms and aid support many of the Arab countries which oppose Israel.

Accident: The chances of nuclear war by accident have increased during the last ten years to the point where some experts believe such a war cannot be avoided for long. Computer technology has largely taken control of decisions which were formerly made by humans, and while in theory only the president can launch nuclear war, computer errors have already brought the world within minutes of such a war on a number of occasions.

272

Accidental war will become more, not less, likely in the future because military planners will be under pressure to program the computers for a "launch on warning" posture. This phrase means exactly what it says: if the computer warns of incoming missiles, it will launch the rataliatory missiles. Since a computer may well signal an attack when there is none, launch on warning could in effect lead to a first strike. This obviously dangerous policy is said to be necessary for deterrence because newer, more accurate missiles could destroy retaliatory capability unless the retaliation were launched with promptness greater than human decision making can achieve.

The so-called hotline between the two superpowers would be useless in an accidental war. It is not a telephone, but a teletype machine which prints its message at sixty words per minute—far too slow to cope with fast-moving events such as a computer-directed missile launch.[9]

Conclusion

It is evident that nuclear weapons have rendered war not merely futile and destructive but dangerous to the entire planet. This new development in technology has not been accompanied by any development in ethics or institutions which can cope with the new realities. Governments still act as though nuclear weapons were merely large artillery shells or overgrown conventional bombs. Without public pressure they will continue to do so—seeking an advantage in the nuclear arms race which will inevitably elude them because advantage is meaningless in this context.

The search for security through armaments is thus exposed as an absurdity. It has always been so, but not as clearly as now. Each new generation of nuclear weapons brings a corresponding response from the other side, leading to a growth in nuclear arsenals beyond any conceivable military use and certainly beyond the bounds of common decency. Yet the nations of the world grow less, not more, secure. There is no safety, only unspeakable danger, in nuclear weapons.

(See also: AREA BOMBING CAMPAIGN, ARMS CONTROL AND DISARMAMENT, CIVIL DEFENSE, COLD WAR, CONVENTIONAL

WAR, DETERRENCE, GOLDEN RULE AND PHOENIX, HIROSHIMA
AND NAGASAKI, JUST WAR THEORY, MIDDLE EAST, MILITARY-
INDUSTRIAL COMPLEX, NATO AND WARSAW PACT, NUCLEAR
FREEZE MOVEMENT, NUCLEAR FREE ZONES, NUCLEAR STRAT-
EGY, SOVIET UNION, UNITED STATES, WAR AND THE ENVIRON-
MENT)

1. Center for Defense Information, "The Cruise Missile Era: Opening Pandora's Box," *Defense Monitor*, Vol. XII, No. 4 (1983), p. 8.

2. This description is adapted from Jonathan Schell, *The Fate of the Earth* (New York: Alfred A. Knopf, 1982), pp. 47–52.

3. *Ibid.*, p. 17–18.

4. Ground Zero, *Nuclear War: What's in it For You?* (New York: Pocket Books, 1982), pp. 125–137.

5. See Barbara Tuchman, *A Distant Mirror* (New York: Knopf, 1978).

6. "American and Soviet Scientists Predict 'Nuclear Winter' in Wake of Blast," *Chronicle of Higher Education*, Vol. XXVII, No. 11 (November 9, 1983).

7. Cf. Schell, Part II, for discussiion of the morality of extinction.

8. Ground Zero, ch. 17.

9. I am grateful to Arthur Kanegis of the Center for Defense Information for this information.

Peacekeeping Forces, Military: The record of military forces whose mission is to preserve order in a war zone— enforcing a cease-fire, for example—has been mixed. Peace-keeping forces have operated extensively in the Middle East conflicts of the last twenty years. In some cases, as in the Sinai following the Camp David accords, they have been suc-cessful. In others, as with the multinational peacekeeping force in Lebanon in 1982–84, they have failed utterly in their mission.

The most successful peacekeeping forces have operated under international auspices, such as the United Nations, and have enforced treaties or cease-fires which were already in place. Often, as in the Sinai, the treaty being enforced is part of a larger rapprochement between the two warring nations. This makes it hard to determine whether the peacekeeping force has actually prevented conflict or whether conflict would not in any case have occurred.

Events in Lebanon during 1982–84, however, demonstrate

the inherent weaknesses of military peacekeeping forces. The Israeli invasion of Lebanon in 1982 took place despite the presence of a United Nations peacekeeping force in southern Lebanon. This force, which was lightly armed and no match for the Israeli army, could not have stopped the invasion. But had it tried to do so, it would have failed in its primary mission and become part of the conflict.

Following the Israeli siege of Beirut and the withdrawal of Palestinian troops from that city, the nominal Lebanese government (which had little popular support) asked the United States, France, and Italy to provide peacekeeping forces to aid the Lebanese army in establishing a stable government. Great Britain later joined the peacekeeping force.

Even for a government with wide popular support this would have been no mean feat. Years of civil war in Lebanon, the occupation of much of the country by foreign troops such as the Palestinians and Syrians, and the added disruption caused by the Israeli invasion, made the government's task nearly impossible. The ethnic resentments and factional disputes which had brought about civil war in the first place had not gone away. The situation required masterly diplomacy, not a token military peacekeeping force.

The Allies quickly established themselves in Beirut, and almost as quickly became an object for attack by the various antigovernment factions. United States operations clearly showed that the purpose of its force was to support the government. The other Allies, while maintaining a more neutral stance, also became identified with the government. Thus the U.S. force found itself under siege, and in late 1983 a suicide attack on the U.S. Marine headquarters, in which an unknown assailant drove a truckload of dynamite past marine guards and detonated the explosive as many marines were sleeping, led to 264 American deaths. There were similar though less destructive attacks on French and Israeli troops.

Far from causing the U.S. to withdraw its peacekeeping force, the Beirut debacle led to increased Reagan administration determination to keep the marines in Lebanon. Even critics of the force argued that pulling the troops out immediately was impossible. Thus the marines, whose peacekeeping function was nil and who had become targets for antigovernment fighters, remained in Lebanon until February 1984, when the factional fighting had become open warfare and the government had all but fallen. The marines were then withdrawn to ships off the Lebanese coast. These ships continued to bombard targets in Lebanon with artillery fire, leading to heavy casualties among the Lebanese civilian population.

Taking sides in a bitter civil war, as the U.S. clearly did in Lebanon, is always unwise and usually disastrous. But the U.S. peacekeeping force failed not only because it took sides, but because it was a military force. Insofar as peacekeeping forces act like military forces—by responding to provocation with violence—they become part of the war and raise the level of the conflict. The U.S. did this in Lebanon by massing ships off the coast, bombarding antigovernment positions with artillery, sending U.S. war plans over Lebanese territory, and bombing targets not shelled by the artillery.

Even peacekeeping forces which act peacefully, however, may become targets. The U.S. Marines, who spent their early days in Lebanon engaging in routine, relatively peaceful patrols, soon found that they had become targets because they were soldiers and thus, in the strange logic of war, legitimate targets. At the same time they represented a hated government. Thus they lost whatever hope they had had of reconciling the various factions in the civil war.

By their very nature military peacekeeping forces represent a paradox which cannot be resolved. Soldiers, who are instruments of war, cannot easily become instruments of peace. They can be trained to keep order, but order is not peace. The reliance on peacekeeping forces represents failure to pursue means of resolving conflicts at their roots; in the long run, peacekeeping forces cannot prevent war because they cannot deal with the causes of the conflict.

In Lebanon the U.S. tendency to use force instead of diplomacy, and its alignment with one faction in a complex situation, made tragedy—or at least failure—inevitable. But even a successful peacekeeping force would not have brought peace. It would have imposed order on Lebanon without building trust and cooperation among the factions. Without

276

these, which no military force can provide, there might have been order, but there would not have been peace.

(See also: CENTRAL AMERICA, MIDDLE EAST, NONVIOLENCE, NONVIOLENT INTERVENTION FORCES, UNITED NATIONS)

Quakers: See American Friends Service Committee

Rapid Deployment Force: The United States Central Command, or Rapid Deployment Force (RDF), is an army of approximately 250,000 combat troops, including ground troops, air transport and supply, artillery, combat air support, and armor. It is composed of troops from more than twenty-five existing units, such as the 82nd Airborne Division, and draws on these units as required when it is in combat. Its budget for fiscal year 1985 was $59 billion.

Military planners developed the Rapid Deployment Force in response to a perceived Soviet threat to Middle Eastern oil supply lines. Its ostensible purpose is to move quickly into an area to counter threats to governments or supplies of strategic materials located there. In theory the RDF would be invited by the government of the threatened nation. In practice it is by no means clear that the United States would actually wait for an invitation. Before the 1983 invasion of Grenada—the only combat use so far of the Rapid Deployment Force—the U.S. deliberately sought an invitation from the governments in the area. In future cases the RDF might simply invade without warning or invitation.

Use of the Rapid Deployment Force against a Soviet attack—the public rationale for its development—would be far more dangerous than is commonly realized. Because it would be lightly armed the RDF could not hold off a full-scale Soviet assault for very long. (Troops assigned to the RDF have nicknamed it the Rapid Dying Force.) The annihilation or

277

defeat of the RDF would function as a kind of nuclear trip-wire, leading to use of tactical nuclear weapons and thus to immediate danger of full-scale thermonuclear war.[1]

A far more likely use of the Rapid Deployment Force is for intervention in a Third World country, as in Grenada. The RDF could invade without debate or congressional authorization, and American casualties would then make it more likely that the U.S. would continue to commit troops to the area. In military affairs it is far harder to stop a war than to prevent one: casualties lead to public anger, which can become public support. And even without public support, the Rapid Deployment Force would make it possible for U.S. intervention to proceed and continue for some time. Whether Congress would invoke the War Powers Act to end the intervention is unpredictable, but the record of the Act in Lebanon and Grenada shows little promise.

Criticism of the RDF in the public media has concentrated not on its purpose but on its "adequacy." Such arguments miss the point. The U.S. invasion of Grenada in 1983 violated international law and was almost universally condemned outside the United States. Without the Rapid Deployment Force the Grenada operation would have been far more difficult to mount quickly. The RDF protects no one. It is a military unit designed to enter other countries and shape events there to conform to the will of the United States. With a force ready at hand, a president will be tempted to intervene where prudence would have dictated otherwise.

(See also: INDOCHINA WAR, MIDDLE EAST, NUCLEAR WEAPONS)

1. For a full discussion of the nuclear tripwire function of the RDF, see Daniel Ellsberg, Introduction, in E. P. Thompson and Dan Smith, *Protest and Survive* (New York: Monthly Review Press, 1981).

Sanctuary Movement: Under U.S. law (the Refugee Act of 1980), immigration authorities are required to accord refugee status to persons who cannot return to their native countries because of persecution or fear of persecution on account of race, religion, nationality, membership in a particular social group, or political opinion. These standards, adopted from the United Nations Convention and Protocol on Refugees, should theoretically have applied to the many people who fled El Salvador and Guatemala during the early 1980s. In both countries, political repression and murder are a way of life.

Granting refugee status to such persons, however, would have been politically embarrassing for the U.S. government, which provided considerable military and economic support to the governments of El Salvador and Guatemala. The U.S. Immigration and Naturalization Service instead argued that Salvadoran and Guatemalan refugees came to the United States not to excape repression but to seek employment. They therefore classified persons from El Salvador and Guatemala as illegal aliens and viewed them as economic refugees. Many were deported.

In response to this policy, in the early 1980s churches from at least twelve major denominations and several synagogues began to provide sanctuary, or help with resettlement, for Salvadoran and Guatemalan refugees. Aid to refugees took the form of providing shelter, food, clothing, health care, assistance in finding employment, and other actions designed to allow refugees to establish themselves in the United States. One researcher estimated that in 1982 more than eighty churches in the Chicago area alone were involved in the sanctuary movement.[1]

Providing sanctuary for Salvadoran and Guatemalan refugees is a violation of U.S. law, punishable by as much as six years in prison and $250,000 fine.[2] A small number of sanctuary workers were prosecuted and imprisoned, but the main thrust of the government's campaign against the sanctuary movement involved attempts to discredit it with allegations of supporting communism, threats of prosecution, and dissemination of misinformation about the U.S. role in Central America.

As the sanctuary movement grows in numbers and effectiveness, the number of prosecutions will likely increase. It is also clear that the government regarded the movement as a serious threat to its Central American policy. The refugees helped by the sanctuary movement were living proof that U.S. claims to be defending democracy in Central America were false.

(See also: CENTRAL AMERICA)

1. Betty R. Nute, "Sanctuary: New Challenge to Conscience," *Friends Journal*, July 1/15, 1983.

2. The maximum penalty specified in the law is $10,000 fine and five years' imprisonment. Under the Comprehensive Crime Control Act and the Criminal Fine Enforcement Act, however, fines for certain felonies were increased to $250,000 as of December 31, 1984, and maximum sentences for certain felonies to six years in prison, effective November 1, 1986.

Solidarity: In August 1980, following several months of economic crisis and strikes, the government of Poland recognized and agreed to the demands of the independent workers' organization, Solidarity. The Gdansk Agreement (so named because it was negotiated and signed in the city of Gdansk) called for greater worker control of economic matters, expansion of free and independent unionism, and greater availability of consumer goods, among other things.

There followed a period of mounting tension which led to rumors of a Soviet invasion of Poland. Soviet displeasure with the independent union—which, if successful, might have led to other independent efforts in Eastern Europe and possibly even the Soviet Union itself—was clear.

In April 1981 Solidarity distributed leaflets outlining a plan for nonviolent defense against a Soviet invasion. The invasion, however, never occurred. Instead, after intense Soviet pressure, the Polish Communist Party declared martial law, outlawed Solidarity and dismissed the government which had signed the Gdansk Agreements. Solidarity is an underground movement whose effective power base is difficult to assess. Its leader, Lech Walesa, who won the Nobel Peace Prize in 1981, remains a well-known and influential figure.

On the face of it, Solidarity was defeated, though this cannot deny the movement's achievements. In a repressive society run by a small elite, Solidarity very nearly transformed the method of making economic decisions. It was the first independent union in an East bloc country to achieve any agreement whatsoever with the government. This, in a system where labor unions are essentially Party agents, was no small feat.

It is also possible that Solidarity's carefully-developed plans for nonviolent defense helped to deter an actual Soviet invasion of Poland. There is no way of knowing. It is likely, however, that the Polish people would have been more willing to resist a Soviet invasion than they were to resist martial law enforced by their own soldiers.

The nonviolent movement in Poland did not end with the government's declaration of martial law. In early 1984, for example, nonviolent pressure from the Catholic church and Solidarity leader Lech Walesa, and from the population at large, forced the government to abandon its plan to remove crucifixes from public places. In Poland, which is more than 90 percent Catholic, this was an issue of major symbolic importance, and it represented a major defeat for the government.

(See also: COMMUNISM, CZECH RESISTANCE, NONVIOLENCE, SOVIET UNION)

South Africa (See Apartheid)

Soviet Union: The Union of Soviet Socialist Republics (U.S.S.R.) is one of the two great contemporary military powers. Its armed forces, numbering just under four million, are second in size only to those of the People's Republic of China. It possesses an immense nuclear arsenal, roughly equal to that of the United States. It dominates Eastern Europe, where it is the major member of the Warsaw Pact alliance.

Because of the Soviet Union's great destructive power, relations between it and the other great military power, the

United States, are crucial to the future of humankind. In the early 1980s those relations became distant and bellicose, with much posturing and little talk of reconciliation. This resulted in part from conflicts of interest and the struggle for power, and in part from a body of mythology which each side has built up about the other. The world views and ideologies of the two sides are radically different, resulting in much misunderstanding and fear and giving the conflict a special bitterness found in religious wars of the past.

It is impossible in a short article to discuss the Soviet Union fully. This article deals with six areas: the Soviet experience of war; the Soviet military; Soviet expansionism; the Soviet mythology regarding the United States; the Soviet Union in American mythology; and Soviet domestic policies.

The Soviet Experience of War

It is likely that no one can understand current Soviet policies and actions without knowing about Soviet experience in World War II. In that war, Germany invaded the U.S.S.R. and was finally forced to withdraw after a series of costly Soviet victories.

World War II on the Eastern Front was fought on a scale which even today is difficult to imagine. The Battle of Stalingrad, one of the most terrible in history, destroyed one-fifteenth of the Germany Army. The Battle of Kursk was the largest tank battle in history. A later battle, called simply the Destruction of Army Group Center, took place on a 350-mile front and resulted in three hundred thousand German casualties in three weeks. In all, twenty million Soviet citizens died, either directly as a result of the fighting, from starvation and disease, or, even worse, by deliberate Nazi policy. Hitler's search for *Lebensraum* meant expansion to the east and deliberate enslavement of Slavic peoples—and the massacre of Jews.

American nuclear strategists misinterpret the Soviet reaction to this history in a particularly grotesque way. They suggest that because the U.S.S.R. has "absorbed" great losses in the past, Soviet policymakers will be willing to do so in a future nuclear war. The truth is the opposite. Soviet policy is often haunted by the World War II experience, the fear of invasion, and the wartime sufferings of the Soviet people. The war memorial in Leningrad—a city besieged by the Germans for four years—is practically a mandatory stop for parties of foreign tourists. World War II is called the Great Patriotic War in the U.S.S.R. and Soviet military planning, much like that in the U.S., is largely based on replays of the earlier conflict.[1]

None of this suggests that the Soviet Union is a peaceable power. On the contrary, it is a great nation with a powerful military, and is thus dangerous, as are all such nations. Within what it considers its sphere of influence, the Soviet Union's policy has been to maintain complete control, using military force or the threat of force. Soviet troops crushed the rebellion in Hungary in 1956. They invaded Czechoslovakia in 1968, removed the liberal Czech government, and installed a more subservient group of rulers. Soviet threats to invade Poland led to the suppression of the Solidarity movement in 1981. And in Afghanistan in 1979 Soviet troops, along with those of the Soviet-installed Afghan government, began a large and bloody counterinsurgency war.

All the same, this terrible record does not mean that Soviet influence is expanding. As detailed below, Soviet influence in the world has actually declined since the 1950s. It is likely that Soviet leaders intervened in the states on their borders for two purposes: to maintain their existing power, and to preserve a buffer zone of client states around Soviet territory. This, in their view, would make war on the Soviet homeland less likely. The Soviet experience of war, instead of making Soviet leaders more peaceable, may have made them more willing to resort to military intervention.

Soviet experience of war may also have influenced Soviet nuclear policy—and not for the good. Soviet leaders, like all national leaders, rationalize their weapons as defensive ones. For them they are a means of preventing another war on Soviet territory. Under the doctrine of deterrence, which the Soviets accept in modified form, nuclear weapons are said to prevent attacks by other nuclear powers. This translates in practice into the nuclear weapons buildup which has been taking place in the Soviet Union since the time of the Cuban Missile Crisis (1962). (See separate article on DETERRENCE.)

The Allied Intervention in Russia, 1918–1919 A little-known historical episode, the Western Allies' attempt to overthrow the Bolshevik regime in 1918–19, continues to make relations between the U.S. and the U.S.S.R. even more difficult than they should be. When it became obvious in 1918 that Russia might not continue in the war on the Eastern Front, the other Allies—Great Britain, Japan, France, the United States, and Czechoslovakia—sent troops to Russian territory. This was actually the second invasion of Russian territory during World War I. (The first was by the Central Powers in 1914.)

The Allied intervention was a military and political blunder far out of proportion to the numbers of troops involved or the damage they did. (The numbers were small, the troops wanted to go home rather than fight, and the Allies were finally compelled to withdraw.) Soviet policymakers, many of whom knew the 1917 revolutionaries or their immediate successors, remember the Allied intervention far better than their Western counterparts. They regard it as a symbol of the unrelenting hostility of the capitalist powers toward their revolution.[2]

Soviet Perceptions and Fears Against this background, the size and power of the Soviet military, while in no way justified, become explicable. Much of the Soviets' military strength is concentrated on the borders of Soviet territory or those of countries in Eastern Europe. The Soviet rationale for the Warsaw Pact alliance holds that it is defensive. Soviet missiles are rationalized as defensive. And so on.

Rationalizations like these are, of course, common among political leaders. In world politics, every new weapon is called defensive, and every aggressive action is justified by some other country's aggression. But it will not do to ignore Soviet perceptions and fears. The Soviet Union is in fact highly vulnerable to U.S. missile attack, and Soviet fears on this score have as much basis as do U.S. fears of a Soviet missile attack. The perceptions themselves exist, and—like American mythology about the U.S.S.R.—they are powerful obstacles to peacemaking.

Paradoxically, this analysis which suggests that peacemaking will be difficult gives far more hope than the standard

American explanation of Soviet behavior: that the Soviets act as they do because they are communists and are therefore uniquely evil and threatening. If Soviet policies result from nameless and ineradicable evil then no action can move the U.S.S.R. toward peace. But if their policies result from ordinary human motives such as fear, historical experience, and adherence to an ideology, then peace is possible because human (and rational) behavior can change.

The Soviet Military Behemoth

The Soviet military is large, powerful, and threatening. It is armed with powerful nuclear and conventional weapons. It has nearly four million active troops and millions more reserves. These facts, and the threat to peace which they represent, are overlaid in American thinking by the myth of the Soviet behemoth—the powerful, efficient army, full of lean, crack troops armed with the latest weapons, which could roll across Europe.

The reality may be quite different. Soviet troops are poorly-fed and poorly-trained. Rates of alcoholism among the troops are extremely high. Soviet military organization is poor and so highly centralized that commanders of individual units cannot make tactical decisions without consulting their headquarters. Soviet soldiers are given no maps so that if their officers should be killed, captured, or disabled, they may actually be unable to proceed. Soviet tanks, the terror of NATO planners, are vulnerable to antitank fire because their fuel tanks are on the outside, a suicidal design seen in no Western tank.

Despite these and other flaws the Soviet military is more powerful than any other save that of the United States. But the Red Army is not the all-powerful threat of American right-wing paranoia. It is not superior to that of the U.S., though the myth that it is helps to fuel the arms race.[3]

Soviet Expansionism

Like every great power the Soviet Union has sought to expand its influence in the world, and it has done so—but on a far smaller scale than Americans fear. A 1980 survey by the

Center for Defense Information in Washington, D.C. shows that Soviet influence in other nations was at its highest in the late 1950s and has since declined. Of 155 countries in the world at the time of the survey, the U.S.S.R. had significant influence in nineteen.[4] The perception of constant Soviet advances and U.S. setbacks is not supported by the facts.

Thus, though Soviet policymakers almost certainly wish to expand their empire, they have had little success in doing so. To say this is not to suggest that the U.S.S.R. is not an expansionist power. Soviet intervention in Afghanistan shows that it will use military force to consolidate its sphere of influence. Such policies, however, are hardly unique to the Soviets. Nor do alleged Soviet gains justify increased U.S. use of military force. Most such gains are either minor or, as in Central America, have little to do with the Soviets.

Soviet Mythology

Soviet citizens, like U.S. citizens, have a highly distorted perception of their primary adversary. Soviet news media picture the U.S. as a warlike, racist society whose aim is the destruction of the U.S.S.R. This portrayal is distorted but no more so than the portrayal of the Soviets by many commentators in the U.S.

American Mythology

United States and to a lesser extent Western policy is dominated by three myths about the Soviet Union. The first is the myth of Soviet military efficiency. The second is the myth of Soviet "geopolitical momentum." And underlying these two myths is a third: the concept of the Soviet Union as implacably revolutionary, mischief-making, and evil. President Reagan's reference to the "evil empire" in 1983 is an example of such demonology.

American fears about the Soviet Union are exacerbated by ignorance. Few Americans speak Russian and even fewer have traveled to the Soviet Union. In recent years Soviet studies have declined both in universities and in the government. In 1984, for example, there were more teachers of English in the Soviet Union than there were students of Russian in the U.S.[5]

Criticism of the Soviet Union on erroneous or exaggerated grounds has made realistic criticism or analysis very difficult. Those, for example, who deplored the Soviet invasion of Afghanistan because they opposed Great Power intervention in the Third World were drowned out in public hysteria over alleged Soviet designs on the oil fields in the Persian Gulf. The effect is to stifle a balanced critical view of the Soviet action.

Such difficulties apply to other criticisms of the U.S.S.R. as well. Too often irrational anti-Communists have preempted the field, leaving more serious critics to choose between seeming too favorable to Soviet actions and seeming to be part of the anti-Soviet hysteria.

Soviet Domestic Policies

There is in fact so much that is wrong with the Soviet Union that one hardly knows where to begin. In foreign affairs it acts like any Great Power—decently when that is in its interest and abominably when that is in its interest. In internal affairs the Soviet Union is a totalitarian state. There is little or no freedom of press or expression; internal travel is restricted; and Soviet citizens must carry internal passports. Emigration is also restricted.

The Soviet economy remains a monument to Stalinist centralization and as such is both inefficient and inflexible. Soviet claims to be a socialist nation have little truth, for economic planning there is controlled not by the public, but by an elite which arrogates to itself special privileges nominally forbidden it by official ideology.

Dissent in the Soviet Union is ruthlessly suppressed, either by imprisonment, by commitment to mental institutions, or, as in the case of the physicist Andrei Sakharov, by internal exile. Except for the abuse of psychiatry, these practices recall the crimes of Stalin, who murdered millions during his bloody years in power.

Indeed in many ways the Soviet Union is also like the Tsarist Russian state which preceded it. Internal passports were first used by Peter the Great. The Tsarist secret police (for whom, ironically, Stalin may once have been an informant)[6] suppressed left-wing revolutionaries, including the

Bolsheviks. The Soviet secret police, in their turn, suppress modern dissenters. It is not a pleasant picture.

Even so, the United States can hardly restore the rights of Muscovites by incinerating them with nuclear missiles, or even by threatening to do so. American policymakers tread on dangerous ground indeed when they suggest that Soviet domestic repression makes it impossible for the two powers to live together. Whatever their differences the U.S. and the Soviet Union *must* talk to and tolerate each other. The alternative is mutual suicide.

(See also: CENTRAL AMERICA, COLD WAR, COMMUNISM, CONVENTIONAL WAR, MIDDLE EAST, MILITARY-INDUSTRIAL COMPLEX, NATO AND WARSAW PACT, NUCLEAR STRATEGY, NUCLEAR WEAPONS AND WAR, TOTALITARIANISM)

1. A recent history of the war on the Eastern Front is Harrison Salisbury, *The Unknown War* (New York: Bantam, 1978).

2. On the Allied intervention in Russia, see John Bradley, *Allied Intervention in Russia* (New York: Basic Books, 1968). See also Richard Goldhurst, *The Midnight War: The American Intervention in Russia, 1918–1920* (New York: McGraw-Hill, 1978).

3. A full discussion of the Soviet military will be found in Andrew Cockburn, *The Threat: Inside the Soviet Military Machine* (New York: Random House, 1983).

4. Center for Defense Information, "Soviet Geopolitical Momentum: Myth or Menace?", *Defense Monitor*, Vol. XI, No. 1 (January, 1980).

5. Center for Defense Information, "U.S.-Soviet Relations: To the Summit and Beyond," *Defense Monitor*, Vol. XIII, No. 2 (1984).

6. H. Montgomery Hyde, *Stalin: The History of a Dictator* (New York: Farrar, Straus & Giroux, 1971), pp. 72–75.

Space and War: The advent of space travel and satellites has revolutionized warfare in ways not generally understood. At present the United States and the Soviet Union make extensive use of satellites for military communications and intelligence-gathering.

In the latter field, space technology has made secrecy in military matters very difficult. From their orbits thousands of miles above the earth's surface, satellite cameras can make clear photographs of automobile license plates. Satellite photography has resulted in detailed topographical maps of enemy territory and of other places where fighting might take place. The military value of satellite technology is so great that in any major conflict each side's forces would try to destroy the other's satellites as a matter of first importance. Thus both sides have tried to develop "killer satellites" whose only purpose is to destroy opposing satellites.

One development has been the proposal to equip satellites with so-called particle beam weapons which would in theory be able to destroy intercontinental ballistic missiles before they reached their targets. The American right wing has argued for some years that the Soviet Union has actually developed and deployed such weapons though the evidence cited in support of this proposition is dubious. President Reagan proposed in mid-1983 to develop antimissile satellites as a kind of "defensive umbrella" over the U.S.

The president's proposal was immediately criticized as destabilizing. Critics argued that the antimissile umbrella would give the U.S. such an advantage in the arms race that the Soviet Union might feel compelled to discharge its nuclear weapons at once.

Such criticism, which assumes that safety lies in mutual terror, hardly merits serious discussion. A much more likely and disturbing result of the president's proposal would be increased militarization of space, which is already heavily used for military purposes. An arms race in space, like an arms race on earth, carries with it an increased risk of war.

Scientists who evaluated the president's proposal showed, with strong supporting evidence and arguments, that the proposal would not in any case work as advertised. In pursuit of the chimera of security through space armaments, however, the U.S. would spend billions or trillions of dollars which it could ill afford—and almost certainly at the expense of social welfare, industrial development, and education.

The absurdity of the president's proposal was nowhere better shown than in his own speech. After proposing the new space technology, he suggested that once the U.S. had developed it the technology could be shared with the Soviet Union so that they could build their own umbrella. If such an arrangement between the two powers were possible at all, then disarmament—a far safer and less expensive solution to the problems of armaments—would also be possible.

Paradoxically space technology could provide the means to

verify a nuclear freeze or disarmament agreement. When each side knows in broad outline what the other is doing, there can be little or no technical barrier to disarmament. Enforcement of an arms agreement could be facilitated by satellite technology which by mutual agreement would be used to assure that neither side violated the agreement.

This more peaceful use of space is unlikely to come about without the political will needed to reach a disarmament agreement. As in most such matters the barriers to peace are not technical but political.

(See also: NUCLEAR FREEZE MOVEMENT)

"Smart" Weapons: For most of the history of warfare human skill has determined whether a weapon—be it spear, bullet, or artillery shell—hit its targets. The weapons themselves were often unpredictable, and this combined with normal human error meant that bullets, shells, and bombs missed their targets more often than they hit.

The inaccuracy of weapons has been troublesome for military commanders, who would prefer an absolutely predictable "kill rate." Thus military technology and strategy have sought to minimize the human factor on the battlefield so that armies can become ever more efficient and destructive. In the eighteenth century soldiers armed with highly inaccurate muskets fired en masse, generally without aiming their weapons at all, to create a lethal area immediately in front of them (in today's terms, a field of fire). The machine gun is the logical development from these massed infantry tactics.

Nothing, however, has so increased the potential deadliness of weapons as modern built-in guidance systems. An artillery shell aimed by traditional methods—that is, a visual spotting of the target and mathematical calculation—may have as little as a 10 percent chance of hitting its target. A missile with a built-in guidance system may have a 90 percent chance of doing so.

Such weapons, called "smart" weapons, range from small missiles to nuclear-armed missiles such as the American cruise missile. Their guidance systems vary. They include remote-control guidance, built-in computer maps of the course to the target, infrared censors, heat sensors, and laser guidance systems. All have in common the ability—at least in theory—to hit a target with uncanny accuracy. Soldiers operating them must understand how to program the weapon but they need not have exceptional skill in aiming.

Since most of these weapons are also highly destructive, smart weapons have increased the danger to soldiers and other targets in modern combat by a factor which is difficult to estimate because most such weapons have not been used in actual combat. The most bizarre of recent developments is a kind of cluster bomb, or bomb which releases hundreds of "bomblets" when it explodes, which combines precision guidance with the ability to render a large area lethal. This new weapon contains bomblets which are designed to destroy armor, ones which destroy buildings, and ones which destroy people. When exploded it covers an area of several hundred square yards with these miniature smart weapons.

Critics of high military technology suggest that smart weapons are unreliable and the money spent on them would be better spent buying larger numbers of cruder but more rugged military hardware. This is a dubious proposition on two counts. First, an army equipped with simple and reliably destructive weapons is not in any way preferable to one equipped with complex and less reliable weapons. Both are expensive, and both can cause untold human suffering.

Second—and far more important—smart weapons are a new development in military technology and their destructiveness has not yet reached its peak. As long as the world relies on armies and weapons, scientists and engineers will try to perfect the guidance systems and increase the dependability of smart weapons until combat will become for all practical purposes infallibly lethal for anyone in the battle zone.

In the meantime smart weapons have, despite their flaws, made combat potentially far more dangerous for participants and bystanders than it was even ten years ago. Though aimed and guided in sophisticated ways, smart weapons destroy indiscriminately when they explode. Worse, though they will almost always hit *a* target, they will not necessarily hit *the* target. A heat-seeking missile may accidentally seek the heat of a civilian airliner rather than an opposing military aircraft. This increases the danger to civilians along with the danger to soldiers.

It is likely that extensive use of smart weapons in a future large-scale war would hasten the descent into nuclear holocaust. This would occur because smart weapons would tend to cancel each other out and cause extremely high casualty rates. Thus, though a smart antitank weapon may destroy tanks almost infallibly, by the very act of firing, the weapon's operator will probably have exposed himself to quick death when a counterweapon seeks the light from his weapon, homes in on it, and destroys his position. Even hours of such combat, let alone days, would lead to appalling casualty rates.

A more immediate problem associated with smart weapons is the high cost of developing, manufacturing, and deploying them. About 85 percent of the projected United States arms expenditure for 1984–1989 ($1.5 trillion) will go toward conventional weapons, many of them smart weapons. Such expenditures can easily cripple even the most advanced economies.

In developing countries governments are also under pressure to buy the most advanced weapons. The Exocet missile, which became popular after the Falklands (Malvinas) War, costs $750,000. Many of its purchasers are developing countries which can ill afford such wasteful spending. In the civil war in Chad the U.S. sold one of the poorest nations in the world a very expensive antiaircraft missile called the Redeye. Chad, where most of the population exists on the minimum of calories required for survival, could not afford such weapons. Yet the government bought them to counter enemy aircraft. From Chad, according to reports in the *Manchester Guardian*, the Redeye may eventually find its way to Northern Ireland for use against British army helicopters. Such arms transfers are frequent in the international arms trade which proceeds uncontrolled, often reselling American or Soviet weapons which were originally sold to client countries as part of Cold War maneuvering. The obscenity of this trade, and of poor countries' use of precious resources for such deadly and expensive weapons, needs no elaboration.

292

The international law of war, which has in any case placed few effective restraints on the behavior of armies in combat, has yet to address the problem of smart weapons. Even if it does, it is unlikely to control the development or use of such weapons unless the nations develop the political will to stop the conventional as well as the nuclear arms race.

(See also: ANTIPERSONNEL WEAPONS, CONVENTIONAL WAR, NATO AND WARSAW PACT)

Stalin: The figure of Joseph Stalin dominates Soviet history from 1917 as no other leader has before or since. Stalin remained in power longer than any other Soviet leader. His terror methods and political purges resulted in the deaths of tens of millions of Soviet citizens.[1] His efforts to force Soviet economic development by central planning and enforced collectivization of farms created problems—an inflexible economic planning bureaucracy, for instance—which still remain unresolved today.

Stalin's reign was characterized by an absolute political dictatorship enforced by mass terror. Stalinist terror was in part the result of Stalin's own personality and in part the result of his ideology. Its effect, however, was to consolidate Stalin's power to such an extent that until his death none dared criticize him. Even after his death, Nikita Khrushchev's public repudiation (in 1956) of Stalinism required an act of great courage.

Separating out the strands of personal paranoia, political opportunism, and Marxism in Stalinist ideology is difficult but it will not do to dismiss Stalin's reign as simply an aberration. Stalin's interpretation of Marxian philosophy, in which the working classes—represented by the Party, represented by Stalin himself—must literally eliminate its oppressors, was one logical interpretation of the concept of class struggle. Other nominal Marxists, such as Pol Pot of Kampuchea, reached similar conclusions years later and enforced similar horrors on their peoples. In both cases, however, the terror reached far beyond the "oppressing classes" to include educated people, writers, other potential opponents, and ordinary citizens who had incurred the government's disfavor for some cause, however trivial. Frequently the children of people Stalin had condemned were exiled to Gulags. Thus ideology became the rationale for pure terror.

Marx himself might have repudiated Stalinism. It is difficult to judge for Marx was intolerant of opposition within the International Workingmen's Association which he headed. Lenin also could not tolerate opposition. Although Stalinism is not a necessary consequence of Marxism, much Marxist thought is unforgiving toward the oppressing classes. It is only a short, logical step from this to wholesale elimination of groups of people.

Stalin's career embodies, as few other historical events, the evils of totalitarian government and violence. The Bolsheviks came to power in one of the bloodiest periods of modern history. They seized power by violence, and they were heirs to the violence of the Romanovs before them. Even before Stalin's reign the Bolsheviks held absolute power and defended it with a growing political terror.

Stalin, who was in all probability psychopathic, inherited this tradition and carried it further than any who came before him. His absolute authority gave him the power of life and death over millions. No human being, least of all one like Stalin, can be trusted with such power, yet absolutist regimes attract most strongly those who, like Stalin, seek power at any cost. In Stalin's ideology and personality absolute authority became unparalleled horror. The crimes of Stalin show that at bottom absolutist government is itself a kind of violence.

(See also: COLD WAR, COMMUNISM/SOVIET UNION, TOTALITARIANISM)

---

1. Authorities differ on the numbers of Stalin's victims. Aleksandr Solzhenitsyn estimates 66 million; Alvin Gouldner, 20 million. Solzhenitsyn, *The Gulag Archipelago* (New York: Harper & Row, 1974–1978); Gouldner, Alvin W., "Stalinism: A Study of Internal Colonialism," *Telos*, 34 (Winter 1977–1978), cited in Leo Kuper, *Genocide* (New Haven & London: Yale University Press, 1981), p. 97. See also Appendix to Robert Conquest, *The Great Terror* (London: Macmillan, 1968).

Terrorism: Deliberate creation of fear through acts of random, or seemingly random, violence is an old political tactic. Governments have frequently used it, though they generally prefer not to call it terrorism. Antigovernment groups of the Right and Left have used political terror extensively. Political assassination ("propaganda of the deed") was widely advocated, though less widely practiced, among nineteenth-century anarchists. Right-wing French terrorists during the Algerian War in the early 1950s attacked civilians directly, detonating bombs in public buildings such as restaurants. Terrorists have also attacked the seat of government itself, as in Guy Fawkes' attempt to dynamite Britain's Parliament in 1605.

Modern terrorists use similar methods. Attacks on third parties, such as the Irish Republican Army bombing of Harrods department store in London, Palestinian hijackings of airplanes and killings, and suicide bombings like the ones on Allied peacekeeping forces in Lebanon in 1983, all illustrate the variety of terrorist tactics.

Spectacular and horrifying though it is, terrorism cannot in fact serve any positive purpose. It directly harms bystanders who have no role in determining policy and often know little or nothing about the supposed goals of the terrorist group. It increases the level of violence in situations which are already violent or, far worse, it can create a violent situation and thus undercut efforts at nonviolent change. Terrorists, who often have little popular support, can make achievement of real change more difficult or nearly impossible—thus harming the very people they claim to represent.

In the nineteenth century anarchists assumed that successful political assassinations would touch off a popular revolution to overthrow all governments. This did not happen. Terrorists find themselves in a similar situation today. Their methods build no popular movement so that eventually terror becomes an end in itself. (It is common, for example, for terrorist demands to center on release of other terrorists being held prisoner for previous terrorist actions. This does not achieve, nor can it achieve, any positive end.)

These arguments notwithstanding, no one can ignore terrorism. Governments, which are in fact the primary instruments of terror, have certainly not done so. Early in the Reagan administration, the U.S. government identified "international terrorism"—including the so-called terrorist conspiracy, whose existence has never been proven—as one of the world's major problems. In many countries, the "fight against terrorism" has become the occasion for intensive political repression so that government terror tactics far outstrip in destructiveness those of the terrorists themselves. In other countries, such as Guatemala and El Salvador, ultra-right-wing terrorists (death squads) operated with the tacit consent or even support of the government, and often with U.S. funding that reached them indirectly. Israeli reprisals against Palestinian terrorists have often consisted of bombing raids against Palestinians—far more destructive in terms of numbers killed than the acts of terror they were avenging. British policies in Northern Ireland, including internment without trial and use of "non-lethal" plastic bullets against crowds, have increased the level of violence in that unhappy country over and above the violence of the Irish Republican Army. Soviet repression of dissent, even of nonviolent opposition, has been harsh and absolute, as in Czechoslovakia (1968) and Poland (1981). In China the state terror of the Red Guards nearly destroyed the fabric of Chinese society. State-sponsored terror extended to entire social classes in Pol Pot's Kampuchea.

One could go on and on. The effort to combat terrorism by repression is itself a form of terrorism and it is doomed to fail. It is based on a crucial error: the belief that terrorists are mere "thugs" or "criminals"; or, worse, that they are simply agents of the Soviet Union or of the "international terrorist conspiracy." Governments further assume that with enough repression terrorism can be defeated and then there will be no problem. Often they will say that attempts to ameliorate the underlying problems amount to "capitulation" to terrorists.

This is not the case. Terrorists do not speak for the people they claim to represent, but terrorism as a phenomenon arises out of social conditions which will continue to breed violence unless they are understood and dealt with. Repression will not in the long run end terrorism. It will cause it to take new and possibly more destructive forms.

It would be far better to examine the roots of terrorism in particular situations and try to find ways to deal nonviolently with the sources of conflict. An example is the work of Lynne Shivers and David Bowman on Northern Ireland.[1] The authors examine the history and social roots of the terror and suggest ways out of the impasse between Protestant and Catholic, the source of much of the violence.

Approaches like these are not simple. They require hard work and real social change. But they promise far more success than repression and the vast apparatus of antiterrorist squads and reprisals which governments have built up in response to terrorist activities.

Public emphasis on the "fight against terrorism" has drawn attention away from the far more destructive policies of the world's governments. The number of people killed by terrorists since World War II is unknown, but it is far less than the twenty-five million killed in wars during that same period. Those killed in an all-out nuclear war might number half a billion immediately and, eventually, most of the human race. Governments which habitually condemn "international terrorism" as the major threat to peace and stability would also do well to examine their own policies.

1. Lynne Shivers and David Bowman, S.J., *More Than Troubles: A Common Sense View in the Northern Ireland Conflict* (Philadelphia: New Society Publishers, 1983).

Third World: Although no single meaning of "third world" is wholly satisfactory, this article will define a Third World country as any nation which is not aligned with either of the two great power blocs and is non-Western in culture. By this working definition, the Third World includes all Latin American and Central American countries, most countries in Asia, most in Africa, and many in the Middle East.

Nearly all Third World countries have in common a history of Western occupation or dominance. Most were included in the great colonial empires of the sixteenth through early twentieth centuries. Many remained under formal Western governance until after World War II, and Western economic hegemony continues in many. Countries such as Saudi Arabia and Brazil are rich in natural resources, making exploitation of these countries highly tempting to Western multinational companies. East bloc countries, particularly the Soviet Union, often compete with the West for influence and access to Third World natural resources, though, as shown in the article on the Soviet Union, with indifferent success.

Many Third World governments are opposed by indigenous guerrilla movements or other antigovernment forces. U.S. policymakers have tended to see such insurgencies as part of an overall Soviet plan to conquer the Third World. This is a serious mistake and has led to tragic consequences—as in the U.S. military intervention in Vietnam. U.S. intervention has also taken the form of military aid, including training government troops, supplying modern weapons, and deploying military advisers in or near the combat zones. Given the repressive nature of some of the governments supported by U.S. aid, the existence of insurgency movements should not be surprising.

Western intervention in the Third World took another and highly destructive form in the late 1970s and early 1980s. Banks in the United States and Europe lent large sums to Third World governments, leading to the accumulation of debts which those governments could not afford to pay. To avoid bankruptcy, many Third World countries turned to the International Monetary Fund, which provided aid conditioned upon economic austerity. Austerity in most Third World countries meant severe cuts in government spending on such domestic necessities as education and economic development—which led in turn to increased suffering for most of the population. At the same time, the high level of government indebtedness to private banks, not only in the Third World but in some Western countries such as Poland, threatened to undermine the world banking system.

Although the most publicized Third World liberation movements have been guerrilla insurgencies, much positive change in the Third World has come about through the use of nonviolence. Gandhi's liberation movement in India remains the largest single successful movement of national liberation. In 1983–85, a number of Latin American countries moved toward democratic governments through nonviolent means. Argentina's military junta, discredited by its performance in the Falklands War, fell from power in 1983 and was replaced by a democratically-elected government pledged to prosecute those in the former regime who had been responsible for the thousands of "disappearances" that had been common in Argentine life. The opposition to the repressive government of Chile in the 1980s was nonviolent and supported by the vast majority of the population. In 1985, Brazil held democratic elections for the first time in twenty-one years; Brazil is also home of the largest nonviolent movement in the world.

In the 1970s and 1980s, those Third World countries which had natural resources began to demand a fair return for their products from the Western industrial powers. This inevitable development led to conflicts, plans for Western military intervention (e.g., to secure oil supplies), and, ironically, hardships for some Third World countries which did not have abundant resources. It is clear, however, that military intervention to secure supplies of resources will fail in the long run. War for oil, for example, is militarily almost impossible, as shown in the article on the Rapid Deployment Force. The facts of economic life in the world have changed irrevocably; the Western industrial powers, including the United States, must adjust.

The problems of the Third World will not be solved by military intervention or bank loans. What is required is a real commitment to economic development founded on the recognition that the industrial nations and the Third World have a common interest in reducing poverty, preventing famine, avoiding national bankruptcies, and controlling population growth. Without justice, there may be—and has been—war. Of the forty active wars surveyed by the Center for Defense Information in 1984, thirty-five were taking place in the Third World.

Many Third World countries have already taken action to prevent nuclear war. In 1984, leaders of six countries—Argentina, Mexico, Tanzania, Sweden, Greece, and India—created the Five Continent Peace Initiative to mobilize global pressure on the "two major nuclear weapon powers to implement their undertaking [in the 1985 Geneva arms control talks] and . . . to produce, at an early date, significant results."[1] This and similar actions demonstrate that the Third World is not solely an arena of East-West conflict, but a group of nations with interests and concerns of their own. The Five Continent Peace Initiative spoke not only for itself, but for all humanity.

(See also: RAPID DEPLOYMENT FORCE, SOVIET UNION, UNITED STATES)

1. Joint declaration of Five Continent Peace Initiative ("Delhi Declaration"), quoted in Christopher Paine, "The 'Other Nations' Speak Up," *Bulletin of the Atomic Scientists*, April, 1985, p. 6.

Thoreau, Henry David: Though known primarily as a naturalist and transcendentalist philosopher, Henry David Thoreau (1817–62) was also involved in the antislavery movement and in the protest against the Mexican War. He began to refuse payment of poll tax in 1842 on the grounds that money raised by the tax went to support slavery, and that to pay the tax was to participate personally in the evil of slavery. By 1848, when he was jailed for his tax resistance, Thoreau was also refusing to support the Mexican War.

Thoreau spent only one night in jail, but the essay that resulted from his experience, "On the Duty of Civil Disobedience" (1849), has become one of the basic documents of nearly all nonviolent movements for social change. Thoreau argued that human laws are not the highest arbiters of behavior. Law, he said, must give place to conscience when there is conflict between the two. A person who refuses to obey an unjust law not only follows the higher law of conscience, he or she becomes an essential agent for social change—in Thoreau's phrase, "a counter friction to stop the machine."

Thoreau was not the first to argue for civil disobedience but his essay has been the most influential. Gandhi read it and adopted parts of Thoreau's philosophy; Martin Luther King, Jr., was also influenced by it. Today "Civil Disobedience" is

300

read in public schools as well as private schools, thus introducing millions of students to the ideas of conscience, civil disobedience, anarchism, and objection to war on principle.

It would be hard to overestimate Thoreau's importance to the peace movement. "Civil Disobedience" at once advocated a more active movement against war (in this case a particular war), and provided a method of action that went beyond letters and petitions and sought to overcome the system's violence directly by refusing to be a part of it. The essay was an antidote to passivity, a call to action which can still move us and whose relevance is undiminished by time.

Important though his work was to the peace movement, Thoreau himself was not a pacifist. He vigorously defended John Brown's guerrilla-style raid on Harper's Ferry in "A Plea for Captain John Brown" (1859). It is likely, however, that if he were alive today Thoreau would say, as he did in 1849, that "it is not too soon for honest men to rebel and revolutionize."

(See also: CIVIL DISOBEDIENCE, GANDHI, MOHANDAS K., KING, MARTIN LUTHER, JR., NONVIOLENCE)

Totalitarianism, Nonviolence and: It is generally recognized that nonviolent action can achieve social change in democratic societies. Critics of nonviolence argue, however, that nonviolence is useless against totalitarian regimes. Pointing to the suppression of nonviolent movements such as the Solidarity movement in Poland, they suggest that the only alternative to tyranny is violent overthrow of the government. Dictatorships, it is argued, are more ruthless in dealing with dissent among their own people than a democratic government would be.

Although the liberalism of democracies is often overstated—in the frequent assertion that the British were unusually civilized in their treatment of Gandhi, for example—it is generally true that a dictatorship will repress dissent with far more violence than a democracy. Nonetheless totalitarian governments are vulnerable to nonviolent resistance because at bottom their power depends upon the obedience of the people they govern. Refusal to obey the government's commands, which is one of the basic techniques of nonviolent action, has been a major factor in most revolutions. This is as true of violent revolutions as of nonviolent ones.

Nonviolence uses this basic weakness of government as one of its starting points. By refusing obedience the people can in effect remove the government's power. To do this successfully their action must be concerted, and it must take place on a large scale. This, however, is equally true of an attempt at violent revolution: in general, such an attempt will fail without popular support or, worse, become a palace revolt leading merely to a reshuffling of leadership but not to real change. Thus the difficulty of nonviolent revolutions is actually the difficulty of *all* revolution. Genuine democratic revolutions are extremely difficult to mount and sustain because they depend on popular support and the willingness of the public to refuse the government's commands.

Nonviolent resistance to East bloc tyranny since World War II has included the East German uprising, 1953; the Hungarian Revolution, 1956, in which a mixture of nonviolent and violent techniques were employed; the Czech Resistance of 1968 (see separate article); and the Solidarity movement in Poland, 1980–81 (see separate article). In addition large-scale Jewish emigration from the Soviet Union has become a form of nonviolent resistance.

In the West the largest nonviolent movement of the 1970s and 1980s was the popular movement in Brazil, a country whose government is a highly repressive dictatorship. The 1978–79 movement to overthrow the shah of Iran was largely nonviolent in tactics. It succeeded in changing the government after months of strikes and mass demonstrations. The aftermath of the Iranian movement, however, raises major questions which will be considered below.

With the exception of Iran, none of these movements has overthrown the government it was resisting. But the record of violent revolutions is far worse. One can point to no successful instances of violent revolution in the East bloc. On the contrary, the most notable resistance movements there have been nonviolent. In the West violent uprisings have been far more likely to lead to protracted and bloody guerrilla wars than to the overthrow of repressive governments. The major exception in the 1980s was the overthrow of the Somoza family dictatorship in Nicaragua. And the success of the Nicaraguan revolution, as judged by its ability to establish political democracy and economic justice, is still an open question—in part because of an anti-Nicaraguan covert war funded by the United States.

In the twentieth century violent revolutions have repeatedly failed to provide liberty and justice for the people in whose name they were made. The violent overthrow of the government of Cambodia led to the appalling regime of Pol Pot, a man who deliberately killed approximately one million of his countrymen. Revolution in Cuba has led to greater economic justice but no political freedom. Worst of all was the Bolshevik Revolution in Russia, which led to a bloody civil war, the horrifying period of Stalin's regime, and a modern Soviet Union which is a dictatorship without economic justice.

It is clear that violent overthrow of a repressive government leads far more often than not to the establishment of an equally repressive and violent government. The aftermath of the Iranian Revolution, which used nonviolent techniques, raises questions about nonviolent revolutions as well. Iran overthrew the tyranny of the shah and replaced it with the tyranny of the Ayatollah Khomeini. In the process it became even more aggressive militarily than it had been under the shah. Iran then became involved in the Persian Gulf War with Iraq, one of the most brutal in Middle Eastern history. How did nonviolent techniques lead to such a tragic result?

There is no simple answer to this question. It is evident, however, that the overthrow of the shah did not result from a movement that was deeply committed to nonviolence. The revolution's slogan, "Death to the shah," hardly bespoke a nonviolent spirit. Thus one lesson of the Iranian Revolution is that nonviolence is *not* a mere technique. Nonviolent methods can be used, as in fact they were used in Iran, out of hatred. But so used, they will ultimately fail. They may achieve overthrow of the government but in the long run a revolution motivated by hatred cannot remain nonviolent.

This clearly occurred in Iran. Khomeini's initial goal—the

destruction of the shah—was violent. His larger goal—establishing a fundamentalist Islamic regime—soon came to mean replacing the shah's violence with the violence of the Islamic revolutionary government. The abandonment of nonviolence was no accident; it was almost certainly part of Khomeini's overall strategy.

That the Iranian Revolution abandoned nonviolence, however, does not mean that nonviolence failed. The end of the shah's regime was achieved by using nonviolent techniques. With leadership committed to nonviolence and democratic change, it is quite possible that the Iranian Revolution would have had a different outcome. This shows not that nonviolence was useless, but that nonviolence cannot achieve justice if it is abandoned and replaced with violence and repression.

(See also: CENTRAL AMERICA, CZECH RESISTANCE, MIDDLE EAST, NAZIS, NONVIOLENCE AND, SOLIDARITY)

United Nations: Critics of the United Nations can point to many shortcomings. The U.N. has given international standing to terrorist groups. It has passed some ill-considered resolutions like the one equating Zionism and racism. It has not, for whatever reasons, prevented war. These are serious failures, and they deserve serious discussion. Without such discussion the U.N. or any other international body cannot become a workable forum for settling international disputes.

What passes for criticism of the United Nations in the United States, however, is neither debate nor serious criticism. It boils down to one complaint: the United Nations does not follow the United States line. Thus U.S. officials berate the U.N. General Assembly as a "useless" or "destructive" forum, when what they mean is that General Assembly resolutions and debate are frequently critical of the United States. They would do far better to realize that the U.S. is not in fact always well-liked in the rest of the world, and to take some of the world's criticism seriously. The administration and many in the Congress prefer to attack the U.N. rather than to use it constructively, though.

This is tragic for the bulk of the U.N.'s work receives little publicity and is of direct and immediate benefit to human-kind. The work of the United Nations International Chil-dren's Emergency Fund (UNICEF) in relieving the suffering of the world's children receives virtually no publicity, save for Halloween collection boxes and Christmas cards. The re-markable Law of the Sea Conference was a major step toward establishing rules for peaceful uses of the sea and conservation of its resources. It received publicity not for its positive achievements but because the Reagan administration rather petulantly refused to abide by its recommendations.

Despite this and other good work a more basic question about the United Nations, and one which its political critics do not raise, remains. Can an organization of sovereign states, each of them committed to use military force for its own purposes, actually maintain peace? The record is discourag-ing: twenty-five million people have died in wars since the U.N. was founded after World War II. United Nations media-tion efforts in conflicts like the Falklands (Malvinas) War were a failure. United States-Soviet arms control negotiations do not involve the U.N. at all.

It is likely that the United Nations will continue to be crippled in its peacemaking efforts as long as nations reserve the right to use military force before seeking mediation, and as long as they undercut or refuse to abide by U.N. mediation efforts. In the nature of things such mediation usually means compromise for both sides, and many national leaders will not agree to such compromises. Worse still are the actions of national leaders such as British Prime Minister Margaret Thatcher: she dispatched a British task force to the Falklands (Malvinas) before mediation had begun—thus making media-tion and compromise far more difficult.

Nonetheless the United Nations remains in principle a useful peacemaking forum. The U.N. Charter, which outlines basic human rights and means of maintaining peace, has be-come the basis for an evolving body of international law which though flawed could become the basis for an international order based on mutual cooperation rather than mutual hostility.

The United Nations has accomplished much which remains unpublicized. It has also served, as has no other organization, as a forum for the ideas and concerns of the Third World. The two United Nations Conferences on Disarmament spoke for the interests of humankind as a whole when they called for general and complete disarmament.

It will not do for the superpowers to dismiss the United Nations. The U.N. remains the major international organization. Its Charter provides the basis for much international law. Its humanitarian work—e.g., its relief work in the Ethiopian famine of 1984–85—has saved thousands of lives. If there were no United Nations, the world would have to develop one.

United States: The United States of America is one of the two largest military powers in the world. Politically, economically, and diplomatically, it is the dominant power in the West. This remains true even though United States per capita income may no longer be the highest in the world and even though foreign technology has in some respects surpassed that of the U.S. This article discusses only the military aspects of American power.

War in U.S. History

It is one of the peculiarities of American history that unlike those of other major military powers the U.S. homeland has not been attacked since the Civil War. Nor has the United States suffered enormous loss in any of its wars since that time. World War II, for example, resulted in the deaths of about three hundred thousand Americans. An appalling loss it is true but the dead on a world scale totaled roughly fifty million, and deaths in the Soviet Union alone totaled about twenty million. Accidents of history and geography account for the relatively low level of American deaths.

Americans have been fortunate. They have not experienced the horrors of war on their own territory. Instead, since the Civil War, American forces have been involved either in expanding white control of Native American territories, often with brutal efficiency, or in wars fought on foreign soil. For Americans wars have mainly been elsewhere. This is true of wars whose motives were dubious, such as the Mexican, Spanish-American, and Indochina wars, and of wars fought for high principles such as World War II.

Thus at least until Vietnam, Americans could easily think of themselves (and did in fact think of themselves) as a powerful giant who fought reluctantly and then only to save the world from evil. This image could plausibly be applied to World War II. It made far less sense when applied to World War I, the Korean "police action," or Vietnam, where U.S. troops were forced to commit acts that American soldiers were supposed to be incapable of committing.

Since World War II the image of our troops as "rescuers" (which was used as recently as the Grenada invasion of 1983) has led to a willingness to intervene militarily in situations where with greater wisdom the United States would have held back. It has created a generally favorable public attitude toward the military and made the American public—at least until Vietnam—less skeptical about war than people in countries which have experienced war directly.

U.S. Military Power

It is fashionable in hardline ideological circles to say that the U.S. "disarmed unilaterally" during the 1970s and is no longer a formidable military power, or was not until the Reagan "rearmament." This notion is utterly false. During the 1970s U.S. defense budgets regularly increased beyond the demands of inflation. The number and efficiency of weapons increased, and military technology reached new heights of diabolism.

The U.S. military has 2.1 million troops. American nuclear warheads, about ten thousand of them, could destroy all of humanity twelve times over. American nuclear submarines, each capable of destroying 160 cities with its missiles, cruise the oceans constantly. American aircraft patrol continually.

United States logistics, or ability to move large numbers of troops and supplies, are the envy of all other armies. Each year, the U.S. spends upwards of $250 billion to support this immense military establishment. Such arms and such expenditure hardly betoken a nation that is disarming.

The Defense of the U.S.

If the sole aim of U.S. military policy were the defense of the United States little of the money now spent on military forces would be required. The U.S. is particularly well-situated for either military or nonviolent defense. It is protected on the east and west by oceans and on the north and south by friendly neighbors. Its territory is vast, a factor which would present major difficulties to an invader. There are few places near it which could act as a staging area for a major invasion. (In any case, invasions across water are rare in history, in part because they are so likely to fail.)

No general would attempt a sea- or airborne invasion on the scale needed to conquer the United States. Pitted against either military defense or civilian resistance, such an invasion would court disaster. The United States is too big and it is too far from most other countries to allow adequate supply lines.

As it happens the bulk of U.S. forces are not defensive. They are trained to fight in the kinds of wars which America has fought for more than a hundred years: wars of intervention. American troops receive jungle training, though few areas in the U.S. are covered by jungle. They receive training in desert warfare, which is likely to be of use primarily in areas like the Middle East or North Africa. Policymakers prepare for war in Europe, in Asia, in the Middle East, and in Central America. They spend little time preparing for the direct defense of the United States—except against nuclear attack, against which there is no real defense.

U.S. Policies

American foreign policy, though extremely complex, has been pervaded by three oversimplified assumptions. First among these is the notion that conflict in the world, whatever its apparent source, is merely a playing-out of the East-West conflict. The Reagan administration carried this assumption to its logical conclusion by asserting that the Soviet Union is the "focus of evil" in the world and treating virtually every uprising as though it were inspired solely by Soviet agents. Many U.S. politicians share this basic assumption.

A second and related assumption is that the Soviet Union is implacably bent upon mischief because of its Marxist ideology. Since the Soviet Union usually behaves like other great powers—well when this suits its interest and despicably when it doesn't—the American tendency to attribute implacable evil to the U.S.S.R. often leads to misunderstanding and miscalculation. It leads also to a tendency to treat all Soviet misdeeds (and they are many) as justification for American abuses.

A third and unstated assumption is that the U.S. and the Soviet Union cannot live together forever. This assumption is the most dangerous of all, but it dies very hard. Yet die it must. If the conflict between the two powers is really mortal and impossible to resolve, then neither will survive.

U.S. Influence

American foreign policy since 1945 has concentrated primarily upon limiting or reducing the influence of the Soviet Union. This goal of "containment" was first articulated by George Kennan (who later repudiated the doctrine) in 1948. In modified form it remains U.S. policy.

If U.S. foreign policy is judged solely by the extent of Soviet influence, containment has been far more successful than the American right wing asserts. As detailed in the article on the Soviet Union, Soviet influence in the world has declined since the 1950s. Whether U.S. policy caused this decline, however, is quite another question. Soviet policies are unattractive to some other countries, and many Third World leaders are skeptical of the motives of both superpowers. Thus the decline in Soviet influence might have taken place whatever the United States did.

Much of what the United States has done in foreign affairs since 1945 has been good. The Marshall Plan, although its rationale depended partly on the containment strategy, was also a major humanitarian program to rebuild a Europe shattered by the most terrible war in history. The Peace Corps and other economic development aid have brought some hope to poor peoples everywhere.

American concentration upon the East-West conflict, however, has led U.S. policy into actions unworthy of a great nation and people. United States dollars and military hardware have, in the name of anticommunism, supported tyrants throughout the Third World, from Syngman Rhee of Korea to Ngo Dinh Diem of Vietnam to Augusto Pinochet of Chile to the murderers in Guatemala. The U.S. is one of the two major arms suppliers in the world (the other is the Soviet Union), and often uses the arms trade as a kind of diplomacy. American troops have intervened in Korea, the Dominican Republic, Vietnam, and Grenada. U.S. intelligence agents have participated in the overthrow of popularly-based governments in Iran, Chile, Guatemala, and other countries. Covert armies funded and supplied by the U.S. began attacking the government of Nicaragua in late 1982.

Many of these actions are self-defeating. Support of dictators contradicts democratic values. United States support for the much-hated shah of Iran led to a severe anti-U.S. backlash when the shah was overthrown in 1979. The U.S. refusal to establish normal relations with Nicaragua could cause the Nicaraguan government to become dependent on the Soviet Union—the opposite of the result intended.

The United States cannot control events in the world. Its attempts to do so have often brought it far more problems than they have solved.

Domestic Effects

At the same time the swollen American military establishment has harmed the United States body politic. Columbia University scholar Seymour Melman has shown that military policies, with their emphasis on technology, have kept many of the best engineers and researchers working on military projects, with the result that the civilian economy is now seriously deficient in many areas. The gigantic military budget is funded at the expense of education, the poor, and social insurance, with the result that the U.S. is among the most backward of all Western countries in those areas. Roads, railroads, bridges, factories, all go without development and repair funds, while expensive weapons systems such as the Trident submarine are funded often without question. These trends were visible twenty years ago, and the United States is now paying full price for its commitment to military superiority.

The U.S. Peace Movement

United States policies on arms and intervention have not proceeded without opposition. The most hopeful development of the last twenty years has been the growth of the peace movement. Much of this growth occurred because of the highly unpopular Indochina War. Since 1980, however, the most successful peace movement strategy has been the campaign for a nuclear freeze. This movement achieved success and popular influence at a time when the government was trying to build support for a renewed arms race. The experience of the nuclear freeze campaign showed that the days when the American public supported military policies without question may have ended.

U.S.-Soviet Relations

The conflict between the United States and the Soviet Union is severe and of long standing. Yet there are grounds for hope that the two nations can learn to live together. According to the U.S. State Department's *Treaties in Force* (January 1, 1983), there are sixty-four bilateral treaties between the U.S. and the Soviet Union, covering a wide range of subjects such as agriculture, copyrights, oceanography, telecommunications, and transportation. The United States and the Soviet Union are also signatories to 102 other multilateral agreements covering subjects such as Antarctica, customs, narcotic drugs, rules of warfare, and tourism.[1] It is clear that where the U.S. and the Soviet Union have interests in common they have often been able to reach mutually acceptable agreements.

311

Peace is one such common interest. Given the stakes involved, it must be the overriding goal of American policy. This does not mean that the U.S. must approve of the Soviet Union, or vice-versa: it will not end the competition between the two powers. But military competition between two nations armed with such destructive power invites only disaster. Peace is possible not because the Soviet Union is "good" (it is not), but because in the long run the only alternative to living together is dying together.

(See also: COLD WAR, CONVENTIONAL WAR, INDOCHINA WAR, MILITARY-INDUSTRIAL COMPLEX, NATO AND WARSAW PACT, NONVIOLENCE, NUCLEAR FREEZE MOVEMENT, NUCLEAR STRATEGY, NUCLEAR WEAPONS AND WAR, SOVIET UNION)

1. Center for Defense Information, "U.S.-Soviet Relations: To the Summit and Beyond," *Defense Monitor*, Vol. XIII, No. 2 (1984), p. 5.

Vietnam: (see INDOCHINA WAR)

War and the Environment: The direct effects of war on natural and human environments are in some respects obvious. Photographs of cities and fields where combat has taken place reveal an unearthly, blasted landscape utterly alien to all normal and healthy life. Trees become stumps without branches, leaves, or identity. Fields are transformed from green to brown. Buildings which were of surpassing loveliness become four walls enclosing emptiness. City blocks littered with broken stones and bricks are themselves corpses even as they are strewn with the human dead and dying.

In the past such landscapes, though horrifying, were for the most part a temporary effect of war. Even the trenches of World War I, a narrow strip which had been shelled and fought over again and again for four years, blossomed with trees and grass again except in the most heavily shelled areas,

312

such as Dead Man's Hill at Verdun, where nothing grew until the government planted trees in the 1930s. Cities such as Tokyo, Hamburg, Rotterdam and even Hiroshima and Nagasaki were able to rebuild almost as though their agonies had never been.

Yet full recovery from the destructiveness of war is seldom possible. Marks from the old trench lines are still visible on some World War I battlefields, and some still hold unexploded shells.[1] Many of the buildings in once-blasted cities are new, but the ones they replaced have been lost forever.

Since World War II developments in military technology have not only increased the environmental damage that armies can do, they have added long-term damage to short-term devastation. A simple example is the plastic land mine. This device, which cannot be detected and retrieved, was used extensively in the Falklands (Malvinas) War. Large areas of the Falkland Islands are now permanently closed to humans and to sheep; the mines are still there and entering these areas is now too hazardous.

On a more complex level the American attempt to "defoliate" the jungles of Vietnam, using the highly dangerous chemical dioxin, has permanently polluted the ecosystem in that unhappy country. Dioxin is so dangerous that in the United States it is considered hazardous waste. Vietnam veterans exposed to the dioxin-based defoliant Agent Orange report a variety of serious illnesses traceable to their exposure, including cancer, liver problems, severe skin problems, and birth defects in their children.

Because modern weapons are so destructive and so indiscriminate in their effects, it is likely that the direct environmental damage associated with war will increase in the future. Modern toxic chemicals, such as nerve gas, are so potent that even very small amounts can kill hundreds of thousands of people and animals. The long-term effects of such poisons on the environment are unknown but are unlikely to be negligible. (Nuclear warfare, which would pollute the environment to an almost unimaginable degree and which could end life on earth, is discussed in NUCLEAR WEAPONS AND WAR.)

Less widely noted than the direct effects of warfare on the environment are its indirect effects. These result from the wastefulness of modern warfare and the expense of equipping a modern army.

Modern armies gain their mobility and destructiveness by using fuel, metals, and other raw materials far more wastefully than the civilian economy. Thus in 1978 the U.S. Defense Department used more energy than the entire country of Sweden.[2] A modern tank uses anywhere from one to four gallons of fuel to travel one mile. The tank itself is made of metal, often using rare or precious metals as part of the alloys that compose it. Armies expect to "lose" tanks—i.e., they expect them to be destroyed—in combat. Because of the peculiar conditions of combat, the materials in a tank may be difficult or impossible to recover. Thus modern combat is the most wasteful of human enterprises.

At the same time the vast quantities of money spent on equipping a modern army are invariably spent at the expense of programs to aid the poor, increase education, and protect the environment. The tank which uses more fuel than thirty civilian automobiles costs tens of millions of dollars. It is built not by ones and twos, but by hundreds or even thousands. It is only a small part of a panoply of environment which includes aircraft, artillery, millions of shells and other ammunition, ships of all sizes, and missiles of all descriptions, sizes, and levels of expense. This equipment is regularly "modernized"—that is, much of it is scrapped and replaced, generally with more complex and more expensive equipment.

Modern warfare, which can destroy the environment quickly and permanently, destroys it with equal finality in peacetime. The difference is that the destruction is slow and difficult to see. Very simply the environment cannot indefinitely survive the combined insults of civilian pollution and waste and military pollution and waste.

(See also: CONVENTIONAL WAR, NUCLEAR WAR)

1. See aerial photographs and photographs of shells removed from the earth in 1982 in the Somme region of France. Lyn Macdonald, *Somme* (London: Michael Joseph, 1983).

2. Center for Defense Information, *Defense Monitor*, Vol. VIII, No. 11 (December, 1979), p. 7.

War and Literature: The literature of war begins in the West with the *Iliad* of Homer. It includes plays, poems, histories, memoirs, novels, and films. Much of it glorifies or distorts war, either for propaganda purposes or because it was written from the command point of view.

The finest writing about war does none of this. It portrays war as the human tragedy that it is. Inevitably, therefore, it makes the case against war more eloquently than much moral and philosophical argument. Yet, as with all good literature, good writing about war does not have argument as its primary purpose. The truth about war and the realities of battle are so terrible that embellishment, argument, and propaganda become superfluous.

The following survey covers only poetry, fiction, memoirs, and histories. It does not pretend to be comprehensive but tries instead to point toward some of the most significant war literature. Further suggestions and publication information on the works below will be found in the bibliography.

Poetry

Until the twentieth century poetry actually written by soldiers was rare. There was a simple reason for this—most soldiers were illiterate. Officers, who were members of the nobility, often wrote poetry, but the poetry of war after the *Iliad* did not reach its full power until World War I. Of antiwar poetry written by civilians, one of the most striking collections is Walt Whitman's "Drum Taps," which was inspired by the poet's experience as a wound dresser in a civil war hospital. It is now a section of Whitman's *Leaves of Grass.*

In World War I, the long periods of idleness in the trenches, coupled with a great interest in poetry among British soldiers at least, led to an outburst of war poetry by well-known poets and unknown writers alike. The poetry of the trenches is uneven but, at its best, unsurpassed.

By common consent the finest of the World War I poets was Wilfred Owen, a British junior officer who was killed in action toward the end of the war. Owen's poems, such as "Dulce et Decorum Est" and "Strange Meeting," were experimental in rhyme and unflinching in their portrayal of the

315

sufferings of the men in the trenches. Other noted World War I poets include Edmund Blunden, Siegfried Sassoon, Rupert Brooke and Robert Graves.

The poetry of World War II is less bitter than that which came out of the trenches. For the most part poets supported the war, but saw its tragedy. Some, like Richard Eberhart, were antiwar in their orientation; others simply portrayed war as they saw it.

In the postwar period, few wars have produced significant poetry in English. An exception is the Indochina War which because of its length and nature led many soldiers to express themselves in verse. Probably the most striking collection to come out of the conflict is a little-known work, *Winning Hearts and Minds*, edited by Larry Rottman, Jan Barry, and Basil T. Pacquet. This powerful book originally could not find a publisher. It was finally published by First Casualty Press, which was founded especially for this purpose by the editors. Major publishers have published relatively little Vietnam poetry.

Histories and Memoirs

Military history is on the whole not literature at all. It not only distorts the truth, and is dense and difficult to read, but much of it treats warfare as a gigantic chess game. There are exceptions well worth reading—not only for their intrinsic merits but as helpful background to war literature.

After a slow beginning John Keegan's *The Face of Battle*, which reconstructs three battles from the point of view of the soldiers, becomes a powerful meditation on violence. Keegan's *Six Armies in Normandy*, though much of it is standard military history, contains an astonishing essay on what it was like to be a child in the West of England during World War II. Keegan's work pioneered the effort to portray battles as the troops saw them. He is among the most compassionate and illuminating of military historians.

A more difficult work to classify but certainly one of the finest prose works to come out of World War II is John Hersey's *Hiroshima*, a portrayal of six Hiroshima survivors originally written on assignment for the *New Yorker*. Whether this book is history or reportage is not material. It is one of the basic books for those who would understand the nuclear age.

Prior to the twentieth century there are few war memoirs written by common soldiers, as noted above. In this century, however, war veterans have produced memoirs which portray battle as vividly as some of the better novels.

Among World War I memoirs, the best are Edmund Blunden's *Undertones of War* and Robert Graves' *Goodbye To All That*. Equally powerful, but of a quite different type, is Vera Brittain's *Testament of Youth*, the only World War I memoir by a woman. Brittain, who served as a nurse at the front, later became a major figure in the British peace movement.

Thirty-five years after his participation in the World War II Allied invasion of Italy, when he felt able to write about it and keep his sanity, Farley Mowat produced a powerful memoir of his combat experience. Titled *And No Birds Sang*, it may be the best such work to come out of World War II.

As yet it is too early to evaluate memoirs from the Vietnam War, and so far few have been published. Two recent works are well worth reading, however. *Home Before Morning*, by Lynda Van Devanter and Christopher Morgan, is, like *Testament of Youth*, the story of a combat nurse. W. D. Ehrhart, a Vietnam-era poet, has also published an account of his combat experience in *Vietnam-Perkasie: A Combat Marine Memoir*. Two works published earlier, *Born on the Fourth of July*, by Ron Kovic and *A Rumor of War* by Philip Caputo are also of high quality.

Novels

With a few exceptions the best war novels are products of the twentieth century. Two exceptions are Tolstoy's *War and Peace*, which depicts (among many other themes) Napoleon's invasion of Russia, and Stephen Crane's *The Red Badge of Courage*. The latter work, which Crane wrote without any direct combat experience, was originally intended as an anti-war novel but Crane's publishers ordered major cuts of its antiwar passages. These are now being restored by scholars.

As with poetry the novel was a major form of expression for veterans of World War I. Though few read like propaganda, most of the novels from the trenches are bitterly antiwar. The most famous are Erich Maria Remarque's *All Quiet on the Western Front*, a horrifying portrait of soldiers in the trenches, their sufferings, and the brutal combat they endured and Ernest Hemingway's *A Farewell to Arms*. Less well-known, but of equal or even greater quality is Siegfried Sassoon's *Memoirs of an Infantry Officer*. Sassoon's book is semiautobiographical; the author, like his protagonist George Sherston, was an officer at the Battle of the Somme. Hemingway's novel about an ambulance driver on the Italian front is considered one of his best.

World War II is the subject of an astonishing amount of writing, including histories, detailed description of weapons, biography, and novels. The bulk of this material is of little value as literature. Among the novels the finest are probably Joseph Heller's *Catch-22* and Norman Mailer's *The Naked and the Dead*.

The literature of the Indochina War is still developing. Among works published to date, Michael Herr's *Dispatches* and John M. del Vecchio's *The Thirteenth Valley* have been well received.

War Resistance: Individual refusal to be part of war has been common throughout history. Collective refusal by large bodies of civilians or by military units has probably been less common but in a number of known cases it has affected the course of major wars.

Governments and their military forces have much to gain from concealing the extent of citizen resistance to their military policies. At the same time historians have until recently concentrated on diplomatic history, history of military weapons and strategy, and set-piece descriptions of battles—that is, on war as seen from the perspective of the rulers.[1] Thus except for pacifist historians[2] they have neglected or even concealed war resistance. This has been particularly true of resistance among soldiers, though works such as David Cortright's *Soldiers in Revolt*, a history of the Vietnam-era resistance in the U.S. military, have begun to redress the balance.

Broadly defined, war resistance is refusal to participate in war or some part of war. Not all war resisters are pacifists, and not all articulate their resistance in moral or religious terms. Yet much war resistance has roots in the religious and humanist traditions which also gave rise to pacifism. These traditions, however much they may rationalize the violence of combat, teach values which clash with the realities of the battlefield. It is not surprising that many people from all religious traditions have found it impossible to enter the military or, once in battle, to do as they are ordered.

At the same time revulsion at the violence of combat, the regimentation of military life, and the impersonal (and frequently foolish) demands of the High Command, occurs more often than is commonly supposed. Armies have developed an elaborate disciplinary apparatus to assure that this revulsion does not hamper military operations. Even so war resistance of this type has resulted in mutinies, collective refusal of orders, and massive desertions. That such actions do not result from simple cowardice is demonstrated by the outright defiance of superiors, with all its attendant risks, which they involve.

Probably the earliest recorded war resister was Maximilian, a Christian in the third century who was executed for refusing to serve in the Roman military.[3] Members of the traditional "peace churches"—Society of Friends, Anabaptists (Mennonites), and Brethren, among others—have frequently refused to be part of war by violating conscription laws, using legal channels provided for conscientious objectors, or even emigrating from countries which have conscription. A somewhat different but related tradition stems from the teachings of Henry David Thoreau and others on civil disobedience. (See separate article on CIVIL DISOBEDIENCE, which has become a major form of war resistance in the nuclear age.)

In addition to civil disobedience, war resistance today takes several forms:

Draft Resistance: In countries which have conscription,

refusal of induction or refusal to register for the draft is a common form of war resistance. European pacifists usually call draft resisters "total resisters" to distinguish them from conscientious objectors who use legal channels for their claims.

In the United States draft resistance became best known during the Indochina War. The Selective Service System recorded over five hundred thousand incidents of resistance from 1964 through 1973. This figure is slightly exaggerated because a draft resister might refuse induction, be called again after charges against him had been dropped because of draft board error, and refuse induction again. Nonetheless it is clear that draft resistance on an unprecedented scale occurred during the Vietnam era. Most of these resisters never faced charges. Selective Service errors were so common that the total number of cases brought to court during the Vietnam era was less than ten thousand.

Draft resisters took their stands for many reasons. Many were opposed not only to war but to the conscription system itself as part of the war machine. Others, who might have qualified for conscientious objector status, believed that it would be wrong for them to do so because such status was given primarily to the articulate, well-off, and well-educated. Still others did not qualify for conscientious objector status because they objected only to the Indochina War.

Selective Service figures, though they exaggerate the number of incidents of resistance, probably also understate the total number of resisters. Most draft resisters simply failed to register for the draft and did not tell anyone. The number of such private resisters will never be known because the draft system had no way to estimate it. Comparisons between draft registration figures and population figures in the relevant age group, however, led to estimates of up to one million silent resisters.

All who refused the draft risked five years in federal prison and $10,000 fine, though these maximum penalties were seldom imposed. Toward the end of the war, more than half of draft sentences were probation. As a condition of probation, the resister was usually required to perform two years' civilian work of national importance.

320

In addition to those who refused to be drafted, the Selective Service System faced major administrative problems in the early 1970s when hundreds of thousands of men filed appeals and requests for reclassification, as was their right under the law. By the time inductions were suspended in late 1972 the draft system was breaking down under the weight of both legal and illegal draft resistance.

In 1980 President Carter proclaimed the start of a new period of registration for the draft. This provoked widespread refusal to register, some of it public and vocal. The majority of men who refused or failed to register for the draft did not make their stands known to the government. By 1983 the Selective Service System estimated that about five hundred thousand men had refused to register as required. Polls commissioned by the system concluded that most of these men had failed to register out of ignorance, but the results were questionable because the pollsters did not ask those polled whether they opposed the draft. Government efforts to enforce the law against draft resisters included computer checks of existing lists of draft-age men (usually lists of licensed drivers purchased from the states); making draft registration a condition for receiving federal student aid and job training; and a large publicity campaign. Court cases challenged these efforts, as well as the whole draft registration program. It is likely that attempts to renew draft inductions would be met with similar resistance. At present the government has no authority to induct, yet even the threat of future induction has led to widespread failure or refusal to register.

War Tax Resistance: Refusal to pay taxes which are used for war is as yet only a small part of the peace movement. Tax resisters argue that the government could not make war without taxes, and that therefore tax resistance is not only a moral stance but in principle an effective one as well. As yet the effect of large-scale tax resistance is untested because such resistance has never occurred. The logic of the position is, however, sound.

War tax resisters in the United States commonly use several methods of refusing to pay their taxes. Some attempt to live below the minimum taxable income—a difficult option not readily available to most people. Others claim a "war crimes deduction" on their income tax returns, arguing that they are not legally required to pay taxes for government violations of international law. Still others claim large numbers of dependents, usually as a form of obvious protest; in one case a tax resister who had claimed the entire population of the world as dependents was acquitted of tax fraud because it was clear that he made the claim in protest. Still other tax resisters fail to file tax returns or simply refuse outright to pay what the government believes they owe.

War tax resisters seldom face imprisonment because the government has a number of recourses—levies on the individual's bank accounts, seizure of property, levies against the individual's salary—short of prosecution. A recent and disturbing development has been the government's effort to fine war tax resisters for filing "frivolous" tax returns. Harassment of this kind is another common Internal Revenue Service tactic.

It is likely that the government will continue to apply the tax laws using harassment and direct seizure of assets, and that the courts will provide little relief for tax resisters. The government, it is clear, accepts the tax resister's argument that large-scale war tax resistance could cripple government military efforts.[4]

A related development in U.S. law is the proposal for a World Peace Tax Fund. This fund would provide a kind of conscientious objector status for taxpayers, who could specify that taxes which normally go to the military should be placed in the fund.

Resistance in the Military: Individual resistance in the military, particularly under fire, has not taken the same forms as civilian resistance. Refusal of orders, refusal to wear the military uniform, absence without leave and desertion, and even application for discharge as a conscientious objector have been the most common forms of military war resistance. The extent of such actions in military history is impossible to ascertain. David Cortright shows in *Soldiers in Revolt* that they were common during the Vietnam era and were a major factor in ending U.S. military involvement in Indochina. The record for other wars includes a good deal of desertion and breakdown of units. Military historians, however, are loath to ascribe a unit's breakdown to "war resistance," preferring to use terms such as "exhaustion," "breakdown of morale," and "failure of command." Thus unit breakdowns may or may not have represented war resistance; it is impossible to know.

This is far less true of mutiny. The largest mutinies of the twentieth century—those in the French and Russian armies in 1917, and those in the German army in 1918—were clearly instances of war resistance, broadly defined. Unit-by-unit refusal to participate in combat was frequent in Indochina.

Because mutinies generally occur when an army is at the end of its tether, historians tend to ascribe them to poor leadership or the imminence of defeat. Such factors precipitate mutiny but rebellion by soldiers can move rapidly in the direction of revolution. This happened in the three major mutinies at the end of World War I. Mutinies by the troops were major factors in the Russian Revolution and in the 1918 attempt at revolution in Germany.[5]

The French army mutinies of 1917, though still largely obscured by official secrecy, reveal the process at work. In 1917 General Robert Nivelle, commander of the French armies, planned and executed a major offensive on the Chemin des Dames. The attack met such fierce resistance that 120,000 French soldiers were killed or wounded in two days. The army mutinied. What had begun as a reaction to poor generalship and senseless slaughter, however, quickly became the beginnings of a revolution. "Regiments elected councils to speak for them, ominously like the *Soviets* that had already seized power in the Russian army, and set off to Paris *en masse*."[6] The authorities suppressed the mutiny by partially meeting the soldiers' demands and by executing those thought to be the leaders.

Far more common than mutiny is the simple act of leaving the military. No military force permits its members to come and go as they wish, and penalties for desertion often include death. Yet absence without leave and desertion have been common in every major war, and not just on the losing side. The best-known instance of large-scale desertion occurred during the Indochina War when the U.S. military recorded 535,000 incidents of AWOL (Absence Without Official

Leave). The number of such incidents varied in direct proportion to the number of American ground troops in Indochina.[8]

Conscientious objectors who are applying for military discharge frequently realize that they can no longer follow military orders. Although in theory these people could be court-martialed, many of them in fact escape it. Some are given quick discharges; others are given nonjudicial punishment. Nonetheless refusing orders or violating military law is a risk, not merely because punishment is possible but because a soldier or sailor is in military custody twenty-four hours a day and subject to informal harassment. A 1983 incident in the navy, when two resisters were tied down and subjected to public humiliation, illustrates what can happen.[9]

Refusal of orders under fire has been far less common than refusal away from combat zones. Collective refusal to enter a combat zone was important in the Vietnam resistance but the pressures of combat all militate against individual, open resistance in battle. A survey by Brig. Gen. S. L. A. Marshall following World War II, however, made the astonishing finding that many soldiers quietly failed to fire as ordered or aimed their weapons over the heads of the enemy. In some units the number taking this action was 75 percent of the unit. It is likely that quiet resistance of this kind has been more common than historians have recognized.[10]

Effects of War Resistance: It is unfair to judge war resistance by its effect in stopping wars. On a large scale it has affected the course of some wars, but it is generally an individual action stemming from religious or moral tradition and from a deep-seated human revulsion at combat. Military training seeks to overcome the normal reaction to battle, and combat itself is so dangerous and frightening that resistance within it is extremely difficult. Thus war resistance has had limited success in halting wars outright.

There is little doubt, however, that war resistance is important for the individual resister and thus ultimately for the peace movement. War resisters frequently go beyond their personal stands to join broader peace efforts. By their actions they set an example for others and show conclusively that opposition to war is not a matter of cowardice. Governments fear them so much that the penalties for war resistance are often harsh out of all proportion to the actions punished. This perception, though unreasonable, is not entirely without foundation. War resisters question the entire war system with their lives and futures. Their contribution to the peace movement is extremely important.

(See also: CIVIL DISOBEDIENCE, COMBAT, CONSCIENTIOUS OBJECTION, CONSCRIPTION, GANDHI, MOHANDAS K., INDOCHINA WAR, KING, MARTIN LUTHER, JR., MILITARY TRAINING, NONVIOLENCE, THOREAU, HENRY DAVID)

1. An exception to this general rule is John Keegan, *The Face of Battle* (New York: Vintage Books, 1977).
2. David Cortright, *Soldiers in Revolt* (Garden City, NY: Doubleday, 1975).
3. See, e.g., Peter Brock, *History of Pacifism in the United States from the Colonial Era to the First World War* (Princeton, N.J.: Princeton University Press, 1968), and *Twentieth Century Pacifism* (New York: Van Nostrand, Reinhold, 1970).
4. Peter Mayer, ed., *The Pacifist Conscience* (New York: Holt, Rinehart & Winston, 1966), pp. 328–329.
5. For a full discussion, see Ed Hedemann, ed., *Guide to War Tax Resistance* (New York: War Resisters League, 1983).
6. Accounts of the Russian Revolution are many. For the aborted German revolution, see Sebastian Haffner, *Failure of a Revolution: Germany 1918/1919* (Library Press, 1973).
7. Alistair Horne, *The Price of Glory: Verdun 1916* (Middlesex, England: Penguin Books, 1964), p. 323. Horne's account of the French mutinies will be found on pp. 320–324. Most recent histories of World War I contain some discussion of the mutinies, but details of the incident are still unavailable.
8. I am grateful to Robert K. Musil of SANE for pointing out this relationship.
9. As reported to the Central Committee for Conscientious Objectors, Philadelphia, 1983.
10. John Keegan, "Men in Battle," *Human Nature*, Vol. I, No. 6 (June, 1978), p. 36.

War Resisters League: Founded in 1923, the War Resisters League is an international, nonsectarian membership organization. It has headquarters in New York and chapters throughout the U.S. Members must sign the following pledge: "War is a crime against humanity. We therefore are determined not to support any kind of war, international or civil, and to strive non-violently for the removal of all causes of war." WRL organizes demonstrations, participates in national action coalitions, promotes draft and war tax resistance, trains activists in civil disobedience, and provides a training program for organizers. War Resisters International, situated in London, coordinates chapters throughout the world. In the U.S., WRL publishes bimonthly *The Nonviolent Activist*. Internationally, it publishes *WRI News*.

Women and Peace: Women have played a major role in the peace movement from its beginnings. Throughout the nineteenth century, women were involved in the early peace societies. In 1854, Fredrika Bremer, a Swedish novelist (1801–65), formed the first Women's Peace League in Europe. French women campaigned against the Franco-Prussian War in 1870. And Bertha von Suttner, an Austrian (1843–1914), wrote an antiwar novel, *Lay Down Your Arms* in 1899 and was awarded the Nobel Peace Prize in 1905.[1]

The slaughter in the trenches of World War I led to the founding of several major peace groups which were still active in the 1980s. Women pacifists initiated and helped to nurture much of this growth in the peace movement. Among the most important groups begun during this period was the Women's International League for Peace and Freedom (subject of a separate article) which by 1985 was the largest women's peace organization. Jessie Wallace Hughan and Tracy Mygatt founded the War Resisters League, which, though not a women's organization as such, advocated feminism as one of its basic principles.

Following World War II, the dangers of nuclear war and atmospheric testing of nuclear weapons led to the growth of a number of new women's peace organizations. Most prominent and lasting of these new groups was Women Strike for Peace, which played a major role in the U.S. protest against the Indochina War and was still active in the 1980s.

Women's role in the protest against the U.S. war in Indochina can hardly be overstated. Both the Women's International League for Peace and Freedom and Women Strike for Peace were active. A third group, Another Mother for Peace, gave the peace movement one of its most enduring slogans:

"War is not healthy for children and other living things." Thousands of women worked at the local, state, and national levels to organize demonstrations, counsel potential draftees and develop support networks for war resisters.

In the late 1970s and early 1980s, the peace movement once again confronted the threat of nuclear war. Women were among the earliest organizers in the antinuclear movement of this period. The nuclear freeze movement grew out of a proposal by Randall Forsberg, an arms control expert. An Australian pediatrician, Dr. Helen Caldicott, became one of the most eloquent and best-known spokespersons for the movement.

The most spectacular women's action in the 1980s was the Women's Peace Camp at Greenham Common Air Base, England. Begun on September 1, 1981, the Greenham Common Camp became a model for peace camps throughout the world.[2] It sought to prevent the deployment of U.S. cruise missiles at the base and, when that failed, remained outside the base in an effort to make use of the missiles impossible through nonviolent resistance.

Greenham Common was significant not only because of its size and the publicity it generated. It represented an attempt by the women's peace movement to develop tactics and styles of leadership that avoided the male dominance many women had experienced in the established peace movement. Greenham Common's collective methods of decision-making were enormously influential in England and throughout Europe. Although the Camp began as a sexually integrated action, the women voted to ask the men to leave in February 1982. Thus Greenham became solely a women's action and remained so.

(See also: CALDICOTT, HELEN, WOMEN AND WAR, WOMEN'S INTERNATIONAL LEAGUE FOR PEACE AND FREEDOM)

1. This summary taken from Lynne Jones, ed., *Keeping the Peace: Women's Peace Handbook* (Salem, N.H.: Merrimack Publishers' Circle, 1983), p. 1.

2. Further discussion of Greenham Common and other peace camps will be found in Lynne Jones, *op. cit.* and in Alice Cook and Gwyn Kirk, *Greenham Women Everywhere: Dreams, Ideas and Actions from the Women's Peace Movement* (Boston: South End Press, 1983). A status report on the camp as of mid-1985 will be found in Ann Snitow, "Holding the Line at Greenham," *Mother Jones*, February/March 1985, p. 30 ff.

Women and War: Warfare has on the whole been a masculine enterprise. This undoubted fact has led to contradictory responses from feminists. Some have sought equal participation with men in war—that is, assignment of military women to combat roles. Since military institutions are built on the assumption that soldiers are male, feminists of this school have had limited success though they are making inroads.

Whether such success is desirable is quite another question. Equality for women is good; but equal partnership in war would do little good for women or anyone else. It would simply make women equal in an oppressive and destructive institution which in many cases has hurt women even more than it has hurt men.

The U.S. military's distinction between combat and noncombat roles is in any case artificial. Women, who are officially supposed to be noncombatants, receive weapons training and frequently are required to carry weapons as part of their duties. An army woman whose job is military police, for example, must carry and be prepared to use firearms. At the same time women with noncombat specialties, such as tank mechanic or even typist, may be caught up in fighting under "deep battle" conditions. In modern combat there is no longer a front line as such. Military installations far behind the battlefront may be attacked with missiles from the air, or even by paratroops or other units trained to penetrate deep into opposing territory.

The controversy over whether or not women should be assigned to combat ignores this central fact of modern warfare, just as it ignores the nature of modern combat. Both sides of the argument assume that combat requires physical strength and other attributes which women are or are not said to have, depending on whether the speaker is for or against women in combat.

This is a gross distortion. Much modern combat, particularly mechanized combat, air combat, and naval combat, is not a matter of strength but of skill at operating complex machinery. To suggest that discussions of combat assignments for women turn on the question of physical strength gives the impression that combat remains at bottom the traditional contest of strength which it once was. This romantic notion gives a false picture not only of combat but of the terrible destructiveness of modern weapons. In fact it would require little or no physical strength to launch nuclear missiles and destroy civilization.

Feminist-pacifists often argue that war is caused by male values and could be ended by adoption of female values. Some hold that these values are culturally based, others that they are biologically based. Biological theorists, who are in the minority, hold little hope for change as long as men hold power. The majority, however, believe that men can and should change.

The idea that there are peculiarly masculine and feminine values is untestable of course, but insofar as it can be evaluated it is poorly supported by the evidence. Women in power behave much as men do. Margaret Thatcher, Indira Gandhi, and Golda Meir were all in power during wars involving their countries. The fact that they were women did not stop them from using their armies.

A small number of women have participated in combat throughout history. This is most common in guerrilla warfare, where armies are frequently staffed by a high percentage of women. Regular armies, however, have had women as combatants (in most cases disguised as men) and some women have distinguished themselves in battle.[1]

None of this proves that feminist-pacifist theory is wrong. In one respect in fact it is almost certainly correct. Military recruitment and training appeal to a young soldier's sense of "manliness" in ways which are both overt and subtle: the soldier quickly learns that if he fails his masculinity will be questioned—generally loudly, publicly, and at length, by his drill instructor. He becomes submerged in a group of soldiers and if he is later involved in combat is likely to fight more to avoid shaming himself before them than to preserve his country.

The military's appeal to a recruit's masculinity, however, is primarily a way to manipulate the recruit and make him follow orders. Young soldiers often have no fully developed sense of themselves. Military training makes use of this fact, just as military recruitment takes advantage of unemployment among youth. Similar tactics are used on female recruits.

Whether military violence is a form of individual violence writ large is a harder question, though crucial to feminist-pacifist theory. Again the evidence is ambiguous. Armies actually reject soldiers who are too violent, those who have committed violent crimes, for example. Military training is designed to inculcate the habit of violence. And many combat veterans experience severe emotional problems because of the contradiction between what they were forced to do in combat and their more gentle impulses.

It is one of the peculiarities of military violence in fact that military operations are not necessarily carried out in anger. Soldiers frequently have less hatred for their opponents than they do for their platoon sergeants. Military operations are planned quite deliberately, and armies which are not under control are frequently losing armies. The calculated nature of warfare makes it far more, and far worse, than machismo. That is almost certainly one element, but one element only in a complex and insane picture.

Much the most potent of the feminist arguments against war is based on the damage that warfare does to women. This argument is not only testable, it has been proven time and again. In modern war civilian casualties—most of them women, children, and the old—usually outnumber military casualties. This was true of World War II, in which cities were bombed and mobile armies destroyed much of the countryside simply by moving. Most of the casualties in the Indochina War were civilians. The war in El Salvador has resulted primarily in civilian deaths. Although casualty figures are always suspect, and though armies seldom keep accurate count of civilian dead and wounded, the toll among civilians in any war today is always very high. This shows clearly that war conflicts with feminist values and the real interests of women.

War hurts women not only because they are in the path of the fighting, but because they are women. It is common for soldiers to assume a kind of "license to rape" civilian women in the combat zone. This license is sometimes applied to military women as well. Male soldiers who rape are probably no more vicious than the general population; some may be less so. The combat situation itself causes men to act in ways

330

which they would not in ordinary life. The solution to this problem in the long run is not tighter command control, but the abolition of war.

Even when there is no war women suffer because of the war system. Soldiers undergoing military training often cannot control the violent impulses which their training unleashes. Rape and sexual harassment are more common in military than in civilian life.[2]

Women also suffer indirectly from preparations for war. Every dollar spent on military force is a dollar which cannot be spent on social welfare, schools, child care, and medical aid for poor people. The destruction of such services hurts all people, but women most of all. Most single parents, who are often badly in need of social services, are women. The military "protects" women and their children at the cost of their health, their education, and even their food.

As the poet Karen Lindsay put it, "Every war is a war against women." This is true not only in wartime, but in peacetime as well.

(See also: AREA BOMBING CAMPAIGN, CHILDREN AND WAR, COMBAT, CONVENTIONAL WAR, MILITARY TRAINING, NUCLEAR WEAPONS AND WAR)

1. A brief survey of the history of women in combat will be found in Helen Rogan, *Mixed Company: Women in the Modern Army* (Boston: Beacon Press, 1981), chs. 4, 6, and 7.
2. Cf. "Rape: A Report," *Magazine Supplement of the Army Times*, January 26, 1976.

Women's International League for Peace and Freedom: Founded in 1915, WILPF is the largest women's peace organization. In the U.S., it is headquartered in Philadelphia, with chapters throughout the country. It seeks to create the conditions for peace, freedom and justice using nonviolent means. Each month it publishes *Peace and Freedom* and *WILPF Legislative Bulletin and Alerts*.

Further Reading

There are many books on war and peace—far too many to include a brief listing. In choosing the following list, I have followed three principles of selection. First, I have tried to include books which are readily available. Second, I have tried to include books which are important or present an important point of view. Third, I have tried to include books which are readable.

Some of the books on this list are out of print; these are marked "OP." Most should be available in libraries. Books marked "PB" are available in paperback. Books marked • are especially recommended.

I have made no attempt to include the many helpful magazine articles in the field. Instead, I have added a brief and highly selective listing of significant periodicals which deal with questions of war and peace.

War in Literature

Novels

Crane, Stephen. *The Red Badge of Courage*, restoration and introduction by Henry Binder. New York: Avon Books, 1982.

Del Vecchio, John. *The 13th Valley*. New York: Bantam, 1982.

Hasek, Jaroslav. *The Good Soldier Schweik*, trans. by Paul Selver. New York: Signet, 1963. PB.

• Heller, Joseph. *Catch-22*. New York: Simon & Schuster, 1961. PB available.

• Hemingway, Ernest. *A Farewell to Arms*. New York: Scribner's, 1929.

• Remarque, Erich Maria. *All Quiet on the Western Front*, trans. by A. W. Wheen. Boston: Little, Brown, 1929. PB: Greenwich, Ct.: Fawcett, 1978.

Sassoon, Siegfried. *Memoirs of an Infantry Officer*. Riverside, N.J.: Macmillan, 1969. PB.

• Tolstoy, Leo. *War and Peace*. Available in many editions and translations.

Trumbo, Dalton. *Johnny Got His Gun*. New York: Bantam Books, 1978. PB.

Vonnegut, Kurt, Jr. *Slaughterhouse-Five*. New York: Delacorte Press, 1969. PB.

Poetry

Bates, Scott. *Poems of War Resistance*. New York: Grossman Publishers, 1969. OP.

• Parsons, I.M., ed. *Men Who March Away: Poems of the First World War*. New York: The Viking Press, 1965.

Rottmann, Larry, Jan Barry, and Basil T. Pacquet, eds. *Winning Hearts and Minds: War Poems by Vietnam Veterans*. New York: East River Press, 1977. PB.

Literary Criticism
• Fussell, Paul. *The Great War and Modern Memory*. New York: Oxford University Press, 1975. PB.

War Memoirs

• Brittain, Vera. *Testament of Youth*. New York: Wideview Books, 1980.
Caputo, Philip. *A Rumor of War*. New York: Holt, Rinehart & Winston, 1977.
cummings, e. e. *The Enormous Room*. New York: Liveright, 1970. PB.
• Ehrhart, W. D. *Vietnam-Perkasie: A Combat Marine Memoir*. Jefferson, N.C.: MacFarland & Co., 1983.
Glasser, Ronald J., M.D. *365 Days*. New York: George Braziller, 1971.
• Gray, J. Glenn. *The Warriors: Reflections on Men in Battle*. New York: Harper & Row, 1967.
Kovic, Ron. *Born on the Fourth of July*. New York: McGraw-Hill, 1976. PB: Pocket Books, 1978.
° Mowat, Farley. *And No Birds Sang*. Boston: Atlantic Monthly Press, 1979.
Van Devanter, Lynda, with Christopher Morgan. *Home Before Morning*. New York/ Toronto: Beaufort Books, 1983.

War in History

Military History
Bradley, John. *Allied Intervention in Russia*. New York: Basic Books, 1968.
Calvocoressi, Peter, and Guy Wint. *Total War: The Story of World War II*. New York: Pantheon Books, 1972.
Fitzgerald, Frances. *Fire in the Lake: The Americans in Vietnam*. Boston: Little, Brown, 1972. PB: Vintage, 1973.
Goldhurst, Richard. *The Midnight War: The American Intervention in Russia, 1918– 1920*. New York: McGraw-Hill, 1978.
• Hastings, Max. *Bomber Command*. New York: Dial Press, 1979.
Horne, Alistair. *A Savage War of Peace: Algeria 1954–1962*. New York: The Viking Press, 1977.
• ——, *The Price of Glory: Verdun 1916*. Middlesex, Eng: Penguin, 1964.
• Irving, David. *The Destruction of Dresden*. New York: Holt, Rinehart & Winston, 1963. OP.
Karnow, Stanley. *Vietnam: A History*. New York: Viking, 1983.

  • Keegan, John. *The Face of Battle: A Study of Agincourt, Waterloo, and the Somme*. New York: Viking Press, 1976. PB: New York, Vintage Books, 1977.
  —— , *Six Armies in Normandy: From D-Day to the Liberation of Paris*. Middlesex, Eng: Penguin Books, 1983. PB
  Kennett, Lee. *A History of Strategic Bombing*. New York: Charles Scribner's Sons, 1982.
  Macdonald, Lyn. *Somme*. London: Michael Joseph, 1983.
  • Pearce, Jenny. *Under the Eagle: U.S. Intervention in Central America and the Caribbean*. Boston: South End Press, 1982.
  • Salisbury, Harrison. *The Unknown War*. New York: Bantam, 1978.
  Shawcross, William. *Sideshow: Kissinger, Nixon and the Destruction of Cambodia*. New York: Simon and Schuster, 1979.

Stone, I. F. *The Hidden History of the Korean War.* New York: Monthly Review Press, 1969. PB only.

Political and Diplomatic History

Caute, David. *The Great Fear: The Anti-Communist Purge Under Truman and Eisenhower.* New York: Simon & Schuster, 1978.

Fay, Sidney B. *The Origins of the World War.* Riverside, N.J.: Macmillan, 1959. PB: Free Press, 1967.

Fleming, D. F. *The Cold War and Its Origins, 1917–1960.* Garden City, N.Y.: Doubleday, 1961, 2 vols.

• Herken, Gregg. *The Winning Weapon: The Atomic Bomb in the Cold War, 1945–1950.* New York: Alfred A. Knopf, 1980.

Knightly, Philip. *The First Casualty: From the Crimea to Vietnam: The War Correspondent as Hero, Propagandist, and Myth Maker.* New York and London: Harcourt, Brace, Jovanovich, 1975. PB.

• Lafore, Laurence. *The Long Fuse: An Interpretation of the Origins of the First World War.* Philadelphia and New York: 1965.

• ——, *The End of Glory: An Interpretation of the Origins of World War II.* Philadelphia and New York: J. B. Lippincott, 1970. PB

• Swomley, John M., Jr. *American Empire: The Political Ethics of Twentieth-Century Conquest.* Riverside, N.J.: Macmillan, 1970. PB.

Taylor, A. J. P. *The Origins of the Second World War.* New York: Atheneum, 1961 (OP). PB: Greenwich, Ct.: Fawcett, 1961.

Blacks in the Military

Barbeau, Arthur, and Forette, Henri. *The Unknown Soldiers: Black American Troops in World War I.* Philadelphia: Temple University Press, 1974.

Motley, Mary Penick. *The Invisible Soldier: The Experience of the Black Soldier, World War II.* Detroit: Wayne State University Press, 1975.

Terry, Wallace. *Bloods. An Oral History of the Vietnam War by Black Veterans.* New York: Random House, 1984.

Genocide, Political Terror, and the Holocaust

The Holocaust

• Dawidowicz, Lucy. *The War Against the Jews, 1933–1945.* New York: Holt, Rinehart & Winston, 1975.

Fleming, Gerald. *Hitler and the Final Solution.* Berkeley, Calif.: University of California Press, 1984.

Hilberg, Raul. *The Destruction of the European Jews.* Chicago: Quadrangle Books, 1971.

Levin, Nora. *The Holocaust.* New York: Schocken, 1973.

• Morse, Arthur D. *While Six Million Died.* New York: Random House, 1968.

Reitlinger, Gerald. *The Final Solution,* (2d Ed.). S. Brunswick, N.J.: Thomas Yoseloff, 1968.

Wyman, David S. *The Abandonment of the Jews.* New York: Pantheon, 1984.

Genocide and Political Terror

Bedoukian, Kerop. *Some of Us Survived: The Story of An Armenian Boy.* New York: Farrar, Straus, Giroux, 1978.

Conquest, Robert. *The Great Terror.* London: Macmillan, 1968.

• Kuper, Leo. *Genocide.* New Haven and London: Yale University Press, 1981.

• Solzhenitsyn, Aleksandr. *The Gulag Archipelago.* New York: Harper & Row, 1974–1978.

Modern War and Its Victims

General

Cunningham, Ann Marie, and Mariana Fitzpatrick. *Future Fire: Weapons for the Apocalypse.* New York: Warner Books, 1983.

Kidron, Michael, and Dan Smith. *The War Atlas.* New York: Simon & Schuster, 1983.

- Kwitny, Jonathan. *Endless Enemies: The Making of an Unfriendly World. How America's Worldwide Interventions Destroy Democracy and Free Enterprise and Defeat Our Own Best Interests.* New York: Congdon and Weed, Inc., 1984.

- Sivard, Ruth Leger. *World Military and Social Expenditures.* Arlington, Va.: Council on World Priorities. Updated annually.

- Wilson, Andrew. *The Disarmer's Handbook of Military Technology and Organization.* Middlesex, Eng.: Penguin, 1983.

Wright, Quincy. *A Study of War.* Chicago: University of Chicago Press, 1942.

Nuclear War

Arkin, William, Thomas B. Cochran, and Milton M. Hoenig. *Nuclear Weapons Datebook.* Cambridge, Ma.: Ballinger Publishing Co., 1984.

- Calder, Nigel. *Nuclear Nightmares: An Investigation into Possible Wars.* New York: Viking Press, 1980.

- Ehrlich, Paul, Carl Sagan, and others. *The Cold and the Dark: Life After Nuclear War.* New York: W. W. Norton, 1984.

Greene, Owen, et al. *London After the Bomb.* New York: Oxford University Press, 1983.

- Ground Zero. *Nuclear War: What's In It For You?* New York: Pocket Books, 1982.

- Hersey, John. *Hiroshima.* New York: Alfred A. Knopf, 1969. PB.

Kaplan, Fred. *The Wizards of Armageddon.* New York: Simon & Schuster, 1983.

- Lifton, Robert J., and Richard Falk. *Indefensible Weapons: The Political and Psychological Case Against Nuclearism.* New York: Basic Books, 1982.

Manno, Jack. *Arming the Heavens: The Hidden Military Agenda for Space, 1945–1995.* New York: Dodd, Mead, 1984.

Scheer, Robert. *With Enough Shovels: Reagan, Bush and Nuclear War.* New York: Random House, 1982.

Schell, Jonathan. *The Fate of the Earth.* New York: Alfred A. Knopf, 1982. PB.

Walker, Paul. *Seizing the Initiative: First Steps to Disarmament.* Philadelphia and Nyack, N.Y.: American Friends Service Committee and Fellowship of Reconciliation, 1983.

Chemical and Biological Warfare

Hersh, Seymour. *Chemical and Biological Warfare: America's Hidden Arsenal.* Indianapolis: Bobbs-Merrill, 1968. OP.

Seagrave, Sterling. *Yellow Rain: A Journey Through the Terror of Chemical Warfare.* New York: M. Evans & Co., 1981.

United Nations Report. *Chemical and Bacteriological Weapons and the Effects of Their Possible Use.* New York: Ballantine Books, 1970.

Guerrilla Warfare

Chaliand, Gerard. *Revolution in the Third World.* Middlesex, Eng.: Penguin, 1978.

Laqueur, Walter. *Guerrilla: A Historical and Critical Study.* Boston: Little, Brown, 1976.

Sully, Francois. *Age of the Guerrilla: The New Warfare.* New York: Parents Magazine Press, 1968.

Central America

Armstrong, Robert, and Janet Shenk. *El Salvador: The Face of Revolution.* Boston: South End Press, 1982. PB

Berryman, Phillip. *The Religious Roots of Rebellion: Christians in the Central American Revolutions.* Maryknoll, N.Y.: Orbis Books, 1984.

Booth, John. *The End and the Beginning: The Nicaraguan Revolution.* Westview, 1981.

Middle East

American Friends Service Committee. *A Compassionate Peace: A Future for the Middle East.* New York: Hill and Wang, 1982.

Avineri, Shlomo. *The Making of Modern Zionism.* New York: Basic Books, 1981.

Eliav, Arie L. *Land of the Hart: Israelis, Arabs, the Territories, and a Vision of the Future.* Philadelphia: Jewish Publication Society, 1974.

Jackson, Elmore. *Middle East Mission: The Story of a Major Bid for Peace in the Time of Nasser and Ben-Gurion.* New York: W. W. Norton, 1983.

Naipaul, V.S. *Among the Believers: An Islamic Journey.* New York: Alfred A. Knopf, 1981.

Oz, Amos. *In The Land of Israel.* New York: Harcourt, Brace, Jovanovich, 1983.

Polk, William. *The Elusive Peace, The Middle East in the Twentieth Century.* New York: St. Martin's Press, 1979.

Women and War

Brownmiller, Susan. *Against Our Will: Men, Women and Rape.* New York: Simon & Schuster, 1975.

• Enloe, Cynthia. *Does Khaki Become You? The Militarization of Women's Lives.* Boston: South End Press, 1983. PB

Rogan, Helen. *Mixed Company: Women in the Modern Army.* Boston: Beacon Press, 1981.

Victims

Grudzinska-Gross, Irena, and Jan Tomasz-Gross, eds. *War Through Children's Eyes: The Soviet Occupation of Poland and the Deportations, 1939–1941.* Stanford, Ca.: Hoover Institution Press, 1981.

• Rosenblatt, Roger. *Children of War.* Garden City, N.Y.: Anchor Press/Doubleday, 1983.

War and Politics

Adams, Gordon. *The Politics of Defense Contracting: The Iron Triangle.* New Brunswick, N.J.: Transaction Books, 1981.

Barnet, Richard J. *Real Security: Restoring American Power in a Dangerous Decade.* New York: Simon & Schuster/Touchstone, 1981.

• Barnet, Richard J., and Ronald E. Mueller. *Global Reach: The Power of the Multinational Corporations.* New York: Simon & Schuster, 1974.

Klare, Michael T. *Beyond the "Vietnam Syndrome": U.S. Interventionism in the 1980s.* Washington, D.C.: Institute for Policy Studies, 1981.

• Myrdal, Alva. *The Game of Disarmament.* New York: Pantheon Books, 1976.

Myrdal, Alva, and others. *Dynamics of European Nuclear Disarmament.* Chester Springs, Pa.: Dufour Editions, 1984.

Indochina War

• Baskir, M. Lawrence, and William A. Straus. *Chance and Circumstance: The Draft, The War, and the Vietnam Generation.* New York: Alfred A. Knopf, 1978. PB

• Bryan, C.D.B. *Friendly Fire.* New York: Putnam, 1976.

337

- Halstead, Fred. *Out Now: A Participant's Account of the American Movement Against the Vietnam War.* New York: Monad Press, 1978
Lewy, Guenter. *America in Vietnam.* New York: Oxford, 1978.
- Lifton, Robert Jay. *Home From the War: Vietnam Veterans Neither Victims Nor Executioners.* New York: Simon & Schuster, 1973.
MacPherson, Myra. *Long Time Passing: Vietnam and the Haunted Generation.* Garden City, N.Y.: Doubleday, 1984.
Patti, L. A. Archimedes. *Why Vietnam?* Berkeley, Ca.: University of California Press, 1980.
- Polner, Murray. *No Victory Parades: The Return of the Vietnam Veteran.* New York: Holt, Rinehart & Winston, 1971.
——. *When Can I Come Home? A Debate on Amnesty for Exiles, Antiwar Prisoners & Others.* Garden City, N.Y.: Anchor Press/Doubleday, 1972.
- Santoli, Al. *Everything We Had: An Oral History of the Vietnam War by Thirty-Three American Soldiers Who Fought It.* New York: Ballantine Books, 1981.
Starr, Paul, and others. *The Discarded Army: Veterans After Vietnam.* New York: Charterhouse, 1973.
Williams, Roger Neville. *The New Exiles: American War Resisters in Canada.* New York: Liveright, 1971.
Zaroulis, Nancy and Gerald Sullivan. *Who Spoke Up?* American Protest Against the War in Vietnam, 1963–1975. (Garden City, N.Y.: Doubleday, 1984.)

The Soviet Union

- Barnet, Richard J. *The Giants: Russia and America.* New York: Simon & Schuster, 1977. PB
Cockburn, Andrew. *The Threat: Inside the Soviet Military Machine.* New York: Random House, 1983.
- Salisbury, Harrison. *Black Night, White Snow: Russia's Revolutions, 1905–1917.* Garden City, N.Y.: Doubleday, 1978.
Smith, Hedrick. *The Russians.* New York: Ballantine Books, 1976.
Suvorov, Victor. *The "Liberators": My Life in the Soviet Army.* New York: W. W. Norton, 1981.

Nazism

Allen, William Sheridan. *The Nazi Seizure of Power.* Revised. New York: Franklin Watts, 1984.
- Bullock, Alan. *Hitler, A Study in Tyranny.* New York: Harper Colophon Books, 1964.
Neumann, Franz. *Behemoth. The Structure and Practice of National Socialism, 1933–1944.* New York: Harper Torchbooks, 1966. PB
Seadle, Michael. *Quakers in Nazi Germany.* Chicago: Progresive Publisher (401 E. 32nd St., Chicago 60616).
- Speer, Albert. *Inside the Third Reich.* New York: Macmillan, 1970.

Human Destructiveness

- Ardrey, Robert. *The Territorial Imperative: A Personal Inquiry into the Animal Origins of Property and Nations.* New York: Bell, 1966.
Cook, Joan Marble. *In Defense of Homo Sapiens.* New York: Farrar, Straus and Giroux, 1975. PB: New York: Dell—Laurel Edition, 1976.
- Fromm, Erich. *The Anatomy of Human Destructiveness.* Greenwich, Ct.: Fawcett, 1973.

338

- Lorenz, Konrad. *On Aggression.* New York: Harcourt, Brace & World, 1966. PB: Harcourt, Brace, Jovanovich, 1974.
- Montagu, M. F. Ashley. *The Nature of Human Aggression.* New York: Oxford University Press, 1976. PB: New York: Oxford, 1978.

Conscientious Objection, War Resistance, and Pacifism

- Bainton, Roland H. *Christian Attitudes Toward War and Peace: A Historical Survey and Critical Re-Evaluation.* New York: Abingdon Press, 1960. PB available.
- Berrigan, Daniel. *No Bars to Manhood.* Garden City, N.Y.: Doubleday, 1970. PB: Bantam, 1971. OP
- Brock, Peter. *History of Pacifism in the United States from the Colonial Era to the First World War.* Princeton, N.J.: Princeton University Press, 1968. PB available.
- ————. *Twentieth Century Pacifism.* New York: Van Nostrand, Reinhold, 1970. PB available.
- Cook Alice, and Gwyn Kirk. *Greenham Women Everywhere: Dreams, Ideas and Actions from the Women's Peace Movement.* Boston: South End Press, 1983.
- DeBenedetti, Charles. *The Peace Reform in American History.* Bloomington, Ind.: Indiana University Press, 1980.
- Deming, Barbara. *Revolution and Equilibrium.* New York: Grossman, 1971.
- Ferber, Michael, and Staughton Lynd. *The Resistance.* Boston: Beacon Press, 1971. OP
- Finn, James, ed. *A Conflict of Loyalties: The Case for Selective Conscientious Objection.* New York: Pegasus, 1968.
- ————, ed. *Protest: Pacifism and Politics.* New York: Random House, 1967. OP
- Galtung, Johan. *There Are Alternatives: Four Roads to Peace and Security.* Chester Springs, Pa.: Dufour Editions, 1984.
- Gaylin, Willard. *In the Service of Their Country: War Resisters in Prison.* New York: Viking, 1970.
- Hesse, Herman. *If the War Goes On . . . Reflections on War and Politics,* trans. by Ralph Manheim. New York: Farrar, Straus and Giroux, 1971.
- Huxley, Aldous. *Ends and Means.* New York: Harper Bros., 1937.
- Jones, Lynne, ed. *Keeping the Peace: Women's Peace Handbook I.* Salem, N.H.: Merrimack Publishers Circle, 1983.
- Lens, Sidney. *Radicalism in America.* New York: Thomas Y. Crowell, 1966.
- Lynd, Alice, ed. *We Won't Go.* Boston: Beacon Press, 1968. OP
- McReynolds, David. *We Have Been Invaded by the Twenty-First Century.* New York: Grove Press, 1970. OP
- McSorley, Richard. *The New Testament Basis of Peacemaking.* Washington, D.C.: Center for Peace Studies, Georgetown University, 1979.
- Mayer, Peter, ed. *The Pacifist Conscience.* New York: Holt, Rinehart & Winston, 1966. OP
- Merklin, Lewis, Jr. *They Chose Honor: The Problem of Conscience in Custody.* New York: Harper & Row, 1974.
- Merton, Thomas, ed. *Breakthrough to Peace.* New York: New Directions, 1962.
- Muste, A. J. *Essays,* ed. by Nat Hentoff. Indianapolis: Bobbs-Merrill, 1967. PB: Simon & Schuster/Touchstone, 1970.
- Nathan, Otto, and Heinz Norden, eds. *Einstein on Peace.* New York: Avenel Books, 1981.
- Polner, Murray, ed. *The Disarmament Catalogue.* New York: Pilgrim Press, 1982.

Schirmer, D. B. *Republic or Empire: American Resistance to the Philippine War.* - Schenkman, 1972.
- Schlissel, Lillian, ed. *Conscience in America.* New York: Dutton, 1968. PB available.

Spaeth, Robert L. *No Easy Answers: Christians Debate Nuclear Arms.* Minneapolis, Mn.: Winston Press, 1983.

Thompson, Dorothy, ed. *Over Our Dead Bodies: Women Against the Bomb.* Salem, N.H.: Merrimack Publishers' Circle, 1984.
- Thoreau, Henry David. "On the Duty of Civil Disobedience." In *Walden and Other Writings.* Garden City, N.Y.: Doubleday, 1970. (Many other editions.)
- Tolstoy, Leo. *Tolstoy's Writings on Civil Disobedience and Nonviolence.* New York: Bergman Publishers, 1967.

Vanderhaar, Gerard A. *Christians and Nonviolence in the Nuclear Age.* Mystic, Ct.: Twenty-Third Publications, 1982.
- Weber, David R., ed. *Civil Disobedience in America: A Documentary History.* Ithaca, N.Y., and London: Cornell University Press, 1978.
- Wittner, Lawrence S. *Rebels Against War—American Peace Movement 1941–1960.* New York: Columbia University Press, 1969.

Yoder, John H. *The Politics of Jesus.* Grand Rapids, Mich.: Wm. B. Eerdmans Publishing Co., 1972.
- Zahn, Gordon C. *Another Part of the War: The Camp Simon Story.* Amherst, Mass.: University of Massachusetts Press, 1979.
- ———. *In Solitary Witness: The Life and Death of Franz Jagerstatter.* Collegeville, Mn.: The Liturgical Press, 1981.

Nonviolence

- Acherson, Neal. *The Polish August: The Self-Limiting Revolution.* New York: The Viking Press, 1982.

American Friends Service Committee. *In Place of War.* New York: Grossman, 1967. OP

Blumberg, Herbert H., and A. Paul Hare. *Nonviolent Direct Action: American Cases: Social-Psychological Analyses.* Washington and Cleveland: Corpus Books, 1968.

Bondurant, Joan. *The Conquest of Violence.* Berkeley, Ca.: University of California Press, 1965. PB
- Boserup, Anders, and Andrew Mack. *War Without Weapons: Nonviolence in National Defense.* New York: Schocken Books, 1975.

Camara, Dom Helder. *Spiral of Violence.* Denville, N.J.: Dimension Books, 1971.
- Cooney, Robert, and Helen Michalowski. *The Power of the People: Active Nonviolence in the United States.* Culver City, Ca.: Peace Press, 1977.

Dellinger, David. *More Power Than We Know: The People's Movement Toward Democracy.* Garden City, N.J.: Doubleday, 1975.
- ———. *Revolutionary Non-Violence.* Garden City, N.Y.: Anchor, 1971. OP
- Gandhi, Mohandas K. *Autobiography: The Story of My Experiments with Truth.* Boston: Beacon Press, 1957.

———. *All Men Are Brothers.* Chicago: World Without War Council, 1972.
- Gregg, Richard. *The Power of Non-Violence.* New York: Schocken, 1959. 2nd Ed.: Nyack, N.Y.: Fellowship, 1959. PB: Schocken, 1959.
- Hallie, Philip. *Lest Innocent Blood Be Shed: The Story of the Village of Le Chambon and How Goodness Happened There.* New York: Harper & Row, 1979. PB

340

- Hedemann, Ed., ed. *Guide to War Tax Resistance*. New York: War Resisters League, 1983.
- ———. *War Resisters League Organizer's Manual*. New York: War Resisters League, 1981.
- Jewish Peace Fellowship. *The Roots of Jewish Nonviolence*. Nyack, N.Y.: Jewish Peace Fellowship, 1970.
- King, Martin Luther, Jr. *Stride Toward Freedom: The Montgomery Story*. New York: Harper & Row, 1958.
——— . *Why We Can't Wait*. New York: New American Library, 1965.
- ———. *The Trumpet of Conscience*. New York: Harper & Row, 1968.
- Lakey, George. *Strategy for a Living Revolution*. New York: Grossman Publishers, 1973.
- Lynd, Staughton, ed., *Non-Violence in America: A Documentary History*. Indianapolis, Ind.: Bobbs-Merrill, 1966. PB available.
McAllister, Pam, ed. *Reweaving the Web of Life*. Philadelphia: New Society Publishers, 1982.
Merton, Thomas. *Faith and Violence*. South Bend, Ind.: Notre Dame Press, 1968. PB available.
Miller, William R. *Nonviolence: A Christian Interpretation*. New York: Association Press, 1964. PB: Schocken, 1966.
- Roberts, Adam, ed. *Civilian Resistance as a National Defence*. Middlesex, Eng.: Pelican, 1969. OP
- Sharp, Gene. *Social Power and Political Freedom*. Boston: Porter Sargent, 1980.
- ———. *The Politics of Non-Violent Action*. Boston: Porter Sargent, 1973. PB
- ———. *Gandhi as a Political Strategist: With Essays on Ethics and Politics*. Boston: Porter Sargent, 1979.
- Shivers, Lynne, and David Bowman, S.J. *More Than Troubles: A Common Sense View in the Northern Ireland Conflict*. Philadelphia: New Society Publishers, 1983.
  - Sibley, Mulford Q. *The Quiet Battle*. Boston: Beacon Press, 1969. OP
Stanford, Barbara, ed. *Peace Making: A Guide to Conflict Resolution*. New York: Bantam, 1976. PB
  - Tolstoy, Leo. *The Kingdom of God Is Within You*, trans. by Leo Weiner. New York: Farrar, Straus and Cudahy, 1961. PB
van Slyck, Philip. *Peace: The Control of National Power*. Boston: Beacon Press, 1964.
Weinberg, Arthur, and Lilia Weinberg. *Instead of Violence*. New York: Grossman, 1963. PB: Boston: Beacon Press, 1965. OP
Woito, Robert. *To End War: A New Approach to International Conflict*. New York: Pilgrim Press, 1982.

Periodicals

- *Bulletin of the Atomic Scientists*, 5801 S. Kenwood, Chicago, IL 60637.
Catholic Worker, 36 East 1st St., New York, NY 10003
CCCO News Notes, Central Committee for Conscientious Objectors, 2208 South St., Philadelphia, PA 19146
Commonweal, 232 Madison Avenue, New York, NY 10016
- *Defense Monitor*, Center for Defense Information, 122 Maryland Ave., NE, Washington, DC 20002
- *Fellowship*, Box 271, Nyack, NY 10960
Friends Journal, 1501 Cherry St., Philadelphia, PA 19102

The Guardian, 33 West 17th Street, New York, NY 10011
In These Times, 1509 North Milwaukee, Chicago, IL 60622
• *Mother Jones,* 625 Third St., San Francisco, CA 94107
The Nation, 72 Fifth Ave., New York, NY 10011
New York Review of Books, 250 West 57th St., New York, NY 10019
Nuclear Times, 298 Fifth Ave., New York, NY 10001
• *Peace News,* 8 Elm Avenue, Nottingham, England
Peacemaker, P.O. Box 627, Garberville, CA 95440
• *The Progressive,* 409 East Main St., Madison, WI 53603
• *Sojourners,* 1309 L Street, NW, Washington, DC 20005
• *War Resisters International Newsletter,* 55 Dawes Street, London SE 17, England

Some Groups That Work for Peace*

American Friends Service Committee, 1501 Cherry Street, Philadelphia, PA. 19102

Amnesty International, 304 West 58th Street, New York, NY 10019

Church of the Brethren World Ministries, 1451 Dundee Avenue, Elgin, Ill. 60120

Catholic Peace Fellowship, 339 Lafayette Street, New York, NY 10012

Catholic Worker, 36 East 1st Street, New York, NY 10003

Center for War/Peace Studies, 218 East 18th Street, New York, NY 10003

Central Committee for Conscientious Objectors, 2208 South Street, Philadelphia, Pa. 19146

Clergy and Laity Concerned, 198 Broadway, New York, NY 10038

Coalition for a New Foreign and Military Policy, 120 Maryland Avenue, NE, Washington, DC 20002

COPRED: Consortium on Peace Education, Research and Development, Kent State University, Kent, Oh. 44242

Episcopal Peace Fellowship, Hearst Hall, Wisconsin Avenue at Woodley Road, NW, Washington, DC 20016

Fellowship of Reconciliation, Box 271, Nyack, NY 10960

Friends Committee on National Legislation, 245 Second Street, NE, Washington, DC 20002

Jewish Peace Fellowship, Box 271, Nyack, NY 10960

Mennonite Central Committee, 21 South 12th Street, Akron, PA 17501

Mobilization for Survival, 853 Broadway, New York, NY 10003

Mothers (and Others) Against the Draft, P.O.B. 2049, Great Neck, NY 11022

Movement for a New Society, 4722 Baltimore Avenue, Philadelphia, Pa. 19143

National Interreligious Service Board for Conscientious Objectors, 550 Washington Bldg., 15th and New York Avenue, NW, Washington, DC 20005

Pax Christi, 6337 W. Cornelia Avenue, Chicago, Ill. 60634

Peacemakers, P.O. Box 627, Garberville, Ca. 95440

Physicians for Social Responsibility, 639 Massachusetts Avenue, Cambridge, Ma. 02139

Religious Task Force, 85 South Oxford Street, Brooklyn, NY 11217

SANE: A Citizens' Committee for a Sane World, 711 G Street, SE, Washington, DC 20003

Southern Christian Leadership Conference, 334 Auburn Avenue NE, Atlanta, GA 30303

War Resisters International, 55 Dawes Street, London SE 17 1EL, England

War Resisters League, 339 Lafayette Street, New York, NY 10012

Women's International League for Peace and Freedom, 1213 Race Street, Philadelphia, Pa. 19107

Women Strike for Peace, 145 South 13th Street, Philadelphia, Pa. 19107

World Goodwill, 866 United Nations Plaza, Suite 566-7, New York, New York U.S.A. 10164

*This listing is adapted from one compiled by War Resisters League. It is current as of July 1984, but addresses may change. My thanks and appreciation to WRL.

Armament and Disarmament Information Unit, The Science Policy Research Unit, University of Sussex, Falmer, Brighton BN1 9RF, England

Campaign for Nuclear Disarmament, 29 Great James Street, London WC 1N 3EY, England

International Fellowship of Reconciliation, Hof van Sonoy 15–17, 1811 LD Alkmaar, The Netherlands

National Peace Council, 29 Great James Street, London WC 1N, England

Pax Christi International, 150 Kerkstraat, 2000 Antwerp, Belgium

Bertrand Russell Peace Foundation, Bertrand Russell House, Gamble Street, Nottingham NG7 4ET, England

Stockholm International Peace Research Institute, Sveavagen 166, S-113 46 Stockholm, Sweden

United Nations Association, 3 Whitehall Court, London SW1, England

War Resisters International, 55 Dawes Street, London, SE 17 England

WMSE Publications, c/o CAAT, 5 Caledonian Road, London N1 9DX, England

World Disarmament Campaign, 21 Little Russell Street, London WC1 4HF, England

World Goodwill, 3 Whitehall Court, Suite 54, London, England SW1A 2EF

Bonne Volonte Mondiale, 1 Rue de Varembé (3e), Case Postale 31, 1211 Geneva 20, Switzerland